The Passes of Colorado:
An Encyclopedia of Watershed Divides

Enjoy!

Gloria Helmuth
Ed Helmuth

The PASSES *of* COLORADO

AN ENCYCLOPEDIA OF WATERSHED DIVIDES

ED HELMUTH & GLORIA HELMUTH

PRUETT

PRUETT PUBLISHING COMPANY
BOULDER, COLORADO

Printed in the United States
10 9 8 7 6 5 4 3 2 1

Library of Congress Cataloging-in-Publication Data

Helmuth, Ed, 1937–
    Passes of Colorado : an encyclopedia of watershed divides / Ed
Helmuth and Gloria Helmuth.
        p.   cm.
    Includes bibliographical references (p.   ) and index.
    ISBN 0-87108-841-X (pb : recycled paper)
    1. Mountain passes – Colorado – Guidebooks. 2. Mountain passes –
Colorado – Encyclopedias. 3. Colorado – Guidebooks. 4. Colorado –
Encyclopedias. I. Helmuth, Gloria. 1940–   . II. Title.
F774.3.H45   1994
917.8804′33 – dc20   93-42044
                                                                         CIP

CONTENTS

PREFACE

From the standpoint of chronology, Spain was the first European power to penetrate the American West. Back in 1540, Francisco Coronado led an impressive expedition north from New Spain but probably did not enter present Colorado. Juan Rivera may have been the first identifiable Spaniard to travel in this state when he reached the Dolores and Gunnison rivers in 1765. Next came Father Dominguez and Father Escalante, who created a trail still visible near Delta.

From the east, other Europeans entered this land. Curiously, 150 years were required for them to get across the Appalachians. But the remaining three-quarters of our country was explored and opened up in an additional span of only fifty years. Never before in recorded human history had a people moved across so much territory in so short a time. When the nineteenth century dawned, we were a nation imbued with the doctrine of expansionism. Some early Americans came west in a search for furs or precious metals. Others hoped to bring Christianity to native people. A few arrived with ideas of progress and romantic imperialism.

Upon entering this vast, unspoiled frontier, how did these pioneers get from one location to another? As in the East, trails and roads were a necessity. In the Colorado territory they encountered massive mountain chains that surpassed anything they had known before. Without doubt, our earliest mountain trails were paths made by migrating animals. In many instances Native Americans, particularly the mountain Utes, followed many of these same paths. For example, one among several so-called Ute Trails extended from South Park down to the later site of Manitou Springs. In 1859 this hunting path became the primary route to the mineral-rich Upper Arkansas Valley followed by the Tabors and many other such argonauts.

Since territorial treasuries lacked the funds necessary to build needed roads, men like Otto Mears and Enos Hotchkiss obtained five-dollar permits that allowed them to construct toll roads. In 1867, Jim Bridger located Berthoud Pass, which became the first nontoll road across the Continental Divide. Since Colorado is a relatively young state, having attained statehood in 1876, a substantial number of our early passes can still be located and followed. Literally hundreds of these pioneer crossings are even now scattered among the several ranges of Colorado's Rockies. Some are difficult to follow, others are easy.

In the years since the end of World War II we have witnessed a nostalgia, a mounting interest in the records of how people sought out passes through the bewildering complexity of our high country. The Colorado Historical Society is seeing a growing interest in our recent past. It exerts a fascination that is completely unrelated to the awe generated by what we call scenery.

In this book, Gloria and Ed Helmuth have compiled the results of several decades spent in rediscovering, researching, and actually exploring many of these nearly forgotten passes. I first met this delightful couple when they enrolled in some classes I taught for the University of Colorado. Since that time we have exchanged bits of information about Colorado's earliest passes and related subjects. For the Helmuths, this rediscovery of our high country trails has been a true labor of love, a great and serious adventure in which you, the reader, are invited to partake to the limits of your indulgence and endurance.

Robert L. Brown
Colorado historian and author

ACKNOWLEDGMENTS

In the years he served as Colorado State Historical Society president, James Grafton Rogers began developing an extensive listing of Colorado places. Colorado mountain passes were included in his work. Rogers continued adding to his passes list up into the 1950s. His lists, in three small black notebooks, now reside at the Colorado Historical Society's library. In 1929 Ralph Brown published, in the *Colorado Magazine*, a list of all the Colorado passes known to him. The works of these two and other researchers have inspired us to continue working to identify, research, and then publish an exhaustive listing on Colorado's passes. We thank Mr. Rogers and Mr. Brown.

Another Mr. Brown, Robert L. Brown, a much-published author, fellow historian, and friend, has encouraged us to record our findings. Tom Noel and other historian friends offered words of encouragement for this and future writing endeavors.

Thanks go to all the librarians who have helped us and continue to provide help: the Colorado State Historical Society, the Denver Public Library's Western History Department, many college facilities, and the state interlibrary loan program. These hard-working researchers gathered the information we requested to feed our ever-increasing appetites for knowledge and facts.

The photos used throughout the text are from the collection of Ed Helmuth, unless otherwise noted.

A thank you goes to Tim and Betty Dannels, Buena Vista neighbors and fellow "pass nuts," who assisted in our research and proofread copy.

Finally, we thank our friends and family, who've accompanied us on our research trips and who've forgone other activities in order to see another pass.

INTRODUCTION

Developing the passes through the Colorado mountains has been an ongoing process ever since prehistoric humans came to the area. Ease of passage from one region to another was desirable for commercial activity from the early days of Indian tribes exchanging food, through the period of fur trapping, into the great mining booms, and up to today's many activities.

As a pass became well-used, it could acquire new characteristics; the trail would become known to many people, it would be given a name, it might become a wagon road, a railroad, or a highway. Use of the mountains changes; new trails or roads are developed that cross previously unused and unnamed areas. Thus, new pass names could be added in the future to this comprehensive listing. Conversely, the use of a pass may decline due to a change in traffic or economic conditions.

This is a book about Colorado's passes. It is a compiled list of passes that have seen use of some kind, and that were given a name. A bit of each pass's history is included with facts about the pass and its location.

WHAT IS A PASS?

We have chosen to define a pass as the point used to cross a ridge that divides two watersheds. "Divide" and "saddle" are other descriptive words sometimes used to identify passes. Most passes are the low point between two higher points and are shaped as a saddle; "divide" describes the water division. Some passes are named "gap," yet meet the criteria of a pass as given here.

Passes are usually at a considerable elevation, and most of them are in the high mountain ranges in the western half of the state. Yet watershed divides do occur in the eastern part of the state, and some have enough significance that they have been named.

Many passes bear the name of a stream or some other physical feature located nearby, such as a mountain. Others are named for prominent people in our state's history.

Any low spot in a mountain range could be considered a pass; however, we recognize in this book only those locations that have had use as a trail, railroad crossing, or roadway, and that have been or are known with a pass name. Other low spots are crossed with roads; however, if no name has ever been associated with such a locale, it is not listed in this work. Some passes are no longer used. If there had once been a use for such crossings and a name had been given, those passes are included.

Now, what a pass is not. A pass is not a gap—a gap is not a pass. A gap is a cut through a rock or mountain barrier that has usually been formed by water. A gap has no watershed division associated with it; rather, the same watershed is present on both sides of the gap.

Some authors consider gaps as passes. Wagon Wheel Gap, in Mineral County, is included in many lists of passes, although there is no change in watershed there. The Rio Grande River runs through the gap and drains both sides toward the east.

The word "gap" is frequently used in the eastern U.S. to name a geographic feature that would be termed a pass in Colorado. Cumberland Gap in the eastern part of Tennessee is a pass by our definition: It is a watershed divide in the Appalachian Mountains.

HOW TO USE THIS BOOK

This text lists passes alphabetically. An index is provided that includes all the passes and any other names by which a pass may have been known. Each pass entry has some basic information about the pass in a section at its beginning. Included in each entry is a map number. Use this number to examine the first map in Appendix 1 on page 259. This will show the general area in the state where the pass is located. To more closely pinpoint the pass, refer to the map whose number is indicated in the pass entry and on the map on page 259. The maps are not completely true to scale—use them only for general location.

To more accurately find the exact location of a pass, use the township and range position given in the basic information portion of the entry, along with supplemental maps, such as the forest service maps of the national forests in Colorado. These maps show townships and ranges along their margins. The township and range designation is an identification system used throughout much of the United States and was introduced to Colorado by the early surveyors sent by the federal government to explore and map the great frontier Out West.

Unfortunately, not all of Colorado was surveyed from the same base. The southwest corner of the state is based on the New Mexico Principal Meridian. Most of the remainder of the state is based on the Sixth Principal Meridian and the 40th Parallel, which is Baseline Road in Boulder. Another small area around Grand Junction has its own unique base also.

A township-range location is ideally a six-mile-square area where the township designation is a north-south location and the range location places it on the east-west line.

Some passes are located and named on state highway road maps. More are located and named on the forest service maps. However, many passes no longer in use or those not commonly known are not located on current maps. To most precisely locate any of the passes, the best aid is the United States Geological Survey (USGS) series of topographical maps. Topo maps show the elevation of an area by a series of lines that connect points of equal elevation. Learning to read these maps takes a bit of practice, but once the system is mastered, the information available is great. Studying the elevation contour lines shows where the low point or pass on a ridge is located.

Topo maps are published in many sizes. We recommend the 7½ minute series and the county series. The 7½ minute series maps cover a smaller area, which enables them to be more precise. However, it takes 1,792 of the 7½ minute series maps to cover the entire state of Colorado; it becomes expensive to collect them all. There are many fewer maps in the county series, even though each county may have up to seven maps to cover it completely.

NOT A GUIDEBOOK

This book is not a driving, hiking, biking, skiing, or other guidebook. We do not attempt to lead the reader through each turn of a trail to end up at the pass summit; therefore, hiking distances and road numbers by which to reach trailheads are not included here. However, we have supplied enough information that, with use of the proper maps, a reader should be able to find the passes listed. That challenge is yours, the same challenge we faced in locating many of the lesser-known passes.

CHANGING ACCESS

An important item to note regards the access listed for each pass. If a pass is described as accessible by foot, often it is only that, particularly those passes in wilderness areas. On other passes, foot trails may be shared with mountain or motorized bikes. If a pass is described as 4WD- or car-accessible, that refers to the accessibility under the best of conditions. If it is extremely wet due to rain or snowmelt, a pass that may be car-accessible in good times may not even be 4WD-accessible. Many 4WD roads are closed due to snow in the winter, and in some years they may not open at all during the summer. To believe that a vehicle can be driven somewhere at any time because a book says so may lead to stuck vehicles and huge towing bills.

Neither are all vehicles created equal. Do not try to take a low-clearance sports car on all car-accessible routes. And a high-clearance pickup truck may be able to negotiate some 4WD routes. Remember, the access described is that for the *best* conditions – don't be embarrassed to turn around and try again another day.

High-country access is constantly changing. New wilderness areas may be established that could close vehicle access that is currently open. United States Forest Service maintenance of forest roads and trails varies year by year. Many roads are maintained only periodically. Four-wheel-drive clubs throughout the state adopt backcountry roads and provide maintenance for them – even occasionally opening roads that previously were impassable.

Another item subject to change is maps. Until recently, the only forest service maps widely available to the public were originally drawn in the 1970s, with revisions for some in the mid-1980s. Recently, the forest service has brought out a new series of maps. References to a pass as named on a forest service map may mean that it is shown on the older series, the newer series, or both. Both series do not necessarily show the same passes or other geographic features. USGS topo maps are constantly under revision. Newer maps may show new roads and may delete roads and trails no longer used or maintained. Another excellent source of Colorado high-country information is the maps of Trails Illustrated, of Evergreen, Colorado.

Other maps are available that have varying degrees of usefulness. A large paperback book, titled *Maps of Colorado – A Complete Set of BLM Land Ownership Maps,* is one we found useful in researching areas not covered by forest service maps. This book of maps covers the entire state. Another book we used is a large paperback, titled *Colorado Atlas and Gazetteer.* It also covers the entire state and includes topographic elevation contours. However, the contours are usually spaced at a three-hundred-foot elevation difference, which is not very precise, although it does lend a sense of the existing elevation changes. Both books are listed in Sources and Suggested Reading, page 287.

DISCLAIMER

A word of caution is needed about reaching many passes. High-country weather is subject to quick changes, and whether one is on foot or in a vehicle, it is not uncommon to get caught in inclement weather at a pass. Take all the necessary precautions given in hiking guides and remember: Just because the pass is listed in this book doesn't guarantee you can reach it the first time you start out for it. Let common sense guide the way; when bad weather arrives, leave and go back another day. And some individuals are subject to high-altitude illnesses. Retreat to lower altitudes if such an attack occurs. Each pass visitor must assume the responsibility for his or her own safety and limitations.

CONCLUSION

The written word cannot begin to describe the beauty of our state as seen from the passes described in this book. The reader is encouraged to seek out each location and to experience firsthand the magnificence and the beauty of Colorado.

If you encounter difficulty in reaching a pass or have questions and comments about any pass described in this text, we would enjoy hearing from you. Write to us in care of our publisher.

The listing of passes in this book is a compilation of more than ten years of research. Studying old maps, digging through library files, visiting individuals in outlying communities, talking to government officials, poring over old newspapers, reading explorers' diaries, and driving or hiking to actual sites resulted in the work presented here. We hope we have covered your favorite pass; they're all special to us.

COLORADO PASSES

A

ALLEN CREEK PASS

Elevation: 10,860 feet
Location: T9N R77W, Map 3
County: Jackson/Larimer
Topo: Rawah Lakes
National forest: Roosevelt and
  Colorado State Forest

Allen Creek Pass is accessible by foot via a trail from the west side; it is on the west edge of the Rawah Wilderness Area. It divides the waters of Allen Creek to the west and McIntyre Creek to the east.

Access to trailheads is complicated due to private land holdings. The trail on the west side is through the Colorado State Forest; no direct access trail exists on the east side. The pass is in the Medicine Bow Mountains.

Allen Creek Pass is not named on forest service or topo maps; James Grafton Rogers located and named it in his listing of Colorado's geographic features.

ALTMAN PASS

Elevation: 11,940 feet
Location: T51N R5E, Map 5
County: Chaffee/Gunnison
Topo: Cumberland Pass
National forest: Gunnison/San
  Isabel
On the Continental Divide
Other name: Alpine

Altman Pass is accessible by foot. It divides the waters of Tunnel Gulch to the north and Middle Quartz Creek to the south.

The pass is named for "Colonel" Henry Altman, an early stage operator. Altman is credited with discovering the pass while looking for a wagon road route between St. Elmo and Pitkin. A stage toll road crossed the pass for a few years in the 1880s.

The narrow-gauge Alpine Tunnel was constructed by the Denver, South Park and Pacific Railway, beginning in 1880, under Altman Pass. The tunnel sloped from an altitude of 11,546 feet to a high point of 11,608 feet, and it was 1,771 feet long. It is the next-highest point ever reached by steam-powered locomotive in the world. It was also the first tunnel under Colorado's Continental Divide. Altitude, weather, and remoteness made the tunnel construction difficult for the laborers, many of whom lived at St. Elmo.

This old photograph, taken by W. H. Jackson in the 1880s, shows the west portal of the well-known Alpine Tunnel under Altman Pass. (*Photograph courtesy Denver Public Library, Western History Department*)

Over ten thousand workers helped on the construction job—and there was no loss of life.

California redwood was brought in to line the tunnel after the engineers discovered the mountain through which they were boring issued loose granite. The first train passed through the tunnel in July 1882. An attempt to reopen the tunnel after a cave-in in 1895 cost four lives. The rail line was abandoned in 1910.

Access on the east side is by 4WD vehicle to the ghost town of Hancock, then by foot along the old railroad grade. The automobile road on the west side follows the old rail-road grade from Pitkin via forest route #839.

A small building near the west portal holds memorabilia about the tunnel. Both tunnel portals have collapsed and are now closed off. These portals were named, appropriately, Atlantic and Pacific.

A good foot trail leads up and over the pass, connecting the portals of the Alpine Tunnel. The pass is on a saddle between Mount Helmers and Mount Poor.

ANDREWS PASS

Elevation: 11,980 feet
Location: T4N R74W, Map 3

County: Grand/Larimer
Topo: McHenrys Peak
In Rocky Mountain National Park
On the Continental Divide

Andrews Pass is accessible by foot, and only from the west side. It divides the waters of Hallett Creek to the west and Andrews Creek to the east.

The pass is named for Edwin B. Andrews, who was, in 1897, an early climber of the glacier located on the east side of the pass. Other geographic features nearby are also named Andrews.

No trails to the pass exist from the east. Hikers use the ridge line to cross the pass above the glacier. Expert ice climbers come down from the top via Andrews Glacier. From the west, hikers climb up the North Inlet trail. The area is known for its spectacular views.

The Alva Adams Water Diversion Tunnel runs under the pass.

ANGEL PASS

Elevation: 11,990 feet
Location: T12S R87W, Map 5
County: Gunnison
Topo: Oh-be-joyful
National forest: Gunnison

Angel Pass is accessible by foot. It is on the west edge of the Raggeds Wilderness Area. It divides the waters of Middle Anthracite Creek to the west and Poverty Gulch to the east.

This pass was used extensively by early settlers as a stock driveway trail between the Slate River area and Paonia. Hikers and mountain bikes in the summer and skiers in the winter now use this pretty pass.

Angel Pass is located northwest of Crested Butte up Poverty Gulch. The Augusta Mine is to the east, Augusta Mountain is to the north, and Richmond Mountain is to the south of the pass.

ANTELOPE PASS

Elevation: 7,899 feet
Location: T2N R80W, Map 2
County: Grand
Topo: Gunsight Pass
On BLM land

Antelope Pass is accessible by passenger car on county road #25. It divides the waters of Hay Gulch to the west and Troublesome Creek to the east.

An old stage road once crossed the pass. The top is an open, wide view that overlooks a valley floor. The mountain to the south is Little Wolford Mountain.

ANTHRACITE PASS

Elevation: 10,280 feet
Location: T12S R88W, Map 5
County: Gunnison/Pitkin
Topo: Marble
National forest: Gunnison/
   White River
Other name: The Gap

Anthracite Pass is accessible by foot on the northern edge of the Raggeds Wilderness Area. It divides the waters of Yule Creek to the north and North Anthracite Creek to the south.

Its earliest known regular use is around 1916; however, the pass was located by the Hayden survey party when they explored here in 1873.

The pass is located west of the Yule Marble Quarry, one-half mile east of Marble Peak, and three miles east of Ragged Mountain. A foot trail ascends from the south, going up North Anthracite Creek. From the north a trail runs from Marble, about four miles away. Anthracite Pass is in the rugged West Elk mountain range.

ANTONE GAP

Elevation: 8,404 feet
Location: T12N R102W, Map 1
County: Moffat
Topo: Beaver Basin
On BLM land

Antone Gap is accessible by 4WD. It divides the waters of Johnson Draw to the north and Beaver Creek to the south.

The pass is located just above Rocky Reservoir and Bishop Hunting Camps. The top is open, flat, and often windy. This area is regularly used for cattle grazing.

Antone Gap is named on the topo map.

ARAPAHO PASS

Elevation: 11,906 feet
Location: T1N R74W, Map 3
County: Boulder/Grand
Topo: Monarch Lake
National forest: Arapaho/Roosevelt
On the Continental Divide

Arapaho Pass is accessible by foot via national forest trails #904 on the east side (Roosevelt National Forest) and #6 on the west side (Arapaho National Forest), in the Indian Peaks Wilderness Area. It divides the waters of Arapaho Creek to the west and the North Fork of Middle Boulder Creek to the east.

The pass is believed to have been used very little by Indians before settlers arrived. A wagon road crossed the pass in the late 1800s and early 1900s. In 1864, an early-day traveler wrote of crossing the pass via a rough and dangerous road. Winter crossings were difficult due to winds and storms. The route was used regularly, though, even as a freight route.

A charter was granted the Overland Wagon Road Company in 1865 to construct a toll road from Denver via Boulder City and Arapaho Pass to the western boundary of Colorado Territory. The Middle and North Park Wagon Road Company, in 1874, announced a plan for a turnpike, which would follow an old path over the pass. In 1904, the state legislative body set aside five thousand dollars to construct a road

Switchbacks on the trail ahead can sometimes discourage hikers. This view is of the west side of Arapaho Pass, northeast of Granby.

across the pass. Boulder County built its share on the east side; Grand County didn't do the west side. Considered for, but not used as, a possible military route, the road on the east side became the easy hiking trail that is still used today.

In the late 1960s, a proposed Boulder-to-Granby tollway, cutting under the Continental Divide at Arapaho Pass, got strong support from West Slope residents. The effort was short-lived, however, and the area was named a wilderness area shortly thereafter.

Arapaho is one of the most-hiked passes in the state due to its proximity to high population centers on the Front Range. The trail up the west side begins at Monarch Lake, and a marker names the top of the pass. Be sure to visit Lake Dorothy while at the top. Looking east on a clear day, you can see the plains far below.

Old mine shafts and equipment add interest for trail users. The Fourth of July Mine, near the top on the east side, was one of the greatest silver mines in the Hessie area. It was discovered in 1875 and closed by 1900.

The trail was upgraded by the Boy Scouts in 1981. An older trail to the top can be seen along the North Fork of the Middle Boulder Creek down in the valley on the east side, below the present trail.

The Arapaho Glacier is located northeast of the pass, on Arapaho Peak. The glacier provides about ten percent of Boulder's water supply.

Earlier in this century, organized climbs to the glacier and the pass were arranged for large groups of people.

Arapaho Pass is on the Continental Divide Trail. If you're fortunate enough to be on the pass on a certain day each summer, you can observe the exchange of tee shirts, a ritual participated in by realtor groups of Grand and Boulder counties. The tee shirts read: "Get Your [picture of donkey here] Over the Pass."

ARAPAHO PASS

Elevation: 8,954 feet
Location: T5N R81W, Map 2
County: Grand/Jackson
Topo: Spicer Peak
On private land
On the Continental Divide

Arapaho Pass is not accessible to the public. It divides the waters of Indian Creek to the north and Diamond Creek to the south.

The earliest documented use of the pass is around 1870, when it was a road. In 1906, five hundred dollars was used to improve the road. Then in 1922, the trail was redefined and rebuilt. By 1923, it had been abandoned in favor of a road over Muddy Pass, and it deteriorated into a trail by 1930.

Captain John Fremont called the pass one of the most beautiful he had ever seen when he visited in 1844. It was used by Arapaho Indians who made hunting trips into North Park from the plains. Utes were believed to have stolen horses in Boulder County and then used the pass to cross back into their homelands.

The pass is on private property. The old trail leading over it can be seen from a forest service road. The Continental Divide Trail skirts the pass, avoiding the private land.

This Arapaho Pass is located north of North Ryder Peak in the Rabbit Ears mountain range.

ARGENTINE PASS

Elevation: 13,207 feet
Location: T5S R75W, Map 6

County: Clear Creek/Summit
Topo: Grays Peak
National forest: Arapaho
On the Continental Divide
Other names: Georgetown,
    Sanderson, Snake River

Argentine Pass is accessible by foot from the west side, via forest service trail #77, and by 4WD from the east side. It divides the waters of Peru Creek to the west and Leavenworth Creek to the east.

Although the pass is close to the Peru mining district, its name is not from the South American word *Argentina*. Rather, the name comes from the Latin word for silver, *argent*.

A wagon team labors past a high snowbank and up the east side of Argentine Pass in this historical photograph. (*Photograph courtesy Denver Public Library, Western History Department*)

A road was constructed over the pass in the 1860s. It was first called Sanderson Pass, after a pioneer family who ran a stagecoach there. In the 1870s it became Snake River Pass, named for the river to its west. In 1867, Stephen Decatur and the Georgetown and Snake River Wagon Road Company began construction of a toll road that carried freight and passenger stagecoaches from Denver after it opened in 1869.

The name of the pass was changed to Argentine when the mining district of East Argentine became a good producer. Both silver and gold were found nearby. Stories are told of accidents on the steep road over the pass when wind, rock slides, the narrowness of the road, and wagon failures caused loss of life.

This area was one of the heaviest ore-producing sections in Colorado. Waldorf, on the east side of the pass, and Argentine, Decatur, and Chihuahua on the west side were thriving mining communities that have passed into oblivion.

William H. Jackson took many photos when he accompanied the Hayden survey party in 1873 to Argentine Pass. Early in the 1900s, an attempt was made to tunnel below the Continental Divide under Mount Edwards, near the pass. That tunnel is now used for a water diversion pipeline.

Argentine Pass was on the dividing line between Spanish and French land ownership on the western North American continent. Some historians claim a marker was found (many years ago) to attest to this boundary point.

The pass is located between Mount Edwards and Argentine Peak. The top is well above timberline and has great views toward Grays and Torreys peaks. Due to height and openness, the top of the pass is a barren and lonely spot. The area is especially prone to electrical storms and bad weather. One-sixth of the state of Colorado is said to be visible from the top, and Mount of the Holy Cross can be seen in the far distance on a very clear day. Many visitors to Argentine Pass today also drive up Mount McClellan, just to the northeast of the pass. Mountain bikers like the challenge of the pass trail.

AVALANCHE PASS

Elevation: 12,100 feet
Location: T11S R87W, Map 5
County: Gunnison
Topo: Marble
National forest: White River
Other names: Coyote, Silver Creek

Avalanche Pass is accessible by foot on forest service trail #1971 in the Maroon Bells–Snowmass Wilderness Area. It divides the waters of the West Fork of Anthracite Creek to the north and Carbonate Creek to the south.

The pass is named for the nearby creek, which in turn is believed to be named for the avalanches that clear out the area each winter.

The earliest known regular use of the pass is around 1926, when it was a pack trail. Today's trail over the pass is well maintained, scenic, and has good views from the top.

AZTEC DIVIDE

Elevation: 6,000 feet
Location: T35N R17W, Map 7
County: Montezuma
Topo: Mud Creek

Public access through private lands

Aztec Divide is accessible by passenger car on county road #21. It divides the waters of Mud Creek to the north and Navajo Wash to the south.

Sleeping Ute Mountain is located to the west of the divide ridge. The pass is a minor crossing in uninspiring, open, sagebrush-covered desert land. Aztec Divide is named on the topo map. ☐

B

BAKER PASS

Elevation: 11,253 feet
Location: T5N R76W, Map 3
County: Grand/Jackson
Topo: Mount Richthofen
National forest: Arapaho/Routt
On the Continental Divide

Baker Pass is accessible by foot via forest service trails #1141 on the north side (Routt National Forest) and #29 on the south side (Arapaho National Forest), in the Never Summer Wilderness Area. The pass divides the waters of the South Fork of Michigan Creek to the north and Baker Gulch to the south.

The pass is named either for Jim Baker, mountain man of the 1830s, or John Baker, mountain man and climber of the 1870s. John was the first person to reach the summit of Baker Mountain. He climbed it in

1875 and filed a claim for a mine on the mountainside.

The earliest known regular use of the pass is around 1905. It has never been anything but a foot trail, and it is currently part of the Continental Divide trail system.

Access to the pass from the east is through Rocky Mountain National Park, up Baker Gulch. From the west, reach the pass by hiking up the Michigan River Valley. The cloud mountains (Mount Nimbus, Mount Stratus, Mount Cirrus, and Mount Cumulus) are just to the east and provide a colorful accent to the ascent.

Baker Pass is located in the Never Summer mountain range.

BASSAM PARK PASS

Elevation: 9,660 feet
Location: T15S R76W, Map 6

County: Chaffee/Park
Topo: Castle Rock Gulch
National forest: San Isabel

Bassam Park Pass is accessible by passenger car on county road #187. It divides the waters of Cottonwood Creek to the west and Cals Creek to the east.

The pass is often mistakenly called "Balsam Pass," but a local historian affirms the name "Bassam" comes from early settlers in the Nathrop area. The correct pronunciation is bass'-am.

The top of the pass is at an offset four-way intersection on the county line and is marked by a cattle guard. The top is open and distinguishable only because the road begins to descend at this point. The pass is a mile and a half north of Bassam Park.

Bassam Park Pass is not named on forest service or topo maps. James Grafton Rogers located and named it in his listing of Colorado's geographic features.

BAXTER PASS

Elevation: 8,422 feet
Location: T5S R103W, Map 4
County: Garfield
Topo: Baxter Pass
On BLM land

Baxter Pass is accessible on the south by passenger car on county road #201, and on the north by 4WD. It divides the waters of Evacuation Creek to the north and West Salt Creek to the south.

The pass is named for C. O. Baxter, of the Barber Asphalt Company of St. Louis. Barber Asphalt developed the gilsonite mines near Dragon, Utah.

An old Ute trail ran through this area. The Indians used the route to go between the Gunnison region and the White River and Green River regions of western Colorado.

Baxter Pass was crossed by the Uintah Railway in the early 1900s and used to move gilsonite from the mining area to a main rail line west of Grand Junction. The line was abandoned in 1939; the gilsonite is now moved via a pipeline over the pass to Mack. This route contained some of the hardest grades any railroad ever attempted to climb. Auxiliary engines were used to push and pull the freight trains to the top of the pass.

A tunnel under the pass was seriously considered in the mid-1910s. About this same time, a small town sprang up near the top of the pass. Both the tunnel and the town died; the tunnel before it started, the town shortly after that.

Today's visitor can drive the old railroad grade. Stay on county roads, because this area contains much private property. The top is accessible from the south by passenger car. Going down the north side, the road has been blocked in recent years by a landslide near McAndrews Lake. When the road is open, it goes through to Bonanza, Utah. A 4WD is required on the north side of the pass, and on the south side when there have been recent rains. The traveler passes natural gas wells and pipeline pump stations, side roads and old buildings — all of which add interest to an otherwise lonely bit of northwest Colorado.

BEAR PASS

Elevation: 12,020 feet
Location: T6S R76W, Map 6
County: Summit
Topo: Keystone
National forest: Arapaho

Bear Pass is accessible by foot, but no established trail currently goes over the pass. It divides the waters of Saints John Creek to the north and the North Fork of the Swan River to the south. Saints John Creek was called Bear Creek in earlier days.

The town site for Saints John was discovered when J. Coley, a prospector, came over Bear Pass from Breckenridge in 1863. He saw silver ore on a mountain about a thousand feet above where he located the town, originally called Coleyville.

Father Dyer used the pass route to carry mail between Montezuma and Breckenridge, beginning in 1865. Later, a pack trail was developed and used for regular mail service between the two points.

Bear Pass is south of the Wild Irishman Mine, southeast of Key-

stone Mountain and on the southwest flank of Glacier Mountain. Topo and forest service maps do not show Bear Pass; it is located and named from historical research.

BEAR CREEK PASS

Elevation: 12,445 feet
Location: T41N, R9W, Map 7
County: San Juan/San Miguel
Topo: Ophir
National forest: San Juan/ Uncompahgre
Other name: South Fork

Bear Creek Pass is accessible by foot on the north side via forest service trail #410. It divides the waters of the Lake Fork of the South Fork of the San Miguel River to the west and the South Fork of Mineral Creek to the east. The pass is named for one of the creeks it heads. On early maps, today's Mineral Creek was called Bear Creek.

Bear Creek Pass was noted by the Hayden survey party in late summer 1874. They traversed fallen timber, bogs, and rock slides to cross this pass.

The pass is a ridge crossing located on a good trail northwest of Silverton and east of San Miguel Peak. It is honored with a poem, "Colorado," by Ethelle Bobier, in which the author extols the views from the top. The pass is not named on forest service or topo maps.

BECKWITH PASS

Elevation: 9,940 feet
Location: T14S R88W, Map 5
County: Gunnison
Topo: Anthracite Range
National forest: Gunnison

Beckwith Pass is accessible by foot on forest service trail #840, and on the north edge of the West Elk Wilderness Area. It divides the waters of Ruby Anthracite Creek to the north and Cliff Creek to the south.

It is named for Lieutenant E. G. Beckwith, of the 1853 Gunnison expedition group. The earliest known regular use of the pass route is around 1900, when it was developed as a pack trail.

The pass is located two miles east of East Beckwith Mountain and is in the rugged West Elk mountain range. A good trail provides easy hiking to the pass. Good views to the south are of the Castles and other unique rock or mountain formations. Horses use the trail for access into the wilderness area.

The pass can be an easy hike — or combined with other passes for a loop trip taking more time and requiring more elevation change.

BELLS GAP

Elevation: 6,347 feet
Location: T27S R67W, Map 10
County: Huerfano
Topo: Black Hills
Public access through private land

Bells Gap is accessible by passenger car on CO69. It divides the waters of Oja Dealaino Arroyo to the west and Butte Creek to the east.

This minor watershed divide is barely off a major highway (I25) but is virtually unknown. It crosses a minor ridge on the road to Gardner. North of the pass is the south face of Greenhorn Mountain, with the tip of Pikes Peak visible to the northeast. The Spanish Peaks are visible to the south.

The top is open and is barren sagebrush-covered land. An old railroad crossed the pass to serve the nearby coal mines. Many old building foundations can be seen, some at the top of the pass.

Bells Gap is named on the topo map.

BERTHOUD PASS

Elevation: 11,315 feet
Location: T3S R75W, Map 3
County: Clear Creek/Grand
Topo: Berthoud Pass
National forest: Arapaho
On the Continental Divide

Berthoud Pass is passenger-car accessible on US40. It divides the waters of the Fraser River to the west and the West Fork of Clear Creek to the east.

The pass is named for Captain Edward Berthoud, who surveyed the area with Jim Bridger for a potential railroad crossing in 1861.

Little or no indication exists that

A bronze tablet placed in 1929 by the Daughters of the American Revolution marks the top of Berthoud Pass.

the area was used as an Indian crossing prior to discovery of the pass by white explorers. Once the pass was marked by a trail, Indians then used the crossing. Federal Indian agents issued supplies to high-country Utes at Empire. As many as fifteen hundred Indians crossed the pass each summer during the years 1865–1867 to receive allotments of cattle, flour, and blankets.

Colorado Governor John Evans and *Rocky Mountain News* publisher William Byers were instrumental in establishing a wagon road over the pass. A Concord stagecoach made the first trip using the new toll road in November of 1874. The first mail contract over the pass was awarded in 1875. The pass was

on the principal route between eastern Colorado and Middle Park during the 1870s and early 1880s. By 1888, local ranchers used the pass to move cattle from one feeding area to another. Around the turn of the century, as other roads developed, use of the pass by stagecoaches and cattle declined. Early-day winter crossings often had to be made at night to avoid the boggy soil conditions at the top that occurred in daylight hours; at night the soil was frozen, allowing for easier traverse.

Telephone service first crossed the pass in 1903. Major road development work began in 1919. By 1924, the road had been improved and was named as part of the "Victory Highway," commemorating American success in World War I. The road was kept open year-round beginning in 1932–33. However, it was not paved until 1938. A celebration of the new paving included a thousand-car caravan on July 3 of that year. Some cars came from the east, some from the west, and all met at the top of the pass. Colorado's oldest ski area opened atop the pass in 1937. Currently under consideration is a four-mile tunnel through the pass as an alternative to fifteen miles of road over the pass summit.

An early-day writer, Chauncey Thomas, is buried near the pass summit. He wrote "Snow Story" in 1900, about a mailman delivering mail during a blizzard on the pass.

BIG HORN PASS

Elevation: 11,340 feet
Location: T38N R1E, Map 8
County: Mineral
Topo: South River Peak
National forest: Rio Grande/
  San Juan
On the Continental Divide

Big Horn Pass is accessible by foot on forest service trail #813, in the Weminuche Wilderness Area. It divides the waters of Lake Creek to the west and the South Fork of the Rio Grande River to the east.

A 1927 Rio Grande National Forest map shows and names this location as Bighorn (one word) Pass. A 1931 listing of state passes designates it as Big Horn Pass. It is located on the Continental Divide between Rock Lakes on the west and Spruce Lakes on the east.

The pass is three miles south of Mount Hope and on the Continental Divide Trail.

BIG HORN PASS

Elevation: 10,670 feet
Location: T5N R73W, Map 3
County: Larimer
Topo: Estes Park
In Rocky Mountain National Park

Big Horn Pass is accessible by foot, but no established trail currently goes over the pass. It divides the waters of the Roaring River to the west and Black Canyon Creek to the east.

This narrow saddle is located between Big Horn Mountain and Mount Tileston. The pass is not named on forest service or topo maps; it was named and located in an early listing of Colorado places.

BIGELOW DIVIDE

Elevation: 9,390 feet
Location: T22S R69W, Map 9
County: Custer
Topo: Deer Peak
National forest: San Isabel

Bigelow Divide is accessible by passenger car on CO165. It divides the waters of South Hardscrabble Creek to the north and Bigelow Creek to the south.

This is a wide, open ridge divide in the Wet Mountain Valley. The pass is just southwest of Round Top Mountain; its top is marked with a state highway marker. The road is known as the Greenhorn Highway.

BISON PASS

Elevation: 11,300 feet
Location: T9S R73W, Map 6
County: Park
Topo: Farnum Peak
National forest: Pike

Bison Pass is accessible by foot via forest service trails #629 on the south side (Ute Creek Trail) and #607 on the north side (Brookside-McCurdy Trail), in the Lost Creek Wilderness Area. It divides the waters of Indian Creek to the north and Ute Creek to the south.

To reach the pass, take either the Lost Creek Trail or the Ute Creek Trail to the top, located adjacent to Bison Peak. The grassy knoll at the pass top gives views toward Antero Reservoir across South Park and onto the mountain ranges behind. The pass is signed; don't be fooled by the false summit south of the actual pass. The pass is one and a half miles southwest of Bison Peak.

Bison Pass is not named on forest service or topo maps. It is shown on Trails Illustrated maps.

BLACK BEAR PASS

Elevation: 12,830 feet
Location: T42N R8W, Map 7
County: San Juan/San Miguel
Topo: Ironton
National forest: San Juan/
  Uncompahgre
Other name: Ingram

Black Bear Pass is accessible by 4WD on forest routes #648 (on the west side) and #823 (on the east side). It divides the waters of Ingram Creek to the west and Mineral Creek to the east.

The Black Bear road was developed to reach the Black Bear Mine in the Ingram Basin, thence the name and the alternate name for this pass. An old wagon road existed in the 1800s, which fell into disuse in the early 1900s.

The alternative name comes from

J. Ingram, who discovered the Smuggler Mine in 1876. Some people believe the pass should be called "Ingram Pass" and the road "Black Bear Road." Neither name has been accepted by the United States Geological Survey Board on Geographic Names. However, the name used most often now, by locals, writers, and visitors, is Black Bear Pass.

Many people, Coloradans and visitors alike, claim this to be their favorite pass in Colorado. It is spectacular, scary, and remote, although on most any summer day when the pass is open a regular traffic jam occurs.

The road was opened to 4WD traffic in 1959 through the efforts of the Telluride Jeep Club. It is very narrow; some 4WDs must turn, back up, and turn again on the switchbacks descending the west side. At the top, the road crosses a rock outcropping, and summer runoff creates a double hazard of wet and rock to drive across. To some drivers, this spot is actually more frightening than the tight switchbacks below.

Note: This is a one-way pass on the west side. Also, rented 4WDs should not be taken over the road. Take a ride with one of the companies in Ouray or Telluride, who drive this every day. Even experienced drivers will find this a frightening drive. The road is open only about a month or six weeks each year due to snow and wet conditions.

The pass is located above Telluride, and one of the reasons the road

The booming community of Telluride nestles close to the western foot of Black Bear Pass.

is so well liked is for its view of the little town in the valley below. Bridal Veil Falls, to the south of the pass, is one of the most photographed natural wonders in our state.

The view of the pass from the east end of Telluride is as awesome as the view of the town from the pass. Looking at the double-Z that climbs straight up the mountain makes most people think they couldn't really have traveled down it. While in town, look for the tee shirts that proclaim, "I survived Black Bear Pass."

BLACK POWDER PASS

Elevation: 12,159 feet
Location: T7S R77W, Map 6

County: Park/Summit
Topo: Boreas Pass
National forest: Arapaho/Pike
On the Continental Divide

Black Powder Pass is accessible by foot, but no established trail currently goes over the pass. It divides the waters of Indiana Creek to the west and French Creek to the east.

The USGS Board on Geographic Names officially named the pass in 1976, accepting the name suggested by the Colorado State Muzzle Loading Association to honor the sport of shooting black powder weapons.

The pass is located between Bald and Boreas mountains. Access to it is from the top of Boreas Pass and around the west side of Boreas Mountain. Only a game trail exists to the pass, but it is an easy hike to follow a drainage ditch and then a broad valley to the pass, which stays in sight, above timberline.

There is no evidence of much historical usage of this pass. Due to the proximity of Boreas Pass, it is very unlikely Black Powder Pass was used regularly. There is a two-track trail along the ditch, indicating some recent vehicular (probably 4WD before it was closed off to vehicles) traffic.

BLACK SAGE PASS

Elevation: 9,745 feet
Location: T49N R5E, Map 5
County: Gunnison
Topo: Sargents
National forest: Gunnison

Black Sage Pass is accessible by passenger car on forest route #887. It divides the waters of Spring Creek to the west and Mountain Spring Creek to the east. The pass is named for nearby Black Sage Peak (a mile north).

The Hayden survey party used this crossing to travel between Pitkin and White Pine. A route over the pass was developed about 1880, when traffic to the mining camps needed a shorter route than what had previously been available. Black Sage Pass made a quicker access, and the road was not difficult to build.

When the railroad arrived at Pitkin, the pass was still used for local freight movement. By then the resort area near Waunita required regular stagecoaches for passengers and supplies. In the late 1890s a stage station atop the pass was still operating. The road has survived and is still a popular drive.

This is a minor crossing in a forested area of a minor ridge line, but it is located in a pretty setting and is easily accessible.

BLACKHAWK PASS

Elevation: 11,970 feet
Location: T40N R10W, Map 7
County: Dolores
Topo: Hermosa Peak
National forest: San Juan

Blackhawk Pass is accessible by foot. It divides the waters of Silver Creek to the north and Straight Creek to the south. The pass is named for nearby Blackhawk Mountain.

This pass is on the Colorado Trail. The foot trail over the pass was constructed in 1986 and is marked by cairns. A small spring issues from a rock cliff just below the pass.

Blackhawk Pass is located on the east flank of Blackhawk Mountain. Good views from the top are of the La Plata Range to the south and Lizard Head to the north. The pass is not named on forest service, topo, or Trails Illustrated maps; it is named and located from Colorado Trail reports.

BLIZZARD PASS

Elevation: 11,822 feet
Location: T14S R69W, Map 6
County: El Paso
Topo: Pikes Peak
On land owned by Colorado
  Springs Water Department

Blizzard Pass is currently not accessible to the public. It divides the waters of the East Fork of Beaver Creek to the west and Boehmer Creek to the east. The pass is named for the blizzard weather conditions that can occur in the vicinity.

A construction camp, located at the pass, was used while the Strickler Tunnel was built.

The pass is named and shown on the *1989 Map of Pikes Peak Region,* by Robert Ormes and Robert Houdek. It is located just west of the Boehmer Reservoir Number 2.

BLOWOUT PASS

Elevation: 11,780 feet
Location: T37N R5E, Map 8
County: Rio Grande
Topo: Jasper
National forest: Rio Grande

Blowout Pass is accessible by 4WD via forest routes #329 (on the north side) and #280 (on the south side). It divides the waters of Bennett Creek to the north and Spring Creek to the south.

This route was used in the late 1800s to move ore from Summitville to Del Norte; later, it was used for freighting.

The pass is located in a remote area. The road climbs up and over the pass, easily defined by the terrain. Sheep and cattle graze all summer atop the pass.

Look for views of Sheep Mountain and Bennett Peak from the top. At the foot of the pass on the south side is the ghost town of Jasper, one of the prettiest little spots in the state.

BLUE HILL

Elevation: 7,660 feet
Location: T5S R86W, Map 5
County: Eagle
Topo: Cottonwood Pass
On BLM land

Blue Hill is accessible by passenger car on county road #10A. It divides the waters of Cottonwood Creek to the west and Gypsum Creek to the east.

This is a minor pass located south of Gypsum and three miles east of Gobbler Knob.

BLUE LAKE PASS

Elevation: 11,020 feet
Location: T8N R76W, Map 3
County: Larimer
Topo: Clark Peak
National forest: Roosevelt

Blue Lake Pass is accessible by foot on forest service trail #959, in the Rawah Wilderness Area. It divides the waters of the West Branch of the Laramie River to the north and Fall Creek to the south.

The pass is not named on forest service or topo maps. It is named on Trails Illustrated maps. Various hiking guides also give information on how to access the pass. However, the trailhead is no longer at the Chambers Lake Campground, as is indicated in most trail descriptions. The trailhead is now on CO14, about one mile south of Chambers Lake.

BLUE LAKES PASS

Elevation: 12,980 feet
Location: T43N R8W, Map 7

County: Ouray
Topo: Telluride
National forest: Uncompahgre

Blue Lakes Pass is accessible by foot on the eastern edge of the Mount Sneffels Wilderness Area. East access is via wildflower-filled Yankee Boy Basin. A 4WD can be driven, on forest route #853.1B, to within about one mile of the pass, then hiking is required.

The pass divides the waters of East Fork Dallas Creek to the north and Sneffels Creek to the south.

In some writings the name is given as Blue Lake Pass; the plural usage in this text is for the three lakes below the pass.

This high pass, adjacent to the over-14,000-foot Mount Sneffels, is on the edge of the Mount Sneffels Wilderness Area.

The pass is on the south shoulder of Mount Sneffels; the first part of the trail to the pass is used regularly in the summer as an access to this popular "fourteener." The San Juan Division of the Hayden survey holds the record for the first ascent of Mount Sneffels, in 1874. Franklin Rhoda, leader of one of the Hayden parties, wrote, "Just to the south of Mount Sneffels was . . . a comparatively low gap, which we felt was passable for good foot-climbers."

The earliest known regular use of the pass was around 1917, as a pack trail. The three Blue Lakes on the west side of the pass are well-known fishing spots, and access to them is shorter from the east, over the pass, than by the long hike required to reach them from the northwest side.

The pass is a narrow, sharp saddle between Gilpin Peak and Mount Sneffels, with rocky ridges extending off each mountain. Look into the Mount Sneffels Wilderness Area to the west, then look northeast to Teakettle Mountain and the little Coffeepot Mountain. A sign marks and names this crossing.

BLUE MESA SUMMIT

Elevation: 8,704 feet
Location: T48N R5W, Map 5
County: Gunnison
Topo: Curecanti Needle
Public access through private land

Blue Mesa Summit is accessible by passenger car on US50. It divides the waters of the Little Cimarron River to the west and Blue Creek to the east.

Captain John Gunnison, in his survey of the Black Canyon of the Gunnison River, crossed over this pass in 1853. He decided the route was too difficult for a railroad. His men had to carry the wagon carts over the mesa summit. It took his group two weeks to cover forty miles. The area was later named Son-of-a-Bitch Hill. Otto Mears built the first road over the summit sometime shortly after 1875. In 1881, settlers poured over Blue Mesa Summit to reach the vacated Ute lands for homesteading.

The drive over the pass today feels more like crossing a wide high ridge. The top is open and lacks great views. It is not named on forest service or topo maps but is marked with a highway department sign and is located south of Morrow Point.

BOLAM PASS

Elevation: 11,340 feet
Location: T40N R9W, Map 7
County: Dolores/San Miguel
Topo: Hermosa Peak
National forest: San Juan
Other names: Barlow Creek,
**   Hermosa, Hermosa Mountain**

Bolam Pass is accessible by 4WD on forest route #578. It divides the waters of the Dolores River to the north and Hermosa Creek to the south.

Bolam Pass shows up on forest service maps beginning about 1951, but evidence of prehistoric Indian use appears near the pass. Prospectors crossed the pass in 1861, and in 1881 it was surveyed for a railroad.

The road over the pass has been known as the Scotch Creek Toll Road and the Rockwood-to-Rico Road. The toll gate was located many years ago near the east end of Hermosa Park. The road was improved to provide access to the Graysill Mine, which was discovered in 1945 and produced vanadium ore. Later, uranium was taken from the mine, which kept the area alive until the 1960s. Now only one building is left to mark this important mining spot. The mine is located just a mile below the pass, on the south side. The road has been maintained to serve hikers and backcountry visitors, who like to explore.

Although the pass is navigable by car most of the time, 4WD is required when the road is wet. The top is covered by trees and the road does not cross in the lowest part of the saddle. Good views of the Dolores River Valley and Lizard Head Peak can be seen from near the top. The Colorado Trail crosses the pass.

BONITO PASS

Elevation: 11,250 feet
Location: T37N R3E, Map 8
County: Rio Grande
Topo: Elwood Pass

National forest: Rio Grande/ San Juan
On the Continental Divide

Bonito Pass is accessible by foot on the Hot Creek Stock Driveway Trail. It divides the waters of Pass Creek to the north and Elwood Creek to the south.

The pass has a good view (*bonito* means "pretty" in Spanish) to the south. An old stock drive way brings livestock into the area for summer grazing. A marker at the top indicates Wolf Creek Pass is seven miles to the north and Park Creek is four miles to the south.

Many logging roads here make it difficult to follow topo, county, or forest service maps. Loggers have also chained off some roads, requiring hiking to reach the Continental Divide trail to traverse the mountains. The pass is just east of Silver Peak.

BOOTH CREEK PASSES

Elevation: 12,060 feet
Location: T4S R80W, Map 6
County: Eagle
Topo: Vail East
National forest: White River

Booth Creek Passes are accessible by foot in the Eagles Nest Wilderness Area. They divide the waters of the Piney River to the north and Booth Creek to the south.

There are actually two crossings: one pass route crosses between

Piney Lake and Pitkin Lake via the Booth Lake trail, and the second route uses an east fork of the creek that comes out of the lake. Spider Mountain lies between the two passes.

Hikers in the Vail vicinity are fond of this area because of the waterfalls and wildflowers—both abound in the Booth Creek Gulch.

These passes were first identified by Ormes in his *Guide to the Colorado Mountains.*

BOREAS PASS

Elevation: 11,481 feet
Location: T7S R77W, Map 6
County: Park/Summit
Topo: Boreas Pass
National forest: Arapaho/Pike
On the Continental Divide
Other names: Breckenridge,
**   Hamilton, Tarryall, Ute**

Boreas Pass is accessible to passenger car when it is open each summer via forest routes #33 on the south side (Pike National Forest) and #10 on the north side (Arapaho National Forest). It divides the waters of Indiana Creek to the west and Tarryall Creek to the east.

The name of the pass has a long evolution. It was first called Ute (in 1859) for the Indians who used it, then Hamilton or Tarryall (in the early 1860s) in honor of the mining communities nearby on the east side. Then, as the Breckenridge mining area grew, the pass assumed the

name of this community on the west side. Later (sometime before 1898), the name Boreas was given it, to describe the severe winds that blow across the pass. "Boreas" is the name of the god of the north wind in Greek mythology.

Early-day travelers included the Indians. Utes from northern Utah came down the Blue River, across the pass, through South Park, and on into southern climates to winter. Thomas Farnham, in his diary, wrote that he crossed the area in his western travels in 1839. Miners discovered this crossing and used the route to go between the South Park and Blue River mines. By the late 1850s, miners used the route, but it was only a footpath. When the mining boom hit the area in 1860, the route became a busy footpath. Skis and snowshoes were used in the winter. The men who used the route recognized the need to improve the road and organized their own work party to do it. Regular stagecoach travel began; as many as six coaches per week were scheduled. By 1868 a good road was in place.

Father John L. Dyer used the pass, and on one of his trips discovered the Warrior's Mark Mine. He was also responsible for starting the little community of Dyersville in Indiana Gulch in 1881. Also in 1881, a narrow-gauge railroad was built over the pass by the Denver, South Park and Pacific division of the Union Pacific Railroad. The trains were used to move ore from the

The remains of old buildings at the rail stop atop Boreas Pass.

Leadville and Breckenridge mines to Denver.

The town at the top was also named Boreas; it served as a railroad stop, telegraph office, and shelter for train crews and passengers. It was the highest post office in the U.S. for many years. (A fire in 1909 erased most of the buildings in the little town.) A snowshed with a passageway to the station had been built at the top to provide protection from the severe winters. Ten more snowsheds provided shelter on the east side of the pass.

One of the important uses for the pass came about in the winter of 1898–1899, when the isolated little hamlet of Breckenridge was snowed in for more than seventy days. Men strapped on snowshoes and headed out over Boreas Pass to reach provisions in South Park. For more than six weeks, workers labored to clear the tracks so the train could again bring in supplies. Finally, in late April 1899, a train broke through and arrived in Breckenridge.

As if snow wasn't enough, late in 1899 a forest fire raged near the top of the pass, destroying some of the snowsheds and threatening a cemetery and animal life.

An amusing story is told about the pass. It seems a circus train was moving from Denver to Leadville and the rail wagons carrying the circus animals could not make it up the Boreas Pass grade. The elephants were removed from their wagon cages and hitched to the train. The added brawn provided by the animals hefted the train up the last three miles to the pass. All reboarded at the top and rode down to Breckenridge.

The railroad did not operate across the pass from 1910 to 1913. Bobcats and mountain lions had set up homes in the tunnel at the top during that time and had to be removed before the tunnel could be used again. The last train moved over the pass and the rail tracks were abandoned in 1937.

The current auto road was built by the U.S. Army Corps of Engineers in 1952, following the old rail route but bypassing the most treacherous feature of the rail route, Windy Point. This road has been entered into the National Register of Historic Places. Boreas Pass is a favorite Sunday-afternoon drive for Front Range residents, particularly when the aspen are wearing fall colors. It is easily accessible from US285 or CO9 and makes an easy round trip from the populated cities on the Front Range. The road takes the traveler by an old water tank, old buildings still standing at the top of the pass, and historic mine diggings. It is closed in the winter.

Today, mountain bikers participate in the Fat Tire Classic over the pass, cross-country skiers use the road, and hikers take a backcountry route between high-country passes via a cairn-marked path.

BOTTLE PASS

Elevation: 11,300 feet
Location: T2S R76W, Map 3
County: Grand
Topo: Bottle Pass
National forest: Arapaho
Other names: Hunter's, Ptarmigan

Bottle Pass is accessible by foot on forest service trail #15. It divides the waters of Crystal Creek to the north and Keyser Creek to the south.

Visitors claim the wind funnels through nearby mountain peaks into a "bottle" at the pass summit.

The earliest known regular use of the pass is around 1880, and it is one of the main trail crossings of the Vasquez mountains.

A good trail leads to the pass. It is used most often as one access to Byers Peak, a popular hiking destination. Bottle Peak is also close by.

BOULDER PASS

Elevation: 11,780 feet
Location: T1S R74W, Map 3
County: Boulder/Grand
Topo: East Portal
National forest: Arapaho/Roosevelt
On the Continental Divide

Boulder Pass is accessible by 4WD. It divides the waters of Ranch Creek to the west and the South Fork of Middle Boulder Creek to the east.

A charter was granted the Overland Wagon Road Company in 1865 to construct a toll road from Denver via Boulder City over the pass to the western boundary of Colorado Territory. Another charter, in 1866, was given to the Middle Park and South Boulder Wagon Road Company to build from mills on South Boulder Creek over the pass into Middle Park. In the late 1860s, the well-used but rough road was considered for a rail route. A tunnel was suggested for the very top. Until the development of other roads, Boulder Pass provided the most open, easy-to-follow route. It was considered the only practicable route for wagons to go and was preferred over the other, more heavily timbered ways that were more suited for animal traffic. One traveler, a photographer who crossed in 1871, told of the steep descent in places on the west side but praised the pretty views from the top.

The east and west sides of the pass use the same access points as does Rollins Pass. Now 4WD-passable, today's road over the pass is rough and rocky. The upkeep on the road was forgotten when railroads, and then auto roads, were built over other passes. Passenger cars often set off from the east side, believing the two-mile route will be as easy as the first hundred yards, which are visible from the main road. It isn't. The pass is not named on forest service or topo maps. It is named on the XYZ maps and identified by a sign on forest route #149. The road over the pass is called the Boulder Wagon Road.

BOULDER-GRAND PASS

Elevation: 12,061 feet
Location: T3N R74W, Map 3
County: Boulder/Grand
Topo: Isolation Peak
In Rocky Mountain National Park
On the Continental Divide

Boulder-Grand Pass is accessible by foot, but no established trail currently goes over the pass. It divides the waters of East Inlet to the west and North St. Vrain Creek to the east.

The pass is named for the two counties it connects. It was used by Indians to cross to and from the plains.

This is one of the most difficult passes to reach. Hikers use the Ouzel Falls Trail route to the top, which is between Mount Alice and Tanima Peak. Rock-scrambling is necessary to attain the top.

BOWEN PASS

Elevation: 11,476 feet
Location: T5N R76W, Map 3
County: Grand/Jackson
Topo: Bowen Mountain
National forest: Arapaho/Routt
On the Continental Divide

Bowen Pass is accessible by foot via forest service trails #1141 on the north side (Routt National Forest) and #118 on the south side (Arapaho National Forest); it is on the west edge of the Never Summer

Wilderness Area. It divides the waters of the Illinois River to the north and Bowen Gulch to the south.

The pass is named for James H. Bourn, who prospected here. He discovered the Wolverine Claim, high up on Bourn Mountain. A mistake in the courthouse records listed the names for the mountain and the pass as "Bowen" rather than "Bourn."

In July 1881, the county road department spent two thousand dollars to develop a road over the pass. In 1882, a mail run between Fraser and Teller City was set up. By 1884, though, this route was given up. The pass is shown and named on a Middle Park map of 1883 but disappears by the 1913 Grand County map because the route over it had been abandoned.

Bowen Pass is a mile west of Bowen Mountain and on the east side of Ruby Mountain in a very narrow gap. Switchbacks are encountered (on the north side) just before the top, which is marked, above timberline, and has good views in every direction. This is a nice hiking area, but it is not well used. Ruby Lake is visible from the top.

BOWMAN PASS

Elevation: 12,241 feet
Location: T11S R83W, Map 5
County: Gunnison/Pitkin
Topo: New York Peak
National forest: Gunnison/
   White River
Other name: Roaring Fork

Bowman Pass is accessible by foot in the Collegiate Peaks Wilderness Area. It divides the waters of Bruin Creek to the north and Bowman Creek to the south.

The pass is named for John Bowman, an early-day resident of an area near a little settlement called Grandview, which was also later named Bowman. He began a stage station there.

Early in 1880, someone placed a crude wooden sign on the pass, reading "This way to the Roaring Fork." The name "Roaring Fork Pass" existed for some time, then "Bowman" came into use.

The pass is above more well-known passes on the same ridge line at Gold Hill. Miners used the crossing to get from the cold, brutal weather of Taylor Park to the more sheltered area near Aspen. The trail has been used as a stock drive way. Thousands of sheep summer on the wide-open hillsides.

A maze of trails near Bowman Pass gives the outdoor enthusiast many opportunities to explore some of Colorado's high country in the Elk mountain range.

BREAKNECK PASS

Elevation: 10,910 feet
Location: T10S R78W, Map 6
County: Park
Topo: Fairplay West
National forest: Pike
Other name: Warmsprings

Breakneck Pass is accessible by 4WD on forest route #175. It divides the waters of Sheep Creek to the west and High Creek to the east.

The first settlers to use the pass encountered great difficulty in going over it because it was so steep; consequently, the common usage of "Breakneck" came into being. The earliest known regular use is around 1910, when a trail was opened into mining digs in Sheep Park.

In a "little" crossing of the "little" Sheep mountain range that runs just in front of the "big" Mosquito Range, this pass leads into Sheep Park. This park is in a valley between the two ranges and hidden from the traveler on US285, only a few miles away. Sheep Park is an appropriate name, because the main use of the area is for grazing sheep.

The area is in a modern development called Warm Springs Ranch. Respect private property and stay on the road all the way to Pike National Forest. The top of the pass is marked with a small road sign. It is located between Sheep Ridge and Round Hill.

Only a few miles off the well-traveled highway, Breakneck Pass makes a good venture into the wooded mountains of central Colorado. The topo map names the pass "Break Neck Pass."

BROWNS PASS

Elevation: 12,010 feet
Location: T14S R81W, Map 5
County: Chaffee/Gunnison
Topo: Mount Yale
**National forest: Gunnison/
San Isabel**
On the Continental Divide

Browns Pass is accessible by foot via forest service trail #1442 from the south; it is in the Collegiate Peaks Wilderness Area. It divides the waters of Texas Creek to the north and the North Fork of Denny Creek to the south.

The crossing was probably used by miners or trappers moving between the supply point at Buena Vista to the eastern reaches of Taylor Park. There are stunning views of the Three Apostles mountains from the top, which is not visible until the very last quarter-mile of the hike. Due to the unusual geographic nature of the Continental Divide here, a panoramic view of many divide peaks can be had from this point.

Today's visitors can make an easy hike to Browns Pass, Hartenstein Lake, Browns Cabin, or Mount Yale —all are available from one trailhead point. This is one of the more popular hiking areas away from the Front Range.

BROWNS PASS

Elevation: 11,372 feet
Location: T10S R78W, Map 6
County: Park
Topo: Fairplay West
National forest: Pike

The mountains known as the Three Apostles are seen here from Browns Pass, west of Buena Vista.

Browns Pass is accessible by 4WD on forest route #176. It divides the waters of Sheep Creek to the west and High Creek to the east. The pass is named for an old prospector of the area (Mr. Brown), who had some claims nearby.

The pass crosses the Sheep mountain ridge between Sheep Mountain and Sheep Ridge and is near timberline. Just west of the top (about one-quarter mile) is a good view of Horseshoe Mountain to the south over Lamb Mountain's west ridge. This view alone is adequate reason for the trip to this pass. The pass is marked by a small sign and is used, other than as a tourist route, for moving sheep into Sheep Park for summer grazing. Lots of columbines, which are getting harder to find in the wild, line the road in late July. Enjoy the cabin ruins atop the pass.

There are forest service gates on this road to contain grazing animals. Be sure to close each gate immediately after using it.

BRUSH CREEK PASS

Elevation: 12,460 feet
Location: T46N R11E, Map 9
County: Custer/Saguache
Topo: Electric Peak
National forest: Rio Grande/
  San Isabel

Brush Creek Pass is accessible by

foot via forest service trails #1356 on the east side and #751 on the west side. It divides the waters of Major Creek to the west and the South Branch of North Brush Creek to the east.

This is one of the minor crossings of the Sangre de Cristo mountain range. It is located above Brush Creek lakes, and may be reached by the North Brush Creek Trail on the east side, and the Major Creek Trail on the west side.

The area is used mostly by hunters. The two Brush Creek lakes are northeast of the pass, which is between Electric Peak (to the southeast) and Lakes Peak (to the northwest). The pass is not named on forest service or topo maps; James Grafton Rogers located and named it in his listing of Colorado's geographic features.

BUCHANAN PASS

Elevation: 11,837 feet
Location: T2N R74W, Map 3
County: Boulder/Grand
Topo: Isolation Peak
National forest: Arapaho/Roosevelt
On the Continental Divide

Buchanan Pass is accessible by foot via forest service trails #2 from the west side (Arapaho National Forest) and #910 from the east side (Roosevelt National Forest), in the Indian Peaks Wilderness Area. It divides the waters of Buchanan Creek to the west and Middle St. Vrain Creek to the east.

The pass is believed to be named for President Buchanan, who signed the bill to create Colorado Territory in 1861.

A road over the pass was surveyed as early as 1881. A rough stage road was in use in the early 1890s. In 1895, Boulder County proposed to improve a wagon road over the pass to the upper forks of the Grand River. They appropriated ten thousand dollars to construct this road, but little of it was spent on road improvements, leaving the road much as it was.

The Boulder, Left Hand and Middle Park Railroad and Telegraph Company began a rail route over the pass. Terrain was smoothed, but no tracks were laid. In November 1897, the Colorado and Northwestern Railroad planned to extend its line over the pass; neither railroad ever finished a route.

In early days, the pass crossing was called The Buchanan Trail. It was one of the two crossings used to go between Middle Park and Boulder County.

In 1967, a proposal to build a toll road and tunnel over and under the pass, to connect the Eastern Slope and the Granby Lake area, was considered in the state legislature. Money for a feasibility study was appropriated, but the project died.

The pass is on the Continental Divide Trail and has good views to the west. The south end of the Granby reservoir can be seen from the top. A permanent snowfield is on the east side of the top. Good trails run to the top from either the west or east side. Sawtooth Mountain is just to the south of the pass. In recent years, University of Colorado research scientists have been studying the destruction of tundra at the pass by voles.

BUCKHORN PASS

Elevation: 7,867 feet
Location: T14S R67W, Map 10
County: El Paso
Topo: Manitou Springs
National forest: Pike and public access through private land

Buckhorn Pass is accessible by passenger car on the Municipal High Drive. It divides the waters of Bear Creek to the north and North Cheyenne Canyon to the south.

To reach this urban-style pass, drive up the North Cheyenne Canyon Road past the Helen Hunt Falls to High Drive. The marker at the top indicates that the road over this pass was constructed by the Colorado Works Administration in 1938. However, the original road over High Drive was built by railroad magnate General Palmer in 1905. This steep climb was an excellent way for early Colorado Springs residents to test the power of their automobiles. Today, all forms of transportation reach this point. It is a good spot for a picnic on a hot summer day: the area is wooded and has scenic views.

The pass is not named on forest service or topo maps. James Grafton Rogers located and named it in his listing of Colorado's geographic features.

BUCKSKIN PASS

Elevation: 12,462 feet
Location: T11S R86W, Map 5
County: Pitkin
Topo: Maroon Bells
National forest: White River

Buckskin Pass is accessible by foot on forest service trail #1975 in the Maroon Bells–Snowmass Wilderness Area. It divides the waters of Snowmass Creek to the west and Minnehaha Gulch to the east.

In 1915 no trail existed over the pass, but backcountry explorers used this crossing to go from Snowmass Lake to Upper Maroon Lake by horseback. Because one horse, a buckskin, refused to take the last steep pitch on the pass, Percy Hagerman named the pass "Buckskin" and decided to recommend that the forest service build a trail over it.

In 1922, Len Shoemaker claimed to name the pass for a buck deer he saw nearby. He later surveyed a route over the pass and in 1923 and 1924 built the trail.

Look for the views in all directions from the pass summit. Often, mountain sheep can be seen in the rocky areas on either side of the top. The pass gives a great view of Snowmass Lake down on the west side.

This is a popular hiking area because it is on a well-defined (and very well used) trail in an easily accessed part of the wilderness area and can be combined with several other passes for a multi-day trip.

BUFFALO PASS

Elevation: 10,320 feet
Location: T7N R83W, Map 2
County: Jackson/Routt
Topo: Buffalo Pass
National forest: Routt
On the Continental Divide

Buffalo Pass is accessible by passenger car on forest route #60, on the southern edge of the Mount Zirkel Wilderness Area. It divides the waters of the North Fork of Fish Creek to the west and Chedsey Creek to the east.

The pass is named for the buffalo the Indians waited for as the animals migrated between the Yampa Valley and North Park. An easy ambush provided winter's meat. The earliest known regular use is around 1865.

Before the highway over Rabbit Ears Pass was developed, this was the main route between North Park and Steamboat Springs. Early drivers used the pass as a challenge for their autos. In the 1930s a major highway was proposed here to traverse northern Colorado, but the project was never started.

A rough 4WD road was improved on the east side by the forest service in 1959. In 1965 more work was done, this time to upgrade the west side of the pass to meet the standards of modern cars.

Buffalo Pass averages close to seven hundred inches of snow each year, which accounts for its lush vegetation.

The pass is on the Continental Divide Trail. A campground at the top is well used on weekends each summer.

BUFFALO PASS

Elevation: 8,768 feet
Location: T6N R79W, Map 3
County: Jackson
Topo: Buffalo Peak
On private land

Buffalo Pass is not accessible. It divides the waters of East Buffalo Creek to the west and Lost Creek to the east.

This is an indistinct crossing in a private area. The pass is on ranch property and not open to the public. It can be seen from a nearby county road.

BUFFALO MEADOWS PASS

Elevation: 11,420 feet
Location: T12S R78W, Map 6
County: Chaffee/Park
Topo: Harvard Lakes
National forest: Pike/San Isabel
Other name: Buffalo

Buffalo Meadows Pass is accessible by foot on forest service trail

#617. It divides the waters of Rough and Tumbling Creek to the north and Fourmile Creek to the south.

The last wild herd of buffalo in the state is said to have lived up here, hence the name.

The trail over the pass was used in mining days as a lower crossing, a shortcut, from South Park to the upper Arkansas Valley. This was around 1870, when it was used as a pack trail. Part of the Hayden survey party camped near the base of the pass while on their 1873–1874 trip through Colorado. They saw mountain sheep on the slopes of the twin Buffalo Peaks. Today, a small herd of bighorn still lives in the top reaches of the nearby peaks. These sheep are probably the descendants of the same sheep Hayden's group saw in 1873.

In one of the grander tall tales of the West, an early-day author wrote that Indians used to drive buffalo up the pass and then, as the buffalo were cornered in the narrow opening at the top, slaughter them. Unfortunately for the story, and fortunately for the grand beasts, there is no such narrow opening in which to trap the buffalo. But it made a good story to send back to the easterners. The author also saw fish, three feet long, leaping five feet in the air out of the creeks in this same area!

Early ranchers northeast of the pass used Buffalo Meadows Pass to move cattle from South Park to the railroad line at Buena Vista.

Good views from the top are of the Collegiate mountain range to the southwest and the Sangre de Cristo mountain range to the southeast. The pass is on the west side of West Buffalo Peak. A long string of beaver ponds marks the west side of the pass. This is an easier hike from west to east, because the east side is very long. At the top, on the east side, is a wide open expanse.

The pass is not named on forest service or topo maps. It is identified as "Buffalo Meadows Pass" in the *History of Chaffee County*.

BUZZARD PASS

Elevation: 8,026 feet
Location: T8S R92W, Map 5
County: Mesa
Topo: Hightower Mountain
National forest: Grand Mesa/
**   White River**
Other name: Hightower Mountain

Buzzard Pass is accessible by 4WD on forest route #270. Two county roads also reach the pass: #330E from the west side, and #342 from the east side. The pass divides the waters of Buzzard Creek to the west and Alkali Creek to the east.

The pass is named for one of the creeks it heads. The alternate name of Hightower Mountain was assigned by Koch in *The Colorado Pass Book*.

The road over this pass is called Silt Cut-off by locals. It runs between Silt and Collbran. The pass is difficult to locate from the east due to the number of ranch roads near the east approach. The pass is two miles southeast of Mud Hill.

The road is passenger-car-accessible when not muddy, otherwise even 4WD is scary. The muddy gumbo soil grabs tires and vehicles slide off the road.

The pass is not named on topo or recent forest service maps. It is named on a 1960s White River forest service map. □

C

CABIN CREEK DIVIDE

Elevation: 10,500 feet
Location: T3N R78W, Map 3
County: Grand
Topo: Corral Peaks
National forest: Arapaho

Cabin Creek Divide is accessible by passenger car on forest route #112. It divides the waters of Corral Creek to the west and the North Fork of Cabin Creek to the east.

The pass is one mile east of Corral Peaks and two miles north of Elk Mountain. This minor crossing of a low ridge north and west of Granby is in a logging area and is identified on the highway (CO125). It is not named on topo or forest service maps.

CALAMITY PASS

Elevation: 9,680 feet
Location: T6N R77W, Map 3
County: Jackson
Topo: Jack Creek Ranch
National forest: Routt

Calamity Pass is accessible by passenger car during the summer months on forest route #740. It divides the waters of the South Fork of the Michigan River to the north and Jack Creek to the south.

The pass is about a mile north of the ghost town of Teller City. A rough road was cut over this pass during mining days to provide access to Gould. The road was never open during winter months. The buildings at Teller City have withstood the harsh winters better than many other ghost towns and perhaps have had less exposure to vandalism. Several buildings remain; interpretive signs describe the life of the town.

Today, Calamity Pass provides snowmobilers a pretty backcountry excursion in the winter months. The route is well defined with diamond markers for cold-weather visitors.

The road over the pass runs from southeast of Rand, providing an interesting shortcut (in mileage, not time) to Gould.

CALICO PASS

Elevation: 12,540 feet
Location: T51N R6E, Map 6
County: Chaffee
Topo: St. Elmo
National forest: San Isabel
Other name: Cyclone

Calico Pass is accessible by foot. It divides the waters of Grizzly Gulch to the north and Cyclone Creek to the south.

A well-used trail once crossed this pass to move miners from the South Arkansas Valley to the mining community around St. Elmo. Today it is a hiker's find and provides access to those wishing to climb high peaks.

The pass is between Grizzly Mountain and Calico Mountain. The trail itself used to be called the Cyclone Creek Trail. The pass is not named on forest service or topo maps. James Grafton Rogers located and named it in his listing of Colorado's geographic features.

CAMERON PASS

Elevation: 10,276 feet
Location: T6N R76W, Map 3
County: Jackson/Larimer
Topo: Clark Peak
National forest: Roosevelt/Routt

Cameron Pass is accessible by passenger car on CO14. It divides the waters of Michigan River to the west and Joe Wright Creek to the east.

The pass was discovered in 1870 by General R. A. Cameron, who also founded Fort Collins, to the east of this pass. Cameron's name was given to the site by Union Pacific surveyors. In 1881, a hotel was built on the pass to accommodate prospectors and miners, who were rushing into North Park looking for gold, silver, and zinc.

About this time is when the "ghost" of Cameron Pass appeared. This ghost, a young woman dressed in animal skins, was thought to be the spirit of an area emigrant's daughter. She stole food from travelers and was seen many times. Finally, on one occasion, several men chased her to a nearby cave, where they found not a wraith but the still-warm body of a young woman who had evidently died of fright and exertion. Examination of the cave revealed that the woman had lived there for some time, subsisting on stolen meat, roots, and leaves.

A toll road over the pass from Fort Collins to Teller City was finished in 1882. A stage line then carried passengers and mail to Teller City and other Jackson County destinations. Improvements were made to the road in 1913 and again in 1926, but it was not paved until the summer of 1978.

In 1940, the Fort Collins Junior Chamber of Commerce, the Mountain Club, and the Poudre Canyon Association formed the Cameron Pass Ski Club and sought to build a ski area near the top of the pass. In

1970, the state considered improving the road to the northwestern part of the state. Neither of these projects came to fruition.

The pass today provides access to many fine hiking trails.

CAMERON MOUNTAIN PASS

Elevation: 9,940 feet
Location: T51N R10E, Map 6
County: Chaffee/Fremont
Topo: Cameron Mountain
Public access through private land
Other names: Ute Trail, Whitehorn

Cameron Mountain Pass is accessible by passenger car during good weather on county road #175. It divides the waters of Railroad Gulch to the west and Willow Creek to the east.

Both the pass and nearby Cameron Mountain are named for Thomas Cameron, who began raising cattle here in 1868. He built an irrigation ditch to provide water to his fields.

Indians first used this old crossing of the range north of the Arkansas River in the Salida area; it was crossed by Governor Juan Bautista de Anza when he explored the area in 1779. Zebulon Pike's exploring party crossed here and celebrated the Christmas of 1806 just under the pass. In the late 1870s and early 1880s, the Denver and Rio Grande Railroad looked at the crossing as a possibility for a direct rail route from Denver, through South Park and into Salida, over the pass. Several small towns on the route were started by gold miners.

A good road was not built until 1936, when the Public Works Administration crews provided the needed manpower to do the job. The original road ran along the creek bottom; the new road was cut out of the hillsides to provide drainage.

The pass provides access between the Arkansas Valley and South Park; it is one and a half miles north of Cameron Mountain and on the Ute Trail Road. The pass is covered mostly with aspen, and there are some pines in an area of private property. There is a cattle guard at the top of the pass.

The ghost towns of Whitehorn (east of the pass) and Turret (west of the pass) are both early mining areas. The pass is not named on forest service or topo maps. James Grafton Rogers located and named it in his listing of Colorado's geographic features.

CAMPION PASS

Elevation: 13,180 feet
Location: T5S R74W, Map 6
County: Clear Creek
Topo: Mount Evans
National forest: Arapaho/Pike

Campion Pass is accessible by passenger car on CO5 (the Mount Evans road), adjacent to the Mount Evans Wilderness Area. It divides the waters of Scott Gomer Creek to the west and Tumbling Creek to the east.

The pass is named for John Campion, a surveyor on the Mount Evans road, who died there in September 1923 of exposure and altitude sickness during a blizzard. His name was assigned to the pass by the Colorado State Highway Department.

The pass is located on the saddle between Mount Evans and Mount Epaulet. The road crosses the pass at a point above the lowest point of the saddle, which makes for an interesting viewpoint down on the pass. The view from the road to the southwest is into South Park; the Continental Divide mountain range is behind that.

This pass is not named on forest service or topo maps. It was identified by the highway department in the mid-1920s and noted in a 1940 listing of Colorado places.

CAPITOL PASS

Elevation: 12,060 feet
Location: T10S R87W, Map 5
County: Pitkin
Topo: Capitol Peak
National forest: White River

Capitol Pass is accessible by foot on forest service trail #1961 in the Maroon Bells–Snowmass Wilderness Area. It divides the waters of Capitol Creek to the north and Avalanche Creek to the south.

The name "Capitol" was assigned to various features by the Hayden

survey party in the 1870s, after the dome-shaped peak nearby. No indication exists of early use of this pass; there was not much mining in the area.

The pass is above Capitol Lake on one side, above Avalanche Lake on the other side, and next to Capitol Peak on the southeast.

Capitol Pass is one of the most difficult Colorado passes to reach. Because this is a difficult one-day hike, Capitol Pass is best combined with other passes for a multi-day loop trip. The trail is well maintained by the forest service but hard hiking. Outfitters provide service into the Capitol Basin. Consider using them.

The pass is not named on forest service or topo maps. It was identified by Len Shoemaker, an Aspen-area forest ranger.

CARIBOU PASS

Elevation: 11,851 feet
Location: T1N R74W, Map 3
County: Grand
Topo: Monarch Lake
National forest: Arapaho
Other name: Arapaho

Caribou Pass is accessible by foot on forest service trail #11 in the Indian Peaks Wilderness Area. It divides the waters of Arapahoe Creek to the north and Meadow Creek to the south.

The pass is named for the Caribou Lode, which was discovered in August 1869. This pass is often confused with another pass nearby, particularly by those who climb it from the west.

The pass is about one-half mile above tree line. From the top, look down on Caribou Lake, then hike a half-mile along a narrow cliff (late in summer only, because snowbanks cover the cliff route earlier each year) to Lake Dorothy.

A rock palisade was built on top of the pass in the late 1800s in order to prepare the area for a road. An old wagon road goes to the pass, which was an alternate crossing from the Middle Park area onto the Front Range. Locals report that this road was used from the east side to get timber from the large stands of trees just over the west side of the pass.

Western access to the pass begins at Meadow Creek Reservoir; eastern access involves climbing to Arapaho Pass, then continuing along a ridge trail to Caribou Pass. Caribou Pass is about a mile north and west of Arapaho Pass and not on the Continental Divide, as is Arapaho.

The pass is on the Continental Divide Trail. It is not named on forest service maps, though it is on the topo, Trails Illustrated, and XYZ maps.

CARNERO PASS

Elevation: 10,166 feet
Location: T43N R5E, Map 8
County: Saguache
Topo: Lake Mountain

National forest: Rio Grande
Other names: Mountain Sheep,
Puerto del Carnero

Carnero Pass is accessible by passenger car on county road #41G. It divides the waters of Houselog Creek to the north and the Middle Fork of Carnero Creek to the south.

The word *carnero* means "sheep" or "mutton" in Spanish. No doubt the name was assigned to this geographic location in honor of the sheep grazing this region.

This pass was well used by Indians. By the time Fremont came this way in 1848, the path was defined and easy to follow. Trappers used the shortcut over Carnero, rather than the longer routes a little farther north, to cross from the Saguache Valley into the San Luis Valley. Wagons crossed here in the 1870s. The road became known then as Lawrence's Road, for one of the men who helped build it.

The pass is two miles west of Sunnyside Park Peak. The top is signed and the pass is named on the current forest service map.

CARSON PASS

Elevation: 12,360 feet
Location: T42N R5W, Map 8
County: Hinsdale
Topo: Finger Mesa
National forest: Gunnison/
** Rio Grande**
On the Continental Divide

Carson Pass is accessible by 4WD via forest route #568 on the north side. Forest service trail #821 provides foot access from the south. It divides the waters of Wager Gulch to the north and Lost Trail Creek to the south.

The pass is named for Christopher Carson, who first discovered silver here in 1881. Later, gold ore discoveries kept the area going when silver was no longer profitable. An old wagon road did cross the pass, connecting the Gunnison River Valley with Lake City.

Can you imagine living at a 12,360-foot altitude? People did — at North Carson and at South Carson, the two ends of the same town that straddle this saddle in the San Juan Mountains. The town was abandoned by 1903 due to winters that kept it cut off from the rest of the world for months at a time and a decline in the mining activity.

The pass is one mile west of Coney Peak and two miles west of Carson Peak. Carson Pass is on the Continental Divide Trail. The Colorado Trail also uses the pass.

CASCADE PASS

Elevation: 12,260 feet
Location: T44N R7W, Map 8
County: Ouray
Topo: Wetterhorn Peak
National forest: Uncompahgre

Cascade Pass is accessible by foot on forest service trail #215. It divides the waters of Cascade Creek to the west and Difficulty Creek to the east.

This is a remote pass that requires a difficult hike in order to reach it. The access is via the Horsethief Trail out of Ouray, which leads to the Bridge of Heaven (a narrow hogback ridge), drops down, then climbs up again to cross the pass.

This pass is not named on topo or forest service maps. It is identified in Ouray-area hiking guides.

CASTLE PASS

Elevation: 11,057 feet
Location: T15S R88W, Map 5
County: Gunnison
Topo: Anthracite Range
National forest: Gunnison

Castle Pass is accessible by foot on forest service trail #441 in the West Elk Wilderness Area. It divides the waters of Cliff Creek to the west and Castle Creek to the east.

The pass is named for the interesting geological formation close by — The Castles — a rugged, rocky, ridgetop section of mountain. Access to the pass, which is south of Storm Ridge, is via the Mill-Castle Trail.

CENTRAL PASS

Elevation: 12,340 feet
Location: T4S R79W, Map 6
County: Eagle/Summit
Topo: Willow Lakes
National forest: Arapaho/
    White River

Central Pass is accessible by foot in the Eagles Nest Wilderness Area. It divides the waters of Big Horn Creek to the west and North Rock Creek to the east.

There was some old mining activity on the east side of the pass but no evidence the pass was used much. No trail exists over it, and bushwhacking is required to reach the pass.

The pass is in the south end of the Gore mountain range and south of Keller Mountain. Central Pass is not named on forest service or topo maps. It is identified in Vail-area hiking guides.

CERRO SUMMIT

Elevation: 7,950 feet
Location: T48N R7W, Map 5
County: Montrose
Topo: Cerro Summit
Public access through private land
Other name: Cedar Divide

Cerro Summit is accessible by passenger car on US50. It divides the waters of Cedar Creek to the west and Squaw Creek to the east.

The Spanish word for "ridge" is *cerro*. And this mesa summit is a big ridge. Antoine Robideau crossed this way in the 1820s as he went from the San Luis Valley to the Western Slope near Delta, where he established his trading post. Captain John Gunnison climbed over Cerro Summit in 1853, when he was exploring the Black Canyon of the Gunnison River area. Otto Mears built a road over the pass shortly after the Ute Agency moved to the Uncompahgre River, in late 1875.

In 1882 the Denver and Rio Grande Railroad – a narrow gauge railway – crossed the pass. Part of the time, the area at the top was used to trade rail cars: one train came from Gunnison and the other from Montrose.

On old highway maps (1910s vintage), the pass is shown as Cedar Divide and the point where the railroad crosses the ridge as Cerro Summit. Now the highway department uses the name Cerro Summit for the road crossing. A small town once existed here as a station for the railroad. By 1920 a good highway had been constructed; it was on the Ocean-to-Ocean and Rainbow highway routes. Cerro Summit is where the view of the Uncompahgre Valley opens up to the traveler coming from the east.

CHALK CREEK PASS

Elevation: 12,150 feet
Location: T50N R6E, Map 5
County: Chaffee
Topo: Garfield
National forest: San Isabel

Chalk Creek Pass is accessible by foot via forest service trail #1422 on the south side; the trail is unnumbered on the north side. It divides the waters of Chalk Creek to the north and the Middle Fork of the South Arkansas River to the south.

Hancock Lake is in the foreground of this view of Chalk Creek Pass.

The pass is named for the creek on its north side. It was used by miners with mules to carry supplies back and forth between prospecting areas in the Monarch and St. Elmo mining districts. The Chalk Creek Toll Road was chartered by Henry Altman to connect Chalk Creek and the South Arkansas by way of the pass. Only a rough wagon road resulted.

This is a picture-perfect mountain pass located above Upper Hancock Lake, which isn't visible until you are upon it. The top is a wide grassy saddle on a ridge that runs off the Continental Divide. Look for mountain goats playing on the rocks to the west of the pass. Van Wirt Mountain is to the west and Sewanee Peak to the northeast. The Continental Divide Trail crosses the pass.

CHAPIN PASS

Elevation: 11,140 feet
Location: T5N R74W, Map 3
County: Larimer
Topo: Trail Ridge
In Rocky Mountain National Park
Other name: Trail Ridge Road

Chapin Pass is accessible by foot. It divides the waters of Chapin Creek to the north and the Fall River to the south.

Three stories exist—take your pick—about the name. The first claims the pass was named for Frederick Hastings Chapin, of Hartford,

Connecticut, who came to Rocky Mountain National Park each summer to hike with other members of the Appalachian Mountain Club. A Mr. Hallett, who lived near Marys Lake by Estes Park, was their guide. He named the pass and a mountain for Chapin. In turn, Chapin named a peak after Hallett.

The second story claims the pass was named for Jennie Chapin by her husband, Dr. Homer James. Jennie ran a general store in Estes Park.

The third story claims the pass was named for a Mr. Chapin who was a guest in the Elkhorn Lodge at Estes Park. Mr. Chapin had the room in the lodge where a hen liked to lay her daily egg. The least they could do for the poor man was to name a feature in the national park for him!

The USGS Board on Geographic Names officially named the pass in 1932.

In the 1910s, a survey was done over Chapin Pass to develop a road connecting Estes Park and Grand lakes. Such a project had been discussed since about 1895. The route was agreed upon and named a state highway. Construction began, only to run into problems that took the route over a higher, wind-blown, open-tundra spur now called Trail Ridge. A trail did go over Chapin Pass, but it's not the main road.

CHILLYCOAT PASS

Elevation: 9,613 feet
Location: T49N R15W, Map 4

County: Mesa
Topo: Snipe Mountain
National forest: Uncompahgre

Chillycoat Pass is accessible by passenger car on forest route #402. It divides the waters of Haley Draw to the north and Big Atkinson Creek to the south.

The pass was named by two cowboys who were moving stock on a blustery winter day. "Chillycoat" replaced their unprintable words, honoring the Chilkoot Pass in Alaska.

This is a shortcut pass on the Divide Road between Monument Hill and T-Bone Spring. The pass is not named on forest service or topo maps; it is identified by local usage.

CINNAMON PASS

Elevation: 12,620 feet
Location: T42N R6W, Map 8
County: Hinsdale/San Juan
Topo: Handies Peak
On BLM land
Other name: Lake Fork

Cinnamon Pass is accessible by 4WD. It divides the waters of Cinnamon Creek to the west and the Lake Fork of the Gunnison River to the east.

The pass is named for Cinnamon Mountain. In turn, the mountain is named for the cinnamon color that shows in the rocks on the mountain. The alternate name of Lake Fork is for one of the rivers the pass heads.

The route over the pass was first

used by Indians, then by Charles Baker when he entered the San Juans in 1860. In 1873, Albert Burrows explored the area; a park at the east end of the pass now bears his name. The mining community of Animas Forks is located on the west side of the pass. Hayden's survey party crossed the pass in 1874. Cairns used for triangulation by these surveyors are still in place at the pass summit.

Mail routes were established over the pass by the mid-1870s. Because the pass was not on the Continental Divide, Washington officials thought the mail should move all year. They awarded a contract for year-round service, which was difficult to accomplish. A good road over the pass was constructed in late 1877 by Enos Hotchkiss, but it was not kept up. Otto Mears had his surveyors consider the route as a potential extension of his railroad empire. A mill was built near the top in 1901.

Now 4WD-accessible and open in the summer only, the Cinnamon Pass road is one of the favorite routes of off-highway enthusiasts. Several ghost towns are still visible there. The road is part of the Alpine Loop Byway, a scenic and historic backcountry designation of the Bureau of Land Management.

The pass is not on the hiking portion of the Colorado Trail, but it is on the mountain-bike detour of the trail.

CLOUDY PASS

Elevation: 5,940 feet
Location: T8N R70W, Map 3
County: Larimer
Topo: Laporte
On private land

Cloudy Pass is not accessible to the public. It divides the waters of Rist Canyon to the north and Long Gulch to the south.

The pass is located on private property west of Fort Collins. It has good views, to the south, of Horsetooth Reservoir and north to tree-covered ridges.

Cloudy Pass is not named on the Roosevelt forest service map. It is named on the topo map.

COAL BANK PASS

Elevation: 10,640 feet
Location: T40N R8W, Map 7
County: San Juan
Topo: Engineer Mountain
National forest: San Juan

Coal Bank Pass is passenger-car accessible on US550. It divides the waters of Coal Creek to the north and Mill Creek to the south.

The pass crosses Coal Bank Hill, which was well used by Indians. By 1877, travelers over the pass were writing accounts of the mining activity and the condition of the road.

Engineer Mountain, one of the most stunning massifs in the Colorado mountains, and two miles away to the west, appears closer than it really is. Potato Hill is two miles to the south.

COBERLY GAP

Elevation: 9,260 feet
Location: T3S R84W, Map 2
County: Eagle
Topo: Castle Peak
On BLM land

Coberly Gap is accessible by 4WD via forest route #54 (on the south side). It divides the waters of Alkali Creek to the north and Milk Creek to the south.

The gap is on the northwest side of Horse Mountain, and three miles east of Castle Peak. Access via the Milk Creek area bypasses private land. On the top are pretty aspens.

Access is only possible in good weather because the soil turns into gumbo when it's wet.

COCHETOPA PASS

Elevation: 10,067 feet
Location: T45N R3E, Map 8
County: Saguache
Topo: North Pass
National forest: Gunnison/
 Rio Grande
On the Continental Divide
Other names: Leroux, Puerto de los
 Cibolas, Saguache, Sawatch, West

Cochetopa Pass is accessible by passenger car on county road #NN14. It divides the waters of

Archuleta Creek to the west and Cantonment Creek to the east.

Cochetopa is a Ute word meaning "gate of buffaloes." The area of the pass is open and would be good buffalo grazing land. The Indians followed the buffalo to obtain meat and hides. The USGS Board on Geographic Names officially named the pass in 1963.

It's important to note that the ridge containing the pass lends itself to many different crossings. And because highway markers were not available to early travelers, it is very likely that any one of a number of places on the ridge may have been crossed by various parties thinking they were at the same place. Rivers or creeks also were not marked, and instructions to "follow up the creek with all the logs in it" would have allowed travelers to follow a creek other than the one the instructor intended.

By the early part of the twentieth century, *Saguache* (an Indian word for "water at the blue earth") was the name most used for the pass.

Cochetopa is the old crossing on the ridge, and a more recent crossing is north of it. The first documented crossing of the pass is that of Governor Juan Bautista de Anza, in 1779. Fur traders and trappers followed soon after. Cochetopa was the first Colorado Continental Divide pass to be crossed by wheeled vehicles. Antoine Robideau brought wagons over the pass as early as 1825. When trappers Pope and

Stover crossed in 1837, they had wagons with them.

Three different exploration parties visited the crossing in 1853: the Gunnison, the Fremont, and the Beale. At this time the pass was known as *Puerto de los Cibolos* (the Spanish word for buffalo is *cibolo*). When Gunnison wrote home, he said he was going through the "Coochu-to-pe Pass."

When U.S. Army Captain Marcy took his men from Wyoming to New Mexico, they crossed what was then the low route, via Cochetopa. In 1858, Colonel Loring explored this area and marked various routes in the vicinity. His rudely cut road was called the "Central Route to the West." A charter was granted by the Colorado Territory legislature in 1861 to the Cañon City, Grand River and San Juan Road Company to build a road from Cañon City via the Sawatch Pass to an intersection with Loring's road from Fort Garland.

John Lawrence built a road over the pass in 1869 to meet the needs of the many freighters wishing to get goods to the Los Piños Ute Reservation and beyond. Regular mail runs were made, by stage, over the pass by 1872. Saguache and Lake City were the main mail terminals on either side.

In 1873, Lieutenant E. H. Ruffner spent some time here studying potential routes to the west. He felt the pass was a logical route, and he heartily recommended it to Washington, D.C.

The Utes lived at the Los Piños Reservation just west of the pass in the 1870s. William Jackson arrived in 1874 to take photos; he was rebuffed by the Utes, so he moved on.

Lawrence turned his road into a toll road in 1875. He charged a dollar per wagon and lesser amounts for animals and foot travelers. Two different railroads sent surveyors to scout out routes over the pass, but nothing ever developed from these survey trips. Although this crossing of the Continental Divide makes the most sense for a railroad, none has ever been built over it.

The pass is in the Cochetopa Hills, near the Continental Divide Trail.

COFFEEPOT PASS

Elevation: 12,760 feet
Location: T12S R85W, Map 5
County: Gunnison/Pitkin
Topo: Gothic
National forest: Gunnison/
   White River

Coffeepot Pass is accessible by foot via forest service trail #1981 on the north side. The trail is unnumbered on the south side. The pass is in the Maroon Bells–Snowmass Wilderness Area. It divides the waters of Conundrum Creek to the north and West Brush Creek to the south.

The USGS Board on Geographic Names officially named the pass in 1973 for a coffeepot found on the pass by some travelers in 1879. They surmised it had been left in 1873 by the Hayden survey party. The pot remained as a marker for many years but is long gone now. The name is sometimes expressed as one word, sometimes as two.

This route was first used by Indians, then by miners in the 1880s to go between the Crested Butte and Aspen areas.

The pass is located between Coffee Pot and Triangle peaks. Castle Peak is to the east. The pass is not named on the forest service map. It is named on the topo and Trails Illustrated maps.

COLUMBIA PASS

Elevation: 12,460 feet
Location: T11S R83W, Map 5
County: Pitkin
Topo: New York Peak
National forest: White River

Columbia Pass is accessible by foot in the Collegiate Peaks Wilderness Area. It divides the waters of New York Creek to the east and Columbia Creek to the west.

The pass is named for one of the creeks it heads, which in turn was named by Harry Halleck, a forest ranger at Aspen in the 1920s.

There is no trail across the pass, but it can easily be bushwhacked. Columbia Pass is a half-mile south of Difficult Peak. It is not named on forest service or topo maps. The pass was identified by Len Shoemaker,

an Aspen-area forest ranger in the 1920s.

COLUMBINE PASS

Elevation: 12,700 feet
Location: T38N R7W, Map 8
County: La Plata
Topo: Columbine Pass
National forest: San Juan
Other name: Chicago Basin

Columbine Pass is accessible by foot on forest service trail #504 in the Weminuche Wilderness Area. It divides the waters of Needle Creek to the west and Johnson Creek to the east.

The earliest known regular use is around 1902, but the route has never been anything but a trail.

This is a difficult hike that can be made easier by taking the narrow-gauge train out of Durango to a drop-off point and riding it back out a day or two later.

The pass is at the head of a glacial cirque with good views in all directions. Many other trails are close. The trail over the pass was improved in 1966, but it can be muddy when wet. Aztec Mountain is west and Hope Mountain northeast of the pass.

COLUMBINE PASS

Elevation: 9,140 feet
Location: T48N R14W, Map 4
County: Montrose
Topo: Starvation Point
National forest: Uncompahgre

Columbine Pass is accessible by passenger car via forest routes #402 and #503. Forest route #402 is also called Divide Road. Columbine Pass divides the waters of Potter Creek to the north and Tabeguache Creek to the south.

The pass is located on the Uncompahgre Plateau. It is believed to be named for the columbine flower, which used to grow in abundance here. Hayden's survey party crossed the plateau in the mid-1870s.

Residents here have desired a real road for many years; low population and remote location have stalled such a project. In 1916 an application was made for an improved road, and some work has been done over the years to upgrade the old route. Now traversed by the Tabeguache Bike Trail, this passenger-car-access road is an old, low crossing on the western plateau. The road can be muddy and difficult when extremely wet.

The top of the pass has trees, is marked, and has corrals where animals can be unloaded or rounded up. A full intersection at the top allows the plateau traveler alternate routes on which to descend. Views while driving to the pass are better than those from the top.

COLUMBINE PASS

Elevation: 8,697 feet
Location: T10N R85W, Map 2
County: Routt
Topo: Hahns Peak
National forest: Routt

Columbine Pass is accessible by passenger car on forest route #129. It divides the waters of Independence Creek to the north and Willow Creek to the south.

The pass is named for the state flower, the columbine. It is three miles north of Steamboat Lake and at the town of Columbine. An early mining camp was started here around 1880.

Columbine Pass was better known in the 1920s, when it was on a more regularly used route. Now it is a back-road route in northern Colorado. Not named on forest service or topo maps, the pass was identified by Colorado Mountain Club members in the 1920s.

COMANCHE PASS

Elevation: 12,700 feet
Location: T44N R12E, Map 9
County: Custer/Saguache
Topo: Horn Peak
National forest: Rio Grande/
San Isabel

Comanche Pass is accessible by foot via forest service trails #746 on the west side and #1345 on the east side. It divides the waters of the Middle Fork of North Crestone Creek to the west and Hiltman Creek to the east.

This route has never been used for more than a riding or hiking trail. Many people combine Comanche Pass with other passes for a loop hike or ride in the beautiful high country of the rugged Sangre de Cristo mountain range.

The pass is between Comanche Peak on the south and Venable Peak on the north. Comanche Lake is to the east.

COMANCHE PEAK PASS

Elevation: 12,500 feet
Location: T7N R74W, Map 3
County: Larimer
Topo: Comanche Peak
National forest: Roosevelt/Rocky
  Mountain National Park

Comanche Peak Pass is accessible by foot on forest service trail #943, on the southern edge of the Comanche Peak Wilderness Area. It divides the waters of Beaver Creek to the north and Cascade Creek to the south.

The pass is named for the rocky Comanche Peak Mountain nearby. It is a wide, broad, rocky area. Walk several hundred yards north and down from the top to get a good view of the Pingree Park Valley below.

Comanche Peak Pass is on the Rocky Mountain National Park northern boundary and is marked by a sign at the trailhead. Watch for ptarmigans, the quiet high-country ground birds, near the top.

CONUNDRUM PASS

Elevation: 12,780 feet
Location: T12S R85W, Map 5
County: Pitkin
Topo: Maroon Bells
National forest: White River

Conundrum Pass is accessible by foot in the Maroon Bells–Snowmass Wilderness Area. It divides the waters of East Maroon Creek to the west and Conundrum Creek to the east.

The USGS Board on Geographic Names officially named the pass in 1972. The name "Conundrum" was first given to a nearby mine; the name was next applied to the creek, then to the pass.

The miners used the very steep and rough trail. A crude wagon road was started up the west side of the pass but never completed.

Look for a hot spring near the trail. Conundrum Peak is two and a half miles east of the top. Because this is a difficult one-day hike, Conundrum Pass is best combined with other passes for a multi-day loop trip.

CONY PASS

Elevation: 12,420 feet
Location: T3N R74W, Map 3
County: Boulder
Topo: Isolation Peak
In Rocky Mountain National Park

Cony Pass is accessible by foot, but no established trail currently goes over the pass. It divides the waters of Ouzel Creek to the north and Cony Creek to the south.

The pass is named for the little animals of the high country known as conies or pikas. They make very loud noises for such a small animal, are often difficult to see, and like to nest in high rocky places on mountains with a southern exposure.

This is a difficult hike in Rocky Mountain National Park that requires rock-scrambling to reach the pass. Both Junco and Cony lakes are worth visiting. The pass is named on the topo map.

COPPER PASS

Elevation: 12,580 feet
Location: T12S R85N, Map 5
County: Gunnison/Pitkin
Topo: Gothic
National forest: Gunnison/
  White River

Copper Pass is accessible by foot via forest service trails #1981 on the north and #981 on the south in the Maroon Bells–Snowmass Wilderness Area. It divides the waters of East Maroon Creek to the north and Copper Creek to the south.

The USGS Board on Geographic Names officially named the pass in 1973. A century before, it had been given the name of Copper Pass by the Hayden survey party for the copper colors of the creek and the lake nearby.

The trail across the pass was built by Len Shoemaker. The trail was constructed to provide an alternative to the steeper trails nearby. This is one of several passes in the Elk mountain range that provided a

means of travel between Aspen and Crested Butte.

The hike is on a good trail on the eastern end of Chicago Mountain; the pass is north of White Rock Mountain and east of Copper Basin and Copper Lake.

COPPER GULCH DIVIDE

Elevation: 7,927 feet
Location: T20S R73W, Map 9
County: Fremont
Topo: Iron Mountain
Public access through private land

Copper Gulch Divide is passenger-car accessible on county road #27.A. It divides the waters of Copper Gulch to the north and Texas Creek to the south.

This easy and low crossing is near the Royal Gorge in central Colorado. In an area of private property, homes are built at the top of the pass. Look for the good views of the Sangre de Cristo range. And watch for the buried gold that's supposed to be in this area.

The divide is between two areas currently proposed for wilderness status by conservation groups. The pass is between Deer Mountain to the west and McClure Mountain to the east.

CORDOVA PASS

Elevation: 11,248 feet
Location: T31S R68W, Map 9
County: Huerfano/Las Animas

Topo: Cucharas Pass
National forest: San Isabel
Other names: Apishapa, Fish

Cordova Pass is accessible by passenger car in good weather, and by 4WD in poor weather conditions, on forest route #415. It divides the waters of Chaparral Creek to the west and Apishapa Creek to the east.

The USGS Board on Geographic Names officially named the pass in 1978. An attempt to change the name back to Apishapa, which had been assigned to the pass in 1941, was withdrawn in 1982. The name "Cordova" comes from a Las Animas County commissioner who was instrumental in building the road over the pass, a road that was completed in 1934. *Apishapa* means "stinking water" in Apache and comes from the brackish water that accumulates along local riverbanks.

The pass makes a good starting point for a hike up West Spanish Peak, which is two miles to the northeast. Look for lots of flowers in the early summer and visit the Apishapa Arch (about five miles down on the east side of the pass).

CORKSCREW PASS

Elevation: 12,217 feet
Location: T42N R7W, Map 8
County: Ouray/San Juan
Topo: Ironton
National forest: Uncompahgre and
  BLM land

Corkscrew Pass is accessible by 4WD on forest route #886. It divides the waters of Cement Creek to the east and Corkscrew Gulch to the west.

The pass is named for Corkscrew Gulch on the west side of the pass and is located on the southwest flank of Red Mountain One, near the old mining town of Gladstone. It's a steep road to reach this pass, but the view from the top is well worth it.

The pass is not named on forest service or topo maps; it is identified by local usage.

COTTON GAP

Elevation: 5,905 feet
Location: T34S R55W, Map 10
County: Las Animas
Topo: Cobert Mesa North
On private land

Cotton Gap is not accessible. It divides the waters of West Carrizo Creek to the north and Gatera Canyon to the south.

It is possible to get close to this water divide but not to it. There are lots of canyons here that would be fun to explore if they were on BLM or forest service land; unfortunately, they are on private land. The pass is named on the topo map.

COTTONTAIL PASS

Elevation: 7,970 feet
Location: T32S R66W, Map 10
County: Las Animas

Topo: Gulnare
**Public access between Colorado
  state land and private land**

Cottontail Pass is accessible by
4WD on county road #41.1. It divides the waters of Sarcillo Canyon
to the west and Burro Canyon to the
east.

The top of the pass is at the
border of the Spanish Peaks State
Wildlife Area. The pass summit is
wooded, has views to the east into
the Colorado plains, and to the west
of the Sangre de Cristos. This is a
pretty little spot.

The pass is named on the topo
and BLM maps.

COTTONWOOD PASS

**Elevation: 12,126 feet
Location: T14S R81W, Map 5
County: Chaffee/Gunnison
Topo: Tincup
National forest: Gunnison/
  San Isabel
On the Continental Divide**

Cottonwood Pass is accessible by
passenger car on county road #306
on the east side (Chaffee County),
and forest route #209 on the west
side (Gunnison County). It divides
the waters of Pass Creek to the west
and the North Fork of Middle Cottonwood Creek to the east.

Cottonwood Pass was *the* route
into the Taylor Park area, and thence
to Aspen and beyond, until the
mid-1880s, when other routes were

opened. Miners, settlers, and freighters all followed the old Indian trail
up and over the fairly open crossing.
One of the reasons Indians used the
crossing was the natural hot springs
found at the eastern base of the pass.
When settlers discovered the springs,
they used them, too. Cottonwood
Springs became a regular stop on
the trail. The snow at the top was
tunneled so that winter travel could
keep moving. The west side of the
pass had a precipitous drop. Goods
would have to be unloaded, then
carried or rope-dropped down, item
by item, when the goods were too
wide for the narrow road.

Buena Vista was a supply point
for the miners. The discoveries of
ores west of the Continental Divide
made the route a logical choice for
travel.

Robert Hughes built the first Cottonwood Pass toll road in the early
1870s. Dave Wood improved the
road and reconverted it to a toll road
over the pass in the late 1870s, but
he went bankrupt in 1882. The pass
was nearly abandoned except for
local traffic at this time. The last
stages to travel the route ran in 1911.
Then it became a rough, unmain-
tained 4WD road.

In 1881, the Buena Vista and
Gunnison Railway Company thought
they would build a railroad over the
pass to link Buena Vista and Crested
Butte. Then the Taylor Park Railroad
Company decided, in 1901, to try
the project. By 1906, talk of a railroad had diminished, and an electric

trolley line was the newest idea—a dam across the Taylor River would provide the power needed. By 1913, all these ideas were dead and buried.

The road was improved in the late 1950s. "Road over pass reopened to traffic for first time in nearly 80 years," said a *Denver Post* headline of August 1959. The forest service spent two years and a quarter of a million dollars rebuilding it. One of the reasons for reopening the road was to provide access for recreational use of Taylor Park.

After asking repeatedly for federal funds for fifty years to pave the road over Cottonwood Pass, Chaffee County finally received monies in 1987 to start the project. The paving was completed in 1990. Gunnison County, as of 1993, has not yet paved the western side of the pass. Today the road is closed each late fall, when snows make it difficult to keep open.

Cottonwood Pass is on the Continental Divide Trail.

COTTONWOOD PASS

Elevation: 8,904 feet
Location: T1N R77W, Map 3
County: Grand
Topo: Hot Sulphur Springs
National forest: Arapaho and public access through private land
Other name: Aspen Divide

Cottonwood Pass is accessible by passenger car on county road #55.

It divides the waters of Gardiner Creek to the west and Eightmile Creek to the east.

An old stage road once crossed the pass. The Denver, Utah and Pacific Railroad considered, in 1880, whether to build a narrow-gauge line over the pass.

The pass looks out over the Fraser Valley. Today's visitor can see the back side of the Indian Peaks Wilderness Area to the east.

The top is not marked, there is some private property nearby, and a forest service firewood area is just on the west side of the pass. This is a pretty backcountry drive, and a shortcut (in miles, not time) off US40 between Fraser and Hot Sulphur Springs.

COTTONWOOD PASS

Elevation: 8,280 feet
Location: T6S R86W, Map 5
County: Eagle
Topo: Cottonwood Pass
Public access through private land

Cottonwood Pass is passenger-car-accessible. It divides the waters of East Coulter Creek to the west and Cottonwood Creek to the east.

The route was used as early as 1873. A wagon road was built over the pass in 1883, between Gypsum and the Roaring Fork Valley.

This Cottonwood Pass was one of the most important passes in our state fifty years ago, but it is almost unknown today. Until the 1940s, when route US24 was designated to go through Glenwood Canyon, the road over Cottonwood Pass carried the Denver–Grand Junction traffic. Then, when the interstate route was to be built along the US6/US24 route, attention was again focused on Cottonwood Pass. Some consideration was given to closing down the Glenwood Canyon route so that construction on the new road could proceed at a faster rate by sending all traffic over the "old" route.

Various factors killed the idea of improving the route over Cottonwood Pass to create a highway, even as a detour route. These factors included the cost of improving the road combined with the fear that after the canyon interstate route reopened, travelers would continue to use this route as a shortcut. Visitors might bypass the Glenwood Springs area, where merchants didn't want to lose the business they got from Aspen-bound skiers and tourists.

The pass road had previously been used as a detour when the Colorado River Canyon road through Glenwood Canyon was closed for improvements in the late 1930s. This Cottonwood Pass road was the only link to eastern Colorado until Glenwood Canyon reopened as US24.

The road is a good shortcut (in miles, not time) between Aspen and Gypsum. Look for good views from several points on the road. Mount Sopris is the single massif to the southwest.

COXCOMB PASS

Elevation: 12,500 feet
Location: T44N R6W, Map 8
County: Hinsdale/Ouray
Topo: Wetterhorn Peak
National forest: Uncompahgre

Coxcomb Pass is accessible by foot on forest service trail #226 in the Big Blue Wilderness Area. It divides the waters of the West Fork of the Cimarron River to the north and Wetterhorn Creek to the south.

The pass is a half-mile west of Coxcomb Peak and is more easily accessed from the north unless combined with other passes. Coxcomb Pass is not named on forest service or topo maps. It is a favorite hiking area for the Colorado Mountain Club.

CROOKED CREEK PASS

Elevation: 9,995 feet
Location: T7S R83W, Map 5
County: Eagle
Topo: Crooked Creek Pass
National forest: White River

Crooked Creek Pass is accessible by passenger car on forest route #400. It divides the waters of Brush Creek to the north and Crooked Creek to the south. It is named for Crooked Creek.

Crooked Creek Pass is located just south of and above Sylvan Lake and the state wildlife area there. This is an interesting area that is well used by hunters but has not yet been discovered by the public.

CROW HILL

Elevation: 8,500 feet
Location: T7S R72W, Map 6
County: Park
Topo: Bailey
Public access through private land

Crow Hill is passenger-car-accessible on US285. It divides the waters of Deer Creek to the north and the North Fork of the South Platte River to the south.

The pass is about three miles northeast of Bailey. It is named on forest service maps, and there is a highway department sign at the top.

CUCHARAS PASS

Elevation: 9,941 feet
Location: T31S R69W, Map 9
County: Huerfano/Las Animas
Topo: Cucharas Pass
National forest: San Isabel

Cucharas Pass is accessible by passenger car on CO12. It divides the waters of the Cucharas River to the north and Guajatoyah Creek to the south. *Cuchara* is the Spanish word for "spoon."

In 1706, Juan de Ulibarri crossed from the Rio Grande toward the Arkansas River via this pass. The earliest known regular use is in 1877, when prospectors moved through.

A ski area is close by, as is the small community of Cuchara, a quiet haven buried in the mountains just west of Walsenburg. The pass is two miles south of South White Peak. The road over the pass has been designated as a scenic and historic byway and named The Scenic Highway of Legends. This route connects Trinidad to Walsenburg over CO12 and through Cuchara and La Veta.

CULBERTSON PASS

Elevation: 8,562 feet
Location: T1N R72W, Map 3
County: Boulder
Topo: Gold Hill
National forest: Roosevelt
Other name: Gold Hill

Culbertson Pass is accessible by passenger car on county road #93 or forest route #327 (the Switzerland Trail Road). It divides the waters of Lefthand Creek to the north and Fourmile Creek to the south.

The pass is just west of the old mining town for which it was once named, Gold Hill. It was still called Gold Hill Pass in 1900 when circulars were distributed by the Colorado and Northwestern Railroad to bring people to the area. Later the pass was named Culbertson.

The road was originally built by the Denver, Boulder and Western Railroad. The pass is on the railroad grade that is part of the old Switzerland Trail through the high country in the western part of Boulder

County. The cut where the pass is located was one of the longest on the railroad and, because of its open, flat expanse, strongly despised by the crews in wintertime.

Watch for lots of bicyclists. The pass is not named on forest service, topo, or Trails Illustrated maps, but it is identified on railroad maps.

CULEBRA PASS

Elevation: 13,500 feet
Location: T34S R70W, Map 9
County: Costilla
Topo: Culebra Peak
On private land

There is no access to Culebra Pass. It divides the waters of North Vallejos Creek to the west and Las Vigas Creek to the east.

The pass is an old stock drive way between private properties in the very southernmost part of the state. It was never a major crossing.

The Culebra Peak topo shows a jeep trail to the pass summit from the east side. The pass is not named on forest service, topo, or any other current maps. It was identified by Luther Bean, San Luis Valley historian.

CUMBERLAND PASS

Elevation: 12,020 feet
Location: T51N R4E, Map 5
County: Gunnison
Topo: Cumberland Pass
National forest: Gunnison

Cumberland Pass is accessible by passenger car on forest route #765. It divides the waters of West Willow Creek to the north and Quartz Creek to the south.

The first road over the pass was built in 1882 using the earlier pack trail so that mines in Tincup could get their ores to the railroad at Pitkin. By 1908 the wagon road was regularly used by residents of the mining areas around Tincup to reach Pitkin. After mining activity slackened, the road remained an access for the few people left in Pitkin and Tincup.

The first automobile crossed the pass in 1905, from Pitkin to Tincup. However, the auto did not make it across on its own. It had to be pulled over the pass by a team of horses! The road was worked on by the Civilian Conservation Corps in 1935 and improved again in the mid-1950s.

At the top of the pass is a small marker describing how "Marshall" met "Eileen" at this place in 1959, and how happy she made him.

The Sawatch mountain range is visible to the east, and Taylor Park is visible to the north from atop the pass. Look for remains of the Bon Ton Mine at the base of the switchbacks that lead to the top from the south side. The pass is one and a half miles northeast of Green Mountain.

A Rand McNally map copyrighted in 1888 names the pass and shows a road over it.

CUMBRES PASS

Elevation: 10,022 feet
Location: T32N R5E, Map 8
County: Conejos
Topo: Cumbres
National forest: Rio Grande

Cumbres Pass is accessible by passenger car on CO17. It divides the waters of Wolf Creek to the west and Cumbres Creek to the east.

Cumbres is the Spanish word for "summit" or "crest." A train station at the top of the pass was also named Cumbres.

Utes lived at the pass before the white man came. Bill Williams, the mountain man, lived with them be-fore he served as a guide for Fremont. In 1848, military units were on the pass, and in the 1870s the Hayden survey party came through. William H. Jackson, the famed photographer, was with the surveyors and took many good photos here. In the fall of 1876, settlers were moving over the pass with wagons. Near the top is evidence of the 1878 forest fire that burned over 26,000 acres of timber.

By 1879 a toll road existed over the pass. Construction work on the Denver and Rio Grande rail line was also in full swing. The railroad was operating by 1881. To keep the railcars moving across the pass in the late 1880s, a rotary snowplow was

Winter in 1909 at the top of Cumbres Pass. (*Photograph courtesy Denver Public Library, Western History Department*)

attached to the train engine during heavy snows. In 1920, consideration was given to building a tunnel under the pass to ease the trip over the top, but it was never built. However, a road over the pass was opened, and the highway was improved in 1923 with grading and graveling.

The railroad tracks were used until 1951, when passenger service was dropped. In 1968 the rail route was abandoned. Then, in 1970, the states of New Mexico and Colorado bought the rail line and began jointly operating the Cumbres and Toltec Scenic Railroad, carrying tourists between Antonito, Colorado, and Chama, New Mexico. This trip has become one of the more popular tourist attractions in the state for visitors and residents alike, and especially for old-railroad enthusiasts. A monument at the pass honors President Garfield.

The pass receives heavy snowfall each winter (an average of 264 inches per year), which makes it difficult to keep the road open. In 1957, two trains with fifty-eight men were snowbound at the top for seven days.

Cumbres Pass is a mile southwest of Neff Mountain. A terminus of the Colorado section of the Continental Divide is at the pass summit.

CUNNINGHAM PASS

Elevation: 12,180 feet
Location: T41N R6W, Map 8
County: San Juan
Topo: Howardsville

National forest: Rio Grande and BLM land
On the Continental Divide
Other name: Rio Grande

Cunningham Pass is accessible by foot on the northwest edge of the Weminuche Wilderness Area. It divides the waters of Cunningham Creek to the west and Deep Creek to the east.

In 1874, settlers were calling the pass Rio Grande, after the river it heads. A 1909 map shows the pass with the name of Rio Grande. The pass was unofficially named for Major Cunningham, who led visitors from Chicago who were considering investments in San Juan–area mines. Both the gulch and pass are named for him.

Prospectors used the crossing as early as 1861. When Lieutenant E. H. Ruffner visited the area in 1873, he felt a road for light wagons could be constructed over this pass. The Hayden survey party, with William H. Jackson as photographer, came here in 1874. A road was cut over the pass to provide service to the Highland Mary mine. By 1875, charters were issued to wagon companies for toll roads across the pass. Mail was carried over the route three times a week; as the population increased, mail delivery changed to a daily service. In 1877, the railroad considered a route over Cunningham Pass to save the thirty-four miles it would take to go to South Fork and then up to Lake City.

The summit of the pass is five hundred feet lower than the better-known nearby Stony Pass; therefore, the route over Cunningham was preferred by many early travelers. These two passes, separated by a mile and a half, are the westernmost point of the Continental Divide in Colorado. Many people once called both passes "Stony." The road over Cunningham Pass was very steep and always muddy. These factors are the reasons the route over Stony eventually became the preferred one.

Cunningham Pass is not named on forest service or topo maps. It is located northwest of the Highland Mary Lakes.

CURECANTI PASS

Elevation: 10,460 feet
Location: T15S R89W, Map 5
County: Gunnison
Topo: Big Soap Park
National forest: Gunnison

Curecanti Pass is accessible by foot on forest service trail #870 in the West Elk Wilderness Area. It divides the waters of Curecanti Creek to the south and Coal Creek to the north.

The pass is named for a minor Indian chief, Curecanti, who happened to be a twin. Curecanti Pass is about a mile southeast of Mount Guero and located in the West Elk mountain range. A long hike is necessary to reach this pass.

CURRANT CREEK PASS

Elevation: 9,470 feet

Location: T14S R74W, Map 6
County: Park
Topo: Dicks Peak
On BLM land
Other name: Thirty-Nine Mile

Currant Creek Pass is accessible by passenger car on CO9. It divides the waters of Threemile Creek to the north and Currant Creek to the south.

An 1875 map by Hayden's survey party shows and names the pass as Thirty-Nine Mile Pass. It is located thirty-nine miles out of Cañon City. This route was regularly used by Indians crossing between the Arkansas River and the South Platte River. Pictographs and well-used rock shelters showing open-fire marks can be found throughout the area. Zebulon Pike came over the pass in 1806. In 1844, Captain John Fremont crossed this way on his explorations.

When Cañon City was laid out in 1859, the residents began to design a road over the pass to Tarryall, a mile or two west of today's Fairplay. It was built in 1860, and traffic soon began to use the route regularly. When mining activity increased in the high country west of South Park, the pass was used as a stock drive way to provide beef on the hoof to mining camps.

At one time, a spur off the Denver and Rio Grande Railroad was proposed to run over the pass. The ghost towns of Balfour and Kester are located near the top. Thirty-Nine Mile Mountain is just behind Kester. □

D

DAGGETT PASS

Elevation: 10,780 feet
Location: T6S R79W, Map 6
County: Eagle
Topo: Red Cliff
National forest: White River

Daggett Pass is accessible by passenger car on forest route #728. It divides the waters of Timber Creek to the north and Turkey Creek to the south.

The pass was named for himself by Orion W. Daggett. He proposed a road route over the pass between Denver and Redcliff. Daggett was the publisher of *The Holy Cross Trail,* the newspaper in Redcliff. He would call his road the Holy Cross Trail, as well.

Daggett Pass is about two miles northwest of Shrine Pass on the same ridge but with a sunnier exposure.

The pass is not named on current forest service or topo maps. It is found on the Holy Cross National Forest map of 1929–1945, which shows a trail over the pass.

DAISY PASS

Elevation: 11,640 feet
Location: T13S R87W, Map 5
County: Gunnison

Topo: Oh-be-joyful
National forest: Gunnison

Daisy Pass is accessible by foot on forest service trail #404. It divides the waters of Poverty Gulch to the north and Oh-be-joyful Creek to the south.

The earliest known regular use of the pass is about 1910, when it provided access to the mines nearby. The trail is now well used by mountain bikers and hikers in the summer and by backcountry skiers in the winter. The pass is between Richmond Mountain to the northwest and Schuylkill Mountain to the southeast in the West Elk mountain range, at the north end of the Ruby range.

DALLAS DIVIDE

Elevation: 8,970 feet
Location: T44N R9W, Map 7
County: Ouray/San Miguel
Topo: Sams
Public access through private land
Other name: Leopard Creek Divide

Dallas Divide is accessible by passenger car on CO62. It divides the waters of Leopard Creek to the west and Cottonwood Creek to the east.

The pass is named for George Dallas, Vice President of the U.S.

A faint trail leads to Daisy Pass, hidden between two rock palisades. (*Photograph courtesy Dannels collection*)

from 1845 to 1849. It was previously called Leopard Creek Divide for the creek on the west side.

The Dominguez-Escalante party crossed this pass in 1776 while exploring in what is today's western Colorado. This route became known as the Old Spanish Trail. Otto Mears opened a toll road to Telluride over the pass in 1882; it was a bad road, but many travelers used it anyway. The Rio Grande Southern Railroad, which Mears also owned, laid track over the pass in 1889 and 1890. When the railroad was functioning, a small town with a post office and train station (also named Dallas Divide) was located at the top. This rail line was abandoned in 1952 and the rails were all gone by mid-1953, but the old railroad grade is still visible over the pass. Autos began crossing the divide here in the early 1900s. In the mid-1940s the road was improved by the state highway department.

Good views of the Sneffels mountain range to the south, and other mountains in the distance, entice the tourist. Although Dallas Divide is a low crossing, it has some of the most spectacular scenery in southwestern Colorado, and many photographers seek out views from the pass. This old mining region has become good ranching country in recent years.

DALY PASS

Elevation: 12,500 feet
Location: T10S R87W, Map 5
County: Pitkin
Topo: Capitol Peak
National forest: White River

Daly Pass is accessible by foot in the Maroon Bells–Snowmass Wilderness Area. It divides the waters of Capitol Creek to the west and West Snowmass Creek to the east.

Daly is a difficult hike; to conserve hiking energy and time, combine it with a loop hike to other passes. The pass is between Mount Daly and Capitol Peak. Hikers must beware—this is rough country. Very experienced hikers rate this as an extremely dangerous place, particularly the area between the pass and Moon Lake. The pass summit is between Capitol Lake and Moon Lake, east of Christiana Peak. Outfitters in the Snowmass area service the pass locale. Consider using them.

The pass is not named on forest service or topo maps. It is identified in some Aspen-area hiking guides.

DANIELS PASS

Elevation: 7,540 feet
Location: T14S R67W, Map 10
County: El Paso
Topo: Manitou Springs
Public access through private land

Daniels Pass is accessible by foot. It divides the watersheds of North and South Cheyenne canyons.

The trail goes over the pass about a quarter of a mile west of the summit on the west side of Muscoco Mountain. The trail is named the Cutler Trail.

The pass is shown in the *Pikes Peak Atlas.* An easy access is available off the Gold Camp Road above Helen Hunt Falls. The saddle is heavily wooded; it's interesting to look down onto the pass and over it into the Colorado Springs valley from the upper reaches of the Bear Creek Road or the Gold Camp Road. Daniels Pass is also shown on the *Ormes 1918 Map of Mountain Trails of the Pikes Peak Region.*

DART PASS

Elevation: 11,660 feet
Location: T1S R74W, Map 3
County: Boulder/Grand
Topo: East Portal
National forest: Arapaho/Roosevelt
On the Continental Divide

Dart Pass is accessible by foot; it is just off the Corona Trail to the east, and in the Indian Peaks Wilderness Area. It divides the waters of Ranch Creek to the west and the South Fork of Middle Boulder Creek to the east.

In 1873, a road was considered for this alternate route between Boulder and Grand counties. Wagons were then using a rough trail. John Rollins resisted efforts to have this road improved, because he controlled a nearby alternative.

The Corona Trail takes off toward the north at the top of Rollins Pass. Dart Pass is on the other side of the first peak. Be sure to look at all the pretty lakes nestled below from atop the pass. Dart Pass may also be reached via the King Lake Trail. King Lake is below the pass, on the east side.

Dart Pass is not named on forest service, topo, XYZ, or Trails Illustrated maps. It is identified from 1870s historic research.

DEAD MAN'S PASS

Elevation: 12,010 feet
Location: T3N R73W, Map 3
County: Boulder/Grand
Topo: Isolation Peak
In Rocky Mountain National Park
On the Continental Divide

Dead Man's Pass is accessible by foot, but no established trail goes over the pass. It divides the waters of East Inlet to the west and North St. Vrain Creek on the east.

This high pass, on the jagged saddle between Tanima and Isolation peaks, was hiked by a party of the Colorado Mountain Club in 1971. They noted the spire that looked like a large cleaver, and they called it Dead Man's Pass. This route had been regularly used by the counselors at Camp Cheley at Rocky Mountain National Park.

The pass is just north of the cleaver. It is not named on forest service, topo, or other current maps. It

is identified by Colorado Mountain Club reports.

DEADMAN HILL DIVIDE

Elevation: 10,269 feet
Location: T10N R75W, Map 3
County: Larimer
Topo: Deadman
National forest: Roosevelt

Deadman Hill Divide is accessible by passenger car on county road #162. It divides the waters of Deadman Creek to the west and the North Fork of the Cache la Poudre River to the east.

The pass is north of the Red Feather Lakes and four miles south of Little Bald Mountain. This area has deep snows in the wintertime and great views north and south.

DENVER PASS

Elevation: 11,900 feet
Location: T43N R7W, Map 8
County: San Juan
Topo: Handies Peak
On BLM land

Denver Pass is accessible by 4WD. It divides the waters of Miners Creek to the west and Burrows Creek to the east.

A well-used road went over this pass at one time between Mineral Point and Animas Forks. The pass is located on the west side of Denver Hill.

Denver Pass is not named on forest service or topo maps. James Grafton Rogers located and named it in his listing of Colorado's geographic features.

DENVER PASS

Elevation: 12,900 feet
Location: T43N R6W, Map 8
County: Hinsdale/San Juan
Topo: Handies Peak
On BLM land

Denver Pass is accessible by foot. It divides the waters of Horseshoe Creek to the west and Schafer Gulch to the east.

This pass saw some use by miners in the late 1800s; there is very little use of the route today.

No formal trail runs to the pass. There are two ways to get to it. For the first route, drive the 4WD road to the south side of Engineer Mountain and hike the ridge south to the pass. For the second route, take the 4WD road to Horseshoe Lake, then hike up to the pass, which is above the lake. The pass is a little less than four hundred feet above the lake.

This Denver Pass is located on the southeast flank of Seigal Mountain and northwest of an unnamed 13,708-foot peak.

DEVIL'S THUMB PASS

Elevation: 11,747 feet
Location: T1S R74W, Map 3
County: Boulder/Grand

Topo: East Portal
National forest: Arapaho/Roosevelt
On the Continental Divide
Other name: Boulder

Devil's Thumb Pass is accessible by foot via forest service trails #7 on the west side (in Arapaho National Forest) and #902 on the east side (in Roosevelt National Forest), in the Indian Peaks Wilderness Area. It divides the waters of Cabin Creek to the west and Jasper Creek to the east.

As early as 1860, William Byers of the *Rocky Mountain News* was writing about a "chimney rock" spire, which is today called Devil's Thumb. He called this rock formation at the pass "The Bowlder."

A pack trail over the pass has existed since the mid-1800s. If any wagons ever went over the pass, they probably did it only once. The top is an extremely steep climb up from each side.

In the 1950s, the 1960s, and again in the 1970s, consideration was given to building a major highway across northern Colorado. One suggested route was to go over or tunnel under Devil's Thumb Pass. Some property owners in the northern part of Grand County preferred the Devil's Thumb route over other alternatives that had been proposed.

An easy hiking access is via the Corona Trail, following the trail that skirts the ridge line on the west side of the Continental Divide. Some rock scrambling is required if you shortcut the trail. Oddly, the

Many passes are named for nearby geographic or geological features, such as Devil's Thumb, shown here.

"Thumb" is not visible from the pass when you get to the trail at the pass, because it blends into the rocks behind it. Technical climbers like to tackle the Thumb.

The trail that comes up from the creek drainage and over the pass crosses the saddle on the south end. The older, original crossing was on the north end of the saddle, at the foot of the thumb rock outcropping. In most years, a snowbank blocks this route, even in summer. Topo maps show this older trail.

From the top, look west toward the Winter Park Ski Area and across the Fraser Valley.

DICK PASS

Elevation: 8,146 feet
Location: T3S R94W, Map 1
County: Garfield
Topo: Thirteenmile Creek
Public access through private land

Dick Pass is accessible by passenger car on county road #252. It divides the waters of Thirteenmile Creek to the north and Fourteenmile Creek to the south.

The top is open with aspen groves up the hillside on either side of the pass. The road over the pass is the older route through this area:

it parallels the newer routes, state roads CO13 and CO789.

This old pass is named on the *New Map of Colorado 1882.*

DIFFICULT PASS

Elevation: 12,020 feet
Location: T11S R84W, Map 5
County: Pitkin
Topo: New York Peak
National forest: Gunnison/
  White River

Difficult Pass is accessible by 4WD. It divides the waters of Difficult Creek to the north and Bowman Creek to the south.

The name was first assigned to the creek, then to the pass, to commemorate the obstructions encountered in the canyon.

An old wagon road was built to provide access to the John Williams mill at the head of Difficult Canyon. After his vein of ore played out, Williams left, and several years later (in the 1920s) Frank Barr moved into the mill. That site then became known as Barr Mill.

To reach the pass, take the Gold Hill Road. Difficult Pass is on the east side of the summit of Gold Hill. The pass is adjacent (on the east side) to the Collegiate Peaks Wilderness Area. It is not named on forest service or topo maps. The pass is identified by early 1900s historical research.

DIX SADDLE

Elevation: 7,470 feet
Location: T5S R71W, Map 6
County: Jefferson
Topo: Evergreen
Public access through private land

Dix Saddle is passenger-car-accessible on county road #120, just off CO74 and up Myers Gulch one and a half miles. It divides the waters of Bear Creek to the north and Turkey Creek to the south.

The top of the pass is not marked. It is located in an area of private homes. There are no outstanding views, but a definite ridge crest is evident.

The pass is not named on the current Arapaho National Forest Service map; it is named on the topo map.

DONNER PASS

Elevation: 10,100 feet
Location: T7N R72W, Map 3
County: Larimer
Topo: Crystal Mountain
National forest: Roosevelt

Donner Pass is accessible by foot on forest service trails #926 and #934. It divides the waters of Buckhorn Creek to the north and Miller Creek to the south.

The pass is next to Signal Mountain and a half-mile southwest of Lookout Mountain. Access to the trail is on the Old Ballard logging road. Some trail signs in the past have read "Danner" Pass. A nice trail, it leads the hiker past a spring and up a wooded lane. Watch for the old sawmill along the trail. The top is wooded, with no views.

DORCHESTER PASS

Elevation: 12,660 feet
Location: T12S R83W, Map 5
County: Gunnison/Pitkin
Topo: Pieplant
National forest: Gunnison/
White River

Dorchester Pass is accessible by foot, but no established trail currently goes over the pass, which is on the border of the Collegiate Peaks Wilderness Area. It divides the waters of Lincoln Gulch to the north and the Taylor River to the south.

After the little settlement named Dorchester was established in the north end of Taylor Park, this route was used to go over the mountain ridge to the Roaring Fork Valley. No indication is left that this route was ever anything more than a trail.

The pass is the easternmost crossing of the Elk mountain range, and on the saddle between Prize Mountain and an unnamed 13,090-foot peak that forms the intersection of Chaffee, Gunnison, and Pitkin counties. The pass is not named on forest service or topo maps. It was identified by Len Shoemaker, an Aspen-area forest ranger in the 1920s.

DOUGLAS PASS

Elevation: 8,268 feet
Location: T5S R102W, Map 4
County: Garfield
Topo: Douglas Pass
On BLM land

Douglas Pass is accessible by passenger car on CO139. It divides the waters of Douglas Creek to the north and East Salt Creek to the south.

The pass is named for the northern Ute, Chief Douglas. Douglas was best known for his involvement in the Meeker massacre of September 1879.

The Dominguez-Escalante party crossed the pass in 1776 while exploring western territory. Father Escalante wrote in his diary that they discovered crude paintings on the canyon walls here. These pictographs are numerous and depict animal and human life from the Fremont Culture archaeological period.

Charlie Goslin of Vernal, Utah, started gilsonite mining operations here around 1897. He was responsible for having the trail improved to road status in order to get to the railroad via a shorter route than had been used earlier.

This area suffers from crumbling mountains. The road often is closed or partially blocked by landslides. The state highway department calls CO139 the most slide-prone highway in the state.

Located in the Book Cliff mountain range, Douglas Pass is between

Grand Junction and Rangely on a good all-weather, paved highway route, which crosses the Roan Plateau. The highway road was improved in 1960. Gas and oil pipelines now cross the pass route.

DOWE PASS

Elevation: 5,780 feet
Location: T4N R70W, Map 3
County: Larimer
Topo: Carter Lake Reservoir
Public access through private land

Dowe Pass is accessible only from the south, by passenger car on county road #47. It divides the waters of Dry Creek to the north and the Little Thompson River to the south.

The top of the pass is at a private development and cannot be crossed. The county road dead-ends at a ranch gate. No spectacular views exist; Dowe Pass is just a saddle in the foothills.

The pass is named on the topo and 1984 Roosevelt forest service maps, but it is not named on the 1990 Arapaho-Roosevelt forest service map.

DUNCKLEY PASS

Elevation: 9,763 feet
Location: T3N R87W, Map 2
County: Rio Blanco
Topo: Dunckley Pass
National forest: Routt

Dunckley Pass is accessible by passenger car on forest route #16. It divides the waters of the East Fork of Williams Fork to the west and Fish Creek to the east.

The pass is named for the five Dunckley brothers—Bob, Richard, Tom, George, and John—who ranched in this area in the 1890s.

An old Ute trail crossed the pass, and a freight road over it was built in the 1890s. This became the major cattle trail from the Williams Fork area to the rail line at Yampa.

The pass is located south of Steamboat Springs, with good views in a nice area. The top is marked and tree-covered, but a good drop-off gives open vistas. The road over the pass is gravel and is at the southeast end of the Dunckley Flat Tops Ridge.

DUNHAM GAP

Elevation: 7,090 feet
Location: T34N R7W, Map 8
County: La Plata
Topo: Bayfield
On private land

There is no access to Dunham Gap. It divides the waters of Hartman Canyon to the west and the Los Piños River to the east.

County Road #502 runs just under the east side of the gap and above the Los Piños River. The gap is the southern low spot on Arrowhead Hill and is on private land. The best view of the gap is from county road #501, the Vallecito Lake Road. This is an interesting geographic feature but an unimpressive pass.

Dunham Gap is named on the topo map.

DURANT GAP

Elevation: 7,330 feet
Location: T34N R7W, Map 8
County: La Plata
Topo: Bayfield
On private land

There is no access to Durant Gap. It divides the waters of Hartman Canyon to the west and Los Piños River to the east.

County road #502 runs just under the east side of the gap and above the Los Piños River. The gap is the northern low spot of a protruding ridge and is on private land. The best view of the gap is from county road #501, the Vallecito Lake Road. The gap is an interesting geographic feature but an unimpressive pass.

Durant Gap is named on the topo and San Juan National Forest maps.

DYKE COL

Elevation: 13,060 feet
Location: T43N R8W, Map 7
County: Ouray
Topo: Mount Sneffels
National forest: Uncompahgre

Dyke Col is accessible by foot. It divides the waters of Wilson Creek to the north and Sneffels Creek to the south.

The col is the crossing between Blaine Basin and Yankee Boy Basin and was used by miners to move between the two areas. It is named for the rhyolite dyke on the west side. Various ores are exposed at the top of the col. Little black diamonds (obsidian?) are scattered around the area.

The pass is between Cirque (to the east) and Kismet (to the west) mountains. Beyond Kismet is Mount Sneffels. No trail exists over the top, but it is easy to crawl up the loose scree and a fun slide down. Don't even think of going up the north side of the pass. Any soil for footsteps must have disappeared long ago. The route is a rope-drop now.

The best front-on views of Mount Sneffels are from around the col. Wear heavy, old pants for this descent!

The pass is not named on forest service or topo maps. It was identified by Ormes in his *Guide to the Colorado Mountains*. □

E

EAGLE PASS

Elevation: 11,770 feet
Location: T36N R11W, Map 7
County: La Plata
Topo: La Plata
National forest: San Juan

Eagle Pass is not currently accessible to the public. It divides the waters of Lewis Creek to the west and Watts Gulch to the east.

This is an old crossing that was used by miners in the La Plata City area to get into Durango. The earliest known regular use is around 1900.

The pass is located in the La Plata Range. At one time, even fairly recently, a 4WD road (forest route #60) went to the pass from the west side. Now a wire, with a "Private Road – No Trespassing" sign attached, blocks the old road above the Golden King Mill.

A mine is located near the blockage in the road. From this point it is possible to pick out a low tree-covered saddle above, on the east,

This old mill continues to deteriorate on the west side of Eagle Pass.

that should be the pass. Eagle Pass is just south of Lewis Mountain, and the road is visible above; it is difficult to see how the road would interfere with the mining operation.

Eagle Pass is not named on forest service maps, but it is named on the topo map.

EAGLE RIVER PASS

Elevation: 11,140 feet
Location: T7S R79W, Map 6
County: Eagle/Summit
Topo: Copper Mountain
On private land

Eagle River Pass is not accessible to the public. It divides the waters of the East Fork of the Eagle River to the west and Tenmile Creek to the east.

A trail dating from the 1870s crossed the pass between the Eagle River Valley and Kokomo. Kokomo and Robinson residents cut a road through the woods for a shorter access to Redcliff, a supply town. Now the pass is buried under tailings from the Robinson Tailings Pond, part of the Climax Molybdenum Mine.

This could be called "The Pass That Was." The pass area is visible from the Climax Public Access Road, a good 4WD road that is well worth the drive just to see the area, but the mining company does not allow access to the pass.

From the north side of Robinson Lake, an old road takes off to the

pass. This road is now posted, with a gate. Even if one did trespass, the pass isn't there anymore. The saddle is completely covered with mine tailings—a sad sight to see. And mountains that had been to the left and to the right of the pass have been worn down by earth-moving equipment, further obliterating the pass.

The pass is a mile southeast of Sheep Mountain, and its west side is above old Camp Hale. It is not named on forest service or topo maps. It is named on XYZ maps.

EAST GAP

Elevation: 7,620 feet
Location: T34N R10W, Map 7
County: La Plata
Topo: Basin Mountain
On the Southern Ute Indian Reservation

East Gap is not accessible to the public. It divides the waters of Basin Creek to the north and Indian Creek to the south.

Good views of the gap are accessible from passenger cars along county road #125, southeast of Hesperus. East Gap is on the east side of a small cone-shaped peak.

The gap is a rolling grassy hillside with some pines on the north side of the top. The old road that goes to the gap is now behind a locked gate. East Gap is named on the topo map.

EAST HIGHTOWER MOUNTAIN PASS

Elevation: 9,390 feet
Location: T9S R91W, Map 5
County: Mesa
Topo: Spruce Mountain
National forest: Grand Mesa/ White River

East Hightower Mountain Pass is accessible by 4WD on forest route #841. It divides the waters of Owens Creek to the west and West Willow Creek to the east.

The crossing is five miles east of Hightower Mountain and one and a half miles south of Van Mountain, in an area with many ranches. The pass is not named on forest service or topo maps. It was identified by Koch in *The Colorado Pass Book.*

EAST LONE CONE PASS

Elevation: 10,890 feet
Location: T41N R12W, Map 7
County: Dolores/San Miguel
Topo: Groundhog Mountain
National forest: San Juan/ Uncompahgre

East Lone Cone Pass is accessible by 4WD on forest route #616. It divides the waters of Beaver Creek to the north and Fish Creek to the south.

The pass is about one mile southwest of Dunn Peak, which is in the Lizard Head Wilderness Area. The name, East Lone Cone Pass, was as-signed by Koch in *The Colorado Pass Book.* East Lone Cone Pass is not named on forest service or topo maps.

EAST MAROON PASS

Elevation: 11,820 feet
Location: T12S R86W, Map 5
County: Gunnison/Pitkin
Topo: Maroon Bells
National forest: Gunnison/ White River

East Maroon Pass is accessible by foot via forest service trails #1983 on the north side and #983 on the south side, in the Maroon Bells–Snowmass Wilderness Area. It divides the waters of East Maroon Creek to the north and Copper Creek to the south.

Travelers of the 1870s used the pass to cross between Gothic and Aspen. At one time a rough wagon road existed up the Copper Creek Valley. Ore was packed to the wagon road in Copper Canyon, then to the mill at Gothic or on to the railroad at Crested Butte. During 1887 a toll road was built from Copper Creek to the junction of the east and west forks of Maroon Creek. An avalanche killed four workmen on this endeavor. The roads over the pass could not withstand the weather and did not survive more than a few years.

The area is subject to snowslides in wet years. A January 1886 slide wiped out a mining camp. But sometimes benefits occur from such slides. A butcher driving beef on the hoof to the new mining town of Aspen in the 1880s got to the pass, where his cattle were stranded in the deep snows. He butchered the animals and buried their carcasses in the snow to preserve them. The next spring he returned, dug up the beef, and took it on to Aspen.

A good hike or horseback trip can be made between Aspen and Crested Butte via East Maroon Pass. The top is above a high-country meadow that can be marshy in a wet year, but the lower trail is good.

The pass is above Copper Basin and Copper Lake (to the south); it is a popular summer hiking destination.

EAST SNOWMASS PASS

Elevation: 12,700 feet
Location: T11S R86W, Map 5
County: Pitkin
Topo: Maroon Bells
National forest: White River
Other name: Snowdrift

East Snowmass Pass is accessible by foot on forest service trail #1977 in the Maroon Bells–Snowmass Wilderness Area. It divides the waters of East Snowmass Creek to the west and Willow Creek to the east.

Len Shoemaker, a forest ranger in the Aspen area, gave the pass two names. He called it Snowdrift for a drift he saw at the top, and East Snowmass for the local term used for natural features in the vicinity and because it divides the waters of East Snowmass and Willow creeks.

The name "Snow Mass" was assigned by the 1873 Hayden survey party when they looked at the mountainous region from Grays Peak. The name has also been given to several other geographic features in the Aspen area.

Willow Lake is below the pass on the south. The pass is not named on forest service or topo maps. It is identified in Aspen-area hiking guides.

ECCLES PASS

Elevation: 11,900 feet
Location: T5S R78W, Map 6
County: Summit
Topo: Vail Pass
National forest: Arapaho

Eccles Pass is accessible by foot via forest service trail #60 (the Gore Range Trail) in the Eagles Nest Wilderness Area. It divides the waters of South Willow Creek to the north and Meadow Creek to the south.

The pass is named for James Eccles, a well-known British climber. It was used by miners from the Frisco area to cross into the valley below Red Peak. Some silver was found in the valley around 1880. A wagon road of sorts existed at one time.

Eccles Pass is a narrow but well-defined saddle between Dillon and Vail. There are excellent views of the Gore Range to the north and lots of pretty but rugged peaks. Meadow Creek Trail accesses the pass from near Frisco. Just north of the pass are two little lakes, now unofficially named Edward's Lake and Lake Gloria by the authors of this book.

ELECTRIC PASS

Elevation: 13,500 feet
Location: T11S R85W, Map 5
County: Pitkin
Topo: Hayden Peak
National forest: White River

Electric Pass is accessible by foot on forest service trail #1984 in the Maroon Bells–Snowmass Wilderness Area. It divides the waters of Conundrum Creek to the west and Castle Creek to the east.

The pass was named in the 1920s by Len Shoemaker, a forest ranger who was knocked to the ground several times by static electricity at the summit. He escaped by rolling down the mountain slopes. The 1873 Hayden survey party also noted the electricity atop the pass.

Miners used the pass in the 1880s. In early days it was called the Panorama Horseback Trail or the Pine Creek Prospector Trail. Mostly it was used by miners leading their animals and packing gold ore to Ashcroft.

Do not attempt to move down into the Conundrum Valley area from the pass, a very dangerous descent. Stay on the trail as shown on the maps. Electric Pass is located above Cathedral Lake, one mile south of Hayden Peak and on a ridge between Hayden and Cathedral

peaks. It is named on the forest service map. The topo map shows the trail that crosses the pass.

ELK BASIN PASS

Elevation: 9,990 feet
Location: T15S R90W, Map 5
County: Gunnison
Topo: Minnesota Pass
National forest: Gunnison

Elk Basin Pass is accessible by foot at the western edge of the West Elk Wilderness Area. It divides the waters of the South Fork of the Minnesota River to the north and North Smith Fork to the south.

The pass is one mile east of Coal Mountain and west of the Chain Mountains. It is not named on the forest service map, but it is on the topo and Trails Illustrated maps.

ELKHEAD PASS

Elevation: 13,220 feet
Location: T13S R80W, Map 5
County: Chaffee
Topo: Mount Harvard
National forest: San Isabel

Elkhead Pass is accessible by foot on forest service trail #1469 in the Collegiate Peaks Wilderness Area. It divides the waters of Missouri Gulch to the north and Pine Creek to the south.

The pass is on the east side of Missouri Mountain and on the west side of Mount Belford. This is a difficult hike on a good hiking trail, but the views make it worthwhile.

ELWOOD PASS

Elevation: 11,660 feet
Location: T37N R3E, Map 8
County: Rio Grande
Topo: Elwood Pass
National forest: Rio Grande/
  San Juan
On the Continental Divide
Other name: Military

Elwood Pass is accessible on the east side by passenger car in good weather on forest route #667. The west side is accessible by 4WD. It divides the waters of Elwood Creek to the west and Iron Creek to the east.

The correct spelling is with one l, not with two, as is sometimes seen.

The pass is named by and for an early settler, T. L. Woodvale. The L and the first part of his last name construct the "Elwood" he used for the pass name.

This area was used by Ute Indians to reach the hot springs at today's Pagosa Springs. It was the first route into the San Luis Valley from the west. In 1876, travelers cut a rough access road through the forest. Then, in 1877, a charter was granted to the Conejos, Pagosa Springs and Rio Grande Toll Road Company, for a toll road up the Alamosa River to the summit and down the western slope to the San Juan River and on to Pagosa Springs. Mail was carried over this road by 1878 between Summitville and Pagosa Springs. In 1880, U.S. soldiers improved the road, which is why it was called Military Pass for a few years. Supplies were hauled over Military Pass to Fort Lewis, at Pagosa Springs.

In August 1896, two Alamosa residents, Frank Spencer and Arthur Flynn, stopped atop the pass. While there, they penned the words to "Where the Columbines Grow." In 1915 the state legislature adopted their poem as the Colorado state song. (Music had been added by that time.) The top of the pass is in a pretty alpine meadow filled with flowers that sway in the wind. It is easy to understand the inspiration for a song about columbines.

In 1911, Elwood Pass was considered for and rejected as a major highway. Again in 1913, consideration was given to making Elwood Pass the state route to the southwestern part of Colorado, but it didn't happen. A natural gas pipeline was laid over the pass in 1961.

Elwood Pass is on the Continental Divide Trail.

EMPIRE PASS

Elevation: 8,760 feet
Location: T3S R74W, Map 6
County: Clear Creek
Topo: Georgetown
Public access through private land
Other name: Union

Empire Pass is accessible by passenger car from the north via county road #252, and by foot from the south. It divides the waters of the West Fork of Clear Creek to the north and Clear Creek to the south.

The pass takes its name from a nearby community. The alternate name, Union, comes from the Civil War, when Union and Confederate sympathizers lived on opposite sides of the pass.

This old crossing is only two miles long and runs between Empire and Georgetown. It was once the main wagon road between the two towns. Now it's a short and easy hike from Georgetown, a short and easy drive from Empire. Look for the rock cribbing along the trail on the south side. Look also for bighorn sheep.

The 1990 Arapaho-Roosevelt forest service map places the brackets showing Empire Pass along I70. It isn't. The south side of the pass is visible from the interstate highway, though.

ENGINEER PASS

Elevation: 12,800 feet
Location: T43N R7W, Map 8
County: Hinsdale/Ouray
Topo: Handies Peak
On BLM land

Engineer Pass is accessible by 4WD. It divides the waters of Bear Creek to the west and Henson Creek to the east.

The road over the pass was built in 1877 by Otto Mears. The first stagecoach from Lake City to Animas Forks crossed the pass in August 1877. The wayside station used by travelers was called Rose's Cabin, and drivers changed their six horses there.

In this remote country it is hard to imagine people actually crossing the pass on foot, especially in the winter. Reverend Darley, who established churches in Ouray and Lake City, once put on his snowshoes and went over the pass in a blizzard. It took him sixteen hours to go from Ouray to Rose's Cabin. Other winter travelers tried to put snowshoes on their burros and head over the pass.

The route over Engineer Pass is considered one of the most enjoyable 4WD roads in the state. The pass is north of Engineer Mountain but not at the highest point on the road. American Flats is the name of the area just east of the top where hundreds of acres of wildflowers and grasses grow each summer. Just west of the saddle, the road climbs up and crawls across a rock face on the west side of Engineer Mountain. The pass road is now part of the Alpine Loop Byway, a scenic and historic backcountry designation by the Bureau of Land Management. □

F

FALL CREEK PASS

Elevation: 12,580 feet
Location: T7S R81W, Map 5
County: Eagle
Topo: Mount of the Holy Cross
National forest: White River

Fall Creek Pass is accessible by foot on forest service trail #2001 in the Holy Cross Wilderness. It divides the waters of Fall Creek to the north and French Creek to the south.

Although there was much mining activity here in the 1880s, there is no indication that the pass trail was ever more than just a pack trail.

The pass can be reached from either the south or north sides and is above Lake Constantine on the north on the Holy Cross Ridge. Views to the east from the top are of the Ten Mile Range. Travel by Hunky Dory Lake, then Seven Sisters Lakes en route to the pass from the south. A good side hike leads to the ghost town of Holy Cross City.

FALL RIVER PASS

Elevation: 11,796 feet
Location: T6N R75W, Map 3
County: Larimer
Topo: Fall River Pass
In Rocky Mountain National Park

Fall River Pass is accessible by passenger car on US34. It divides the waters of the Cache la Poudre River on the west and Fall River on the east. The pass is named for Fall River.

Indians first used the pass. In 1915 the Arapahos were still crossing the open area they called the Dog Trail. They used dogs to haul their goods, particularly in the winter when the travois would skid easily across the snow. Trappers and prospectors next used the route.

Discussion of a plan to connect Grand Lake and Estes Park by a road over the high country began in 1895. By 1912 the need for the road had increased to the point that Larimer County commissioners and Rocky Mountain National Park officials ordered a survey to the summit of the Fall River divide from the south. In early 1913 the route was considered a state highway.

Work began on the road, the first part of which was built with convict labor. In 1919 a misunderstanding arose about just where the road was to cross the divide. The surveying had been done over a more northern route, which the county and state preferred, but the road was actually being constructed over Fall River Pass, the route preferred by the park officials. These officials preferred the six-hundred-foot-higher, but more scenic, crossing, and they prevailed. The road was completed within the year.

On September 14, 1920, the road was opened between Grand Lake and Estes Park. It provided service between the two communities until another road was developed over Trail Ridge in 1932. The Fall River road follows a valley up to the pass on each side, while the later route runs atop a ridge.

From 1952 to 1968, the road was completely closed above Chasm Falls. Then, in 1968, the road was re-opened all the way through. It is now a one-way, uphill-only road. Snow prevails late into spring in the valley up Fall River Pass. The pass is located where the dirt-base Fall River Road enters US34 at the Visitor's Center on Trail Ridge Road.

Fall River Road runs along the rock formation called "Face of the Indian." The road is closed after Labor Day each year. In the winter, skiers and snowshoers use the trail.

FANCY PASS

Elevation: 12,380 feet
Location: T7S R82W, Map 5
County: Eagle
Topo: Mount Jackson
National forest: White River

Fancy Pass is accessible by foot on forest service trail #2006 in the Holy Cross Wilderness Area. It divides the waters of Cross Creek to the north and Fancy Creek to the south. The pass is named for Joseph Fancy, an 1880s miner.

This pass was originally just a ridge with no opening. Miners used dynamite to blast a gap.

In the 1880s, when mining activity was heavy in the high country of the Holy Cross Ridge, big timbers and the bulky, heavy mill machinery needed at the Treasure Vault Mill were brought over the pass. To get the goods over the sheer cliffs on the west side, ropes were used to lower the machinery item by item. Pins, much like those today's rock climbers use, were pounded into the rocks to pass ropes through and help support the weight. Mules were used to carry as much of the weight as they could hold.

A road once ran over the pass and down to Holy Cross City. This road was built by the Treasure Vault Mining Company when they wanted to get their mill to Holy Cross City. Their competition, the Gold Park Milling and Mining Company, had denied Treasure Vault the use of Gold Park's road. So Treasure Vault made its own.

The pass is above Fancy Lake. An elevation gain of eight hundred feet is required in the half-mile from the lake to the pass summit. From the top, the views to the east are of the Ten Mile Range. To the west, the Cross Creek Valley leads down to Minturn. The pass is the crossing of the southern part of the Holy Cross Ridge. The top is usually filled with snow.

A ranger crosses through the narrow opening atop Fancy Pass in this historical photograph. (*Photograph courtesy Denver Public Library, Western History Department*)

FAWN CREEK PASS

Elevation: 10,180 feet
Location: T2S R75W, Map 3
County: Grand
Topo: East Portal
National forest: Arapaho

Fawn Creek Pass is accessible by passenger car on forest route #149. It divides the waters of the South Fork of Ranch Creek to the north and Jim Creek to the south.

The South Fork of Ranch Creek was called Fawn Creek in earlier days and on early maps. Thus, the pass was named for one of the creeks it heads.

A water tank and a wye were constructed for the railroad at this minor pass. Many railroad workers lived at the camp town called Arrow, which was near Fawn Creek Pass.

The present-day car route crosses the wide part of the saddle. The pass is part of the old railroad route through this backcountry, located east of Winter Park.

The pass is not named on current forest service or topo maps. It is shown and named on the 1912 Central City fifteen-minute quad map and on XYZ maps.

FLINT PASS

Elevation: 11,630 feet
Location: T6N R74W, Map 3
County: Larimer
Topo: Comanche Peak
In Rocky Mountain National Park

Flint Pass is accessible by foot, but no established trail goes over the pass. It divides the waters of the South Fork of the Cache la Poudre River to the east and Hauge Creek to the west.

Roger Toll named the pass in 1927 in honor of the flint chips he found atop it, which suggest that Indians made arrowheads here.

A trip into the high country here lends itself to a backpack excursion. Allow extra time and combine a hike to Flint with hikes to nearby passes.

FLOYD HILL

Elevation: 7,920 feet
Location: T4S R72W, Map 6
County: Clear Creek
Topo: Squaw Pass
Public access through private land

Floyd Hill is accessible by passenger car on I70. It divides the waters of Clear Creek to the north and Beaver Brook to the south.

The pass is not named on the topo or Arapaho National Forest Service maps. There is a highway department sign at the top.

FOREST CANYON PASS

Elevation: 11,300 feet
Location: T5N R75W, Map 3
County: Larimer
Topo: Fall River Pass
In Rocky Mountain National Park

Forest Canyon Pass is accessible by foot. It divides the waters of the

Cache la Poudre River to the west and the Big Thompson River to the east.

The area was originally known as Willow Canyon because of the number of willows there. But lots of conifers also grow along the slopes of this high valley, so Forest Canyon is as appropriate a name as any other.

This pass is visible from Trail Ridge Road. The top is flat, open, and at the edge of timberline. An old indistinct road from the early 1900s provides a hiking trail. Look for bighorn sheep, elk, and deer.

The pass is on the old Ute Trail through Rocky Mountain National Park.

FREMONT PASS

Elevation: 11,318 feet
Location: T8S R79W, Map 6
County: Lake
Topo: Climax
Public access through private land
On the Continental Divide
Other names: Alicante, Arkansas, Tenmile

Fremont Pass is passenger-car-accessible on CO91. It divides the waters of Tenmile Creek to the north and the Arkansas River to the south.

The pass is named for Captain John Fremont, the explorer who passed this way in 1844 but who did not go over the pass. Fremont Pass was part of the western boundary of the Louisiana Purchase of 1803 dividing French land from Spanish property in North America.

In 1872 the pass was called Arkansas Pass. A town and mine named Alicante existed for a few years at the foot of the pass.

The pass was still called Tenmile by federal agencies as late as the 1930s, but the railroad was calling it Fremont's Pass (as did Ingersoll in his book *Crest of the Continent*) in 1885. An 1898 map shows the pass as Tenmile.

Ore was found on the pass in August 1879. It was thought then to be graphite. Only after World War I did the discovery become important, but it was molybdenum, not graphite.

In 1880 the Denver and Rio Grande ran an extension line (the Blue River Extension) between Leadville and Kokomo. The South Park Railroad crossed in 1884; there were then two railroads traveling over the pass. Snow closed the rail lines nearly every winter.

In 1936 three high passes in the state were kept open each winter— one of these was Fremont. In 1947 the highway was still a dirt road for the eight miles that traversed the top.

In 1936 a small ski area began operating on the Chalk Mountain side of the pass. It closed about the same time the mining company town, Climax, was moved to Leadville, in the early 1960s.

In 1937 the narrow-gauge track over the pass was changed to standard gauge. In 1988 the Leadville, Colorado and Southern Railroad

Company opened for tourist excursions. The line now runs from Leadville toward Fremont Pass.

The pass is today best known for the Climax Mine at its top. The Mount of the Holy Cross is visible from several points just north of the pass along the highway.

Fremont Pass is on the Continental Divide Trail. The Ten Mile Range borders the pass on the east side. This area is believed to be the cloudiest place in Colorado. Climax Mine logs 729 hours (on the average) of measurable precipitation each year.

FRENCH PASS

Elevation: 12,046 feet
Location: T7S R77W, Map 6
County: Park/Summit
Topo: Boreas Pass
National forest: Arapaho/Pike
On the Continental Divide

French Pass is accessible by foot via forest service trail #651 on the south side (in Pike National Forest) and by an unnumbered trail on the north side (in Arapaho National Forest). It divides the waters of French Gulch to the north and French Creek to the south.

The pass is named for French Pete, a trapper and French Canadian, who found some of the crossings that later became roads.

Indians used the pass to cross to and from the Blue River. In 1860, a forest fire on both sides of the pass wiped out several mining camps and caused injuries. By 1861, wagons were crossing here, indicating some road construction had been done.

History books printed in 1867 mention the crossing. French Pass was well used when the boom miners started streaming into the Blue Valley looking for gold. Miners improved the pass crossing into a regular wagon route in the 1880s. French Gulch, just to the north, is the site of the "Ten Years' War," a legal battle for control of the rich ores of the valley.

French is one of the oldest passes in the area; it used to be the best way to travel between South Park and Summit County. The pass is on the Colorado Trail, located between Bald Mountain and Mount Guyot. Hikers use the old wagon road, then follow a trail to the open top. This is not a well-known or highly used area.

FRIGID AIR PASS

Elevation: 12,380 feet
Location: T11S R86W, Map 5
County: Gunnison
Topo: Snowmass Mountain
National forest: White River
Other name: Fravert

Frigid Air Pass is accessible by foot on forest service trail #1974 in the Maroon Bells–Snowmass Wilderness Area. It divides the waters of the North Fork of the Crystal River to the north and the East Fork of the Crystal River to the south.

The pass is named in honor of the cold winds that nearly always blow over the summit. The alternate name, Fravert, comes from the Fravert Basin, located below the pass.

Frigid Air Pass is in the Elk Mountains. This is a good hike on a good trail, and it can be combined with other passes, as well.   □

G

G GAP

Elevation: 6,875 feet
Location: T10N R100W, Map 1
County: Moffat
Topo: G Spring
On BLM land

G Gap is 4WD-accessible in good weather; some low draws may be dangerous in rainy conditions. It divides the waters of East Dry Creek to the west and Dry Fork Sand Wash to the east.

Located in the canyon lands of northwest Colorado, this pass's top is covered in sagebrush and piñon; it's dry and hot in the summer. It is

The northwestern corner of Colorado has many interesting and unusual views, such as this one near G Gap.

out in the middle of nowhere, but getting there makes for a good drive, with interesting rock formations to observe en route.

The pass allows hiking access to various roadless areas in the Vermillion Basin, areas that are now being considered for wilderness status by conservation groups. G Gap is named on the topo map.

GAME PASS

Elevation: 9,780 feet
Location: T4N R73W, Map 3
County: Larimer
Topo: Longs Peak
On private land

Game Pass is accessible by foot, but no established trail currently goes over the pass. It divides the waters of two gulches off Tahosa Creek. The pass location is south of the present trail to the top of Twin Sisters Peak.

Game Pass is not named on current maps. It is shown on the 1911 *Map of Long's Peak and Vicinity,* by William Cooper and Dean Babcock.

GARNER PASS

Elevation: 12,700 feet
Location: T46N R11E, Map 9
County: Custer/Saguache
Topo: Electric Peak
National forest: Rio Grande/
** San Isabel**

Garner Pass is accessible by foot

on forest service trail #752. It divides the waters of Garner Creek to the west and North Lake Creek to the east.

West access is up Garner Creek Draw. The pass top is between Cottonwood Peak and Thirsty Peak. The trail continues east to Rainbow Lake. The Rainbow Trail provides access to the trailhead from the east.

The pass is not named on forest service or topo maps. It was identified by Ormes in his *Guide to the Colorado Mountains.*

GEORGIA PASS

Elevation: 11,585 feet
Location: T7S R76W, Map 6
County: Park/Summit
Topo: Boreas Pass
National forest: Arapaho/Pike
On the Continental Divide
Other names: Jefferson, Swan River

Georgia Pass is accessible on the south side by passenger car in dry weather via forest route #54, and by 4WD the rest of the time. The north side is accessible by 4WD, and then only for very experienced drivers via an unnumbered route. The pass divides the waters of the South Fork of the Swan River to the north and Michigan Creek to the south.

Georgia Pass is on the dividing line of the old Utah and Kansas territories, from which Colorado Territory was carved. When Captain John Fremont passed through in 1844, he bypassed the area because the Arapaho were already present. A few early settlers decided to take another route as well whenever Indians were present in the pass. Both Utes and Arapahos used the crossing extensively.

The pass was used before the Civil War by trappers and prospectors. It was heavily used in the 1859 mining boom as miners from the east swarmed over to reach the wealth in the Blue Valley.

The *Rocky Mountain News* reported when an early attempt at a road had been made: in January 1861, eight wagons crossed the pass. It took twenty men to shovel the snow ahead of the wagons. A charter was granted for a toll road over the "Swan River" Pass in November 1861. When Hayden's surveyors visited in 1873 they made note that the pass was easy to cross via the established wagon road.

Don't even think about taking a passenger car down the north side, and think two or three times about a 4WD. Several descents into the Swan River Gulch are not road-like.

The pass top is an open, grassy saddle with fine views. The area is now well used by mountain bikers. The Colorado Trail crosses the pass.

GILL CREEK DIVIDE

Elevation: 8,400 feet
Location: T15S R101W, Map 4
County: Mesa

Topo: Snyder Flats
National forest: Uncompahgre

Gill Creek Divide is accessible by 4WD via forest route #417. It divides the waters of West Creek to the north and Gill Creek to the south.

The pass is located just off Divide Road, atop a plateau.

GLACIER PASS

Elevation: 12,300 feet
Location: T6S R76W, Map 6
County: Park/Summit
Topo: Boreas Pass
National forest: Arapaho/Pike
On the Continental Divide

Glacier Pass is accessible by foot, but no established trail goes over the pass. It divides the waters of Missouri Gulch to the west and Jefferson Creek to the east.

The pass is on the west side of Glacier Peak. Although there is only foot access, it is possible to get within about a quarter-mile of the pass by 4WD on the Glacier Ridge Trail.

Look for the good views to the east into the Jefferson Creek Valley. The pass is not named on forest service or topo maps, but many years ago a forest service sign marked the way to it.

GOLDEN GATE PASS

Elevation: 7,754 feet
Location: T3S R72W, Map 3

County: Gilpin
Topo: Ralston Buttes
Public access through private land
Other name: Guy's Hill

Golden Gate Pass is accessible by passenger car via county road #70. It divides the waters of Tucker Gulch to the east and Guy Gulch to the west.

Utes first lived in this area. Next came the trappers and settlers. The old town of Gate City was located nearby. Gate City was probably along the old wagon road that became today's US6. The old road to Central City went up over this pass rather than up the valley of Clear Creek. In early days the route was called Guy's Hill for the geographic feature nearby.

The pass is located southeast of Golden Gate Canyon State Park. It is not named on current forest service or topo maps, but this is an old crossing that was well used in early mining days.

GORE PASS

Elevation: 9,524 feet
Location: T1N R82W, Map 2
County: Grand
Topo: Gore Pass
National forest: Arapaho/Routt
Other names: Elkhorn, Toponas

Gore Pass is accessible by passenger car on CO134. It divides the waters of Pass Creek to the north and Blacktail Creek to the south.

The pass is named for Sir St. George Gore, a young Irish baronet who hunted here as early as 1854. Edward Berthoud claims to have named the pass after Sir Gore in 1861, when Berthoud, Jim Bridger, and their party crossed here while scouting a rail route west. H. M. Vaile, Commissioner of Indian Affairs, claimed he named the pass after Sir Gore in 1863, on a trip from Denver to the Great Salt Lake, when he crossed the pass.

Two other theories about the name exist. One is that the pass is named for the wedge shape (a "gore") of the pass area. And Gannett, of Hayden's survey party, thought the name was for George Gore, who was a Denver gunsmith of some renown.

"Gore Pass" shows on the Mountain Men's Middle Park map of 1859. A 1908 Clason map shows the location as Toponas Pass. A road over the "Toponas Summit" was improved in 1908. In 1839 the Farnham party camped on the pass, which was a trail by 1866, an improved wagon road by 1874, and a highway by 1956.

On June 21, 1861, an overland mail route from the Missouri River to California was begun, and it crossed the pass. In November 1861 a charter was issued to the Colorado and Pacific Wagon, Telegraph and Railroad Company for a wagon road over "Gore's Pass." By 1865, Gore Pass was being touted as "the western gate through which the trade of the continent will flow . . ." In 1866, a mountain traveler wrote in the *Rocky Mountain News* about following the old Indian trail over the "Elkhorn Pass." In January 1867, the Colorado and California Wagon Road Company was issued a charter for a toll road. Then, the Gore's Pass and White River Wagon Road Company charter was issued late in 1867 for a road that had opened in 1865.

A pioneer had built a home atop the pass sometime before 1872. By 1879 a regular stage route was running from Georgetown to Empire to Berthoud Pass and Hot Sulphur Springs via the Gore Pass road. Some accounts in the late 1800s tell of a "crazy man" who lived in a cabin at the pass. He was said to wear a stovepipe on his head in which he had a live fire to keep evil spirits away.

In 1880 the Denver, Utah and Pacific Railroad proposed to build a narrow gauge line over the pass; in 1881 the Denver and Rio Grande surveyed the pass for their rail route. But neither rail line was ever built. Before plans to build a railroad were scrapped, though, a land developer began speculating in properties along the route.

Gore Pass was the favored route of early pioneers. It was well used as a cattle drive until the railroads were in place in 1888. Stages were still running in 1906 from Kremmling over Gore Pass and on to Steamboat Springs during warm weather; by 1908, when the railroad reached

Toponas, this service was discontinued. A state highway map of 1916 shows an auto road over the pass, but by 1923 it was still not fit for motorized vehicles. In the 1930s, travelers began asking for improvements in the road over Gore. When heavy snows fell on US40 farther north, Gore Pass was a better road choice because it is a low crossing. But the Gore route was always in such poor condition that it was rarely chosen for travel. Gore Pass was more heavily traveled when it was used in 1960 as the detour for US40.

The pass is tree-covered, with a campground at the top. It is a pretty area but lacks spectacular views.

GRAHAM PASS

Elevation: 12,540 feet
Location: T11S R82W, Map 5
County: Lake/Pitkin
Topo: Independence Pass
National forest: San Isabel/
  White River
On the Continental Divide

Graham Pass is accessible by foot in the Collegiate Peaks Wilderness Area. It divides the waters of Grizzly Creek to the west and Graham Gulch to the east.

The pass is named for Benjamin Graham, a prospector who used it in the 1860s and 1870s.

The pass was first used to reach Hurst's mining camp, near the old mining camp of Ruby.

Upper access to the pass is via McNasser Gulch; lower access is up Graham Gulch (although this particular trail is not shown on some newer maps). The pass is one and a half miles northwest of Grizzly Peak.

Graham Pass is not named on forest service or topo maps. Len Shoemaker named the pass in his histories.

GRANITE PASS

Elevation: 12,085 feet
Location: T4N R73W, Map 3
County: Larimer
Topo: Longs Peak
In Rocky Mountain National Park

Granite Pass is accessible by foot on the trail to Longs Peak. It divides the waters of Alpine Brook to the east and Boulder Brook to the west.

The USGS Board on Geographic Names officially named the pass in 1911.

The pass is on the shoulder of Battle Mountain. It is hiked by everyone who climbs Longs Peak, but rarely do peak climbers stop to enjoy it.

GRASSY GAP

Elevation: 7,050 feet
Location: T5N R87W, Map 2
County: Routt
Topo: Mount Harris
On Colorado state land

Grassy Gap is passenger-car-accessible on county road #27. It divides the waters of Grassy Creek to the north and Fish Creek to the south.

The pass was named by cowboys in the late nineteenth century for the good grazing it offered. A wagon road was built over the pass in the late 1800s. This is now a main route for local ranchers and miners. Even though the terrain features a lot of sagebrush and open country, the pass is an interesting break in the vista.

The pass is named on the Routt National Forest Service map.

GRASSY PASS

Elevation: 11,220 feet
Location: T8N R76W, Map 3
County: Larimer
Topo: Rawah Lakes
National forest: Roosevelt

Grassy Pass is accessible by foot on forest service trail #961 in the Rawah Wilderness Area. It divides the waters of Rawah Creek to the north and the North Fork of the West Branch of the Laramie River to the south.

Because there are lots of flowers here, this is a pretty hike. Watch for mosquitoes.

GRASSY PASS

Elevation: 12,620 feet
Location: T7S R82W, Map 5
County: Eagle

Topo: Mount Jackson
National forest: White River

Grassy Pass is accessible by foot, but no established trail currently goes over the pass, which is in the Holy Cross Wilderness Area. It divides the waters of Cross Creek to the east and Lime Creek to the west.

The pass is between Strawberry Lakes and Blodgett Lake; it is two miles northwest of Savage Peak. Look for some of the many pretty lakes here.

This Grassy Pass is not named on forest service or topo maps. It was identified by Ormes in his *Guide to the Colorado Mountains.*

GREAT DIVIDE

Elevation: 6,800 feet
Location: T9N R95W, Map 1
County: Moffat
Topo: Bald Mountain
Public access through private land
Other name: Iron Springs Divide

Great Divide is passenger-car-accessible on county road #6. It divides the waters of Little Snake River to the north and the Yampa River to the south.

In 1918 and in the 1930s, this pass was called Iron Springs Divide, but no road was shown on maps of that period, just a geographic ridge line.

The Great Divide Homestead Colony was established here in about 1915 to try dry-land farming in the northwestern part of the state.

By 1918, one cabin had been built; in the twenties many homes were constructed. Miles of barbed wire were strung to fence in the extensive grazing lands. A magazine named *Great Divide* was started to promote the venture. It lasted through the thirties, then began to decline.

The divide itself is southwest of the old town of Great Divide. Lots of antelope graze nearby. The pass is named in the BLM maps book.

GREENHILL DIVIDE

Elevation: 9,340 feet
Location: T23S R69W, Map 9
County: Custer
Topo: Saint Charles Peak
National forest: San Isabel

Greenhill Divide is passenger-car-accessible via CO165. It divides the waters of Middle Creek to the north and Willow Creek to the south.

The top is not marked. It is wide and open, on the Greenhorn Highway, and located in the Wet Mountain Valley. The pass is two miles east of St. Charles Peak.

GRIZZLY PASS

Elevation: 12,756 feet
Location: T5S R76W, Map 6
County: Clear Creek/Summit
Topo: Grays Peak
National forest: Arapaho
On the Continental Divide
Other names: Irwin, Quail

Grizzly Pass is accessible by foot, but no established trail currently goes over the pass. It divides the waters of the North Fork of the Snake River to the west and Grizzly Gulch to the east.

The pass is named for nearby Grizzly Gulch. The alternate name of "Irwin" comes from Richard Irwin, a miner who proposed the wagon road for the pass.

The XYZ maps show the spot as Irwin Pass with an alternate name of Quail Pass. In the high country here, ptarmigan are more likely to be found than quail; perhaps some early traveler didn't know the difference.

In 1867 a wagon road was planned for the pass by the Georgetown and Breckenridge Wagon Road Company. It would have run between Georgetown and Breckenridge. Edward Berthoud filed for permission to continue the Colorado Central Railroad from Georgetown over this pass.

The Ten Mile Wagon Road Company in 1878 began building a road from Bakerville up the Grizzly Gulch toward Irwin Pass. W. A. H. Loveland had ideas of building over a pass just north of Grizzly. His route won out and is now a major crossing while Grizzly has been almost forgotten, except by historians.

Used by early prospectors, miners, and settlers, this route was discovered earlier than were most other routes through this section of the mountains.

One of the earliest known attempts to tunnel under the Continental Divide occurred at the pass. A promoter, Mark Pomeroy, proposed to drill between the upper end of Peru Creek and the upper end of Grizzly Gulch (near Grizzly Pass).

The pass is between Grizzly Peak to the south and an unnamed 13,117-foot peak to the north. Grizzly Pass is not named on current forest service or topo maps. It is named on the XYZ maps.

GUANELLA PASS

Elevation: 11,669 feet
Location: T5S R74W, Map 6
County: Clear Creek
Topo: Mount Evans
National forest: Arapaho/Pike
Other name: Geneva

Guanella Pass is passenger-car-accessible via county road #381. It divides the waters of South Clear Creek to the north and Duck Creek to the south.

The pass is named for Byron Guanella, a Clear Creek County commissioner from Empire. He was a big supporter of building a road over the pass.

Buffalo used the crossing to move from the Clear Creek Valley to South Park. Therefore, Indians too used the pass to follow their food supply. There are reports that some early prospectors were killed by Indians in this region.

The pass was noted by Edward

Berthoud, Jim Bridger, and their scouting party in 1861, while they were looking for railroad crossings.

The road over the pass used to be called the Geneva Park Trail. This road was greatly improved in 1962. The Cabin Creek hydroelectric plant is on the north access to the pass.

Several hikes take off from the top, which is open, has good vistas, and makes a fine day trip from the big cities of the Front Range. This is a good place to see the fall colors and there are lots of campgrounds. Watch for ptarmigan near the pass.

GUNSIGHT GAP

Elevation: 7,980 feet

Location: T5N R101W, Map 1
County: Moffat
Topo: Skull Creek
On BLM and private land

There is no access to Gunsight Gap. It divides the waters of Wolf Creek to the north and Miller Creek to the south. It can be located by driving up the Watson Draw Road and is obvious when one views the "gunsight bead" within the saddle on the ridge. The pass is named in the BLM maps book and on the topo map.

GUNSIGHT PASS

Elevation: 8,332 feet
Location: T3N R80W, Map 2

Anyone who has ever looked down the barrel of a rifle will understand why this pass is named Gunsight Gap.

County: Grand
Topo: Gunsight Pass
On BLM land
Other name: Gunshot

Gunsight Pass is accessible by passenger car on county road #2. It divides the waters of Antelope Creek to the west and Troublesome Creek to the east.

A stage road was built over the pass many years ago, but it was never used for much more than local traffic. The area is now used for cattle grazing.

The forest service's 1985 Routt map shows an old access on the east side of the pass that is no longer usable. Ascend the west side: At the top, take the road that descends south (not east) to bypass the private land holdings. Newer maps show the correct route.

GUNSIGHT PASS

Elevation: 12,090 feet
Location: T13S R87W, Map 5
County: Gunnison
Topo: Oh-be-joyful
National forest: Gunnison

Gunsight Pass is 4WD-accessible on forest route #585 on its north side. The south-side access is closed by a molybdenum mine. The pass divides the waters of Oh-be-joyful Creek to the north and Coal Creek to the south.

The pass is identified by the rock notch in the ridge and is located next to Mount Emmons, at the southeast end of Scarp Ridge. Snow can be found near the top throughout the summer except in dry years.

This pass is best known for the large number of switchbacks on its north approach.

GUNSIGHT PASS

Elevation: 12,167 feet
Location: T51N R3E, Map 5
County: Gunnison
Topo: Fairview Peak
National forest: Gunnison
Other names: Gun Site, Gunsight Notch

Gunsight Pass is accessible by foot on forest service trail #428. It divides the waters of Brush Creek on the north and Gold Creek on the south.

The pass was formed in about 1900 by John Gardiner, who blasted the hole through Fossil Ridge in order to have a shortcut route for his pack train. He named it Gun Site Pass.

This Gunsight Pass is located between Broncho (some maps say Bronco) and Square Top mountains. It overlooks Lamphier Lake, to the south.

GUNSIGHT PASS

Elevation: 12,170 feet
Location: T35N R2E, Map 8
County: Archuleta
Topo: Summit Peak

A narrow notch provides access from one side of the ridge line to the other on this Gunsight Pass, northwest of Pitkin.

**National forest: Rio Grande/
San Juan
On the Continental Divide
Other name: Gunshot**

Gunsight Pass is accessible by foot, but no established trail currently goes over the pass. It divides the waters of Fish Creek to the west and the Middle Fork of the Conejos River to the east.

The USGS Board on Geographic Names officially named the pass in 1967. It is the southernmost named pass on the Continental Divide. The Continental Divide Trail goes near but not over it. The pass is a half-mile southeast of Snow Peak. Watch for ptarmigan in the area.

GUNSIGHT PASS

**Elevation: 12,380 feet
Location: T39N R5W, Map 8
County: Hinsdale
Topo: Rio Grande Pyramid
National forest: San Juan**

Gunsight Pass is accessible by foot via forest service trail #813 in the Weminuche Wilderness Area. It divides the waters of Rincon La Osa to the north and Flint Creek to the south.

The pass is on the Continental Divide Trail even though it is not on the Continental Divide. The trail drops off the Divide and goes over this crossing, which is located on a ridge spur off the Continental Divide.

This Gunsight Pass is south of 12,892-foot Ute Peak and above timberline. Ute Lake is north of the west-side-access trail. The pass is not named on forest service or topo maps. It is well marked in Continental Divide hiking guidebooks.

GYPSUM GAP

**Elevation: 6,125 feet
Location: T43N R17W, Map 7
County: San Miguel
Topo: Gypsum Gap
On BLM land**

Gypsum Gap is passenger-car-accessible on CO141. It divides the waters of Disappointment Creek to the south and Gypsum Creek to the north.

The gap is in open country on the road between Naturita and Dove Creek. It is named on the topo map, in the BLM maps book, and on some highway maps.   □

HAGERMAN PASS

Elevation: 11,925 feet
Location: T9S R81W, Map 5
County: Lake/Pitkin
Topo: Homestake Reservoir
National forest: San Isabel/
White River
On the Continental Divide
Other names: Cooke, Fryingpan,
Frying Pan, Saguache

Hagerman Pass is accessible by 4WD on forest route #105. It divides the waters of Ivanhoe Creek to the west and Busk Creek to the east. The pass is named for James Hagerman, a Colorado Midland Railroad president.

Hagerman Pass was first known as Cooke Pass when Douglas City, at the east end of the pass, supplied materials to mining camps on the west end. The Hayden survey party in 1873 called it the Frying Pan Pass.

The first tunnel under the pass, the Hagerman Tunnel, built in 1885, was at 11,528 feet. It was 2,060 feet long, opened to traffic in 1887, closed in 1893, reopened in 1897, and abandoned in 1899. It was used a total of only eight years.

The second tunnel, the Busk-Ivanhoe Tunnel (named for the two creeks it connected), was started in 1890 and opened in 1893 at a 10,953-foot elevation. It carried rail traffic until 1897, when the Colorado Midland went back to using the Hagerman Tunnel. The Hagerman Tunnel was converted to an auto route and renamed Carlton Tunnel in 1922; it was abandoned to through traffic in 1943.

In 1899 the railroad went back to using the lower Busk-Ivanhoe Tunnel. That winter was severe, and the line, even with a tunnel, was very difficult to keep open.

The Carlton Tunnel allowed vehicular traffic in the 1920s and 1930s. An alternating east-to-west/west-to-east configuration was used because the route was one-lane. In 1943 the state highway department closed the tunnel after a cave-in near the west end. State Highway 104 ran through the Carlton Tunnel until it was closed. The tunnel was named for Albert Carlton, the last owner of the Colorado Midland Railroad.

A water pipeline had been laid through the tunnel, and when the highway department closed the tunnel the pipeline was purchased by the High-Line Canal company, and they renovated the tunnel. The water pipeline through the Carlton Tunnel is still used.

Today, a third tunnel under the pass, the Boustead, is a water diversion route under the Continental Divide. It is used to carry West Slope water to the east slope of the mountains.

The Colorado Midland was the first railroad to use a standard-gauge track over the high Rockies, which ran over Hagerman Pass.

The pass is on the Continental Divide Trail.

HALFMOON PASS

Elevation: 11,650 feet
Location: T6S R81W, Map 5
County: Eagle
Topo: Mount of the Holy Cross
National forest: White River

Halfmoon Pass is accessible by foot on forest service trail #2009 in the Holy Cross Wilderness Area. It divides the waters of East Cross Creek to the west and Notch Mountain Creek to the east.

Edward Berthoud investigated the pass in about 1879 for potential rail routes through the high country.

The saddle is north of Notch Mountain and is reached by following an old stock trail. It's a relatively short hike, rocky and tough at the end. Look for the good view of the Mount of the Holy Cross. The trail is heavily used, especially on summer weekends, by hikers to the Mount of the Holy Cross. Only the last one-third mile of the hike is in the open; the first part is in trees.

HALFMOON PASS

Elevation: 12,490 feet
Location: T42N R2E, Map 8
County: Mineral/Saguache
Topo: Halfmoon Pass
National forest: Rio Grande

Halfmoon Pass is accessible by foot via forest service trails #912 and #914 from the north and #790 from the south, at the southern edge of the La Garita Wilderness Area. It divides the waters of Twin Peaks Creek to the north and West Bellows Creek to the south.

The pass is above the Wheeler Geologic Area, the onetime national monument established in 1908 by Theodore Roosevelt. Because the area was small, had poor access, and was isolated from other areas belonging to the park service, it was returned to forest service administration in 1950.

Ute Indians used the area of the rock formations. Before the early 1900s, the only white people to see the geologic site were probably sheepherders moving their animals. A forest service ranger heard rumors about the strange rock shapes and went in to investigate.

The area was named in honor of Lt. George M. Wheeler, an explorer of the area in the late 1870s, although there are no indications he ever saw the formations that now bear his name.

It takes about two and a half hours to drive the fourteen miles, by 4WD, into the geologic area. From the point where the road is blocked off it is a half-mile into the formations, then another couple of miles

The spirelike rocks of the Wheeler Geologic Area provide additional incentive to hike this Halfmoon Pass.

from the formations to the pass summit. Allow plenty of time for the trip and the hike.

HALSEY PASS

Elevation: 12,100 feet
Location: T11S R86W, Map 5
County: Gunnison
Topo: Snowmass Mountain
National forest: White River

Halsey Pass is accessible by foot, and is just inside the Maroon Bells–Snowmass Wilderness Area. It divides the waters of two forks of the Crystal River: the North Fork to the north and the East Fork to the south.

The pass was used by miners who

crossed between Lead King Basin and Schofield. Now used by hikers and sheepherders moving their flocks, the crossing is at the head of Hasley Basin. The pass is just northeast of an unnamed 12,480-foot peak. Note the discrepancy between the names of the pass and of the basin. Just one of life's little puzzles!

Halsey Pass is not named on forest service or topo maps, although the topo shows the trail over the pass. It was identified by Len Shoemaker.

HANCOCK PASS

Elevation: 12,120 feet
Location: T50N R5E, Map 5

A snakelike road winds up the west side of Hancock Pass.

County: Chaffee/Gunnison
Topo: Garfield
National forest: Gunnison/
  San Isabel
On the Continental Divide

Hancock Pass is accessible by 4WD on forest route #299. It divides the waters of Chalk Creek to the north and Middle Quartz Creek to the south.

The earliest known regular use of the pass was around 1888, as a mining route. The USGS Board on Geographic Names officially named the pass in 1962. Before that, no name had been assigned, but a road of sorts went over the pass anyway.

The west side of the pass is steep, rough, and narrow in places. On the east side, the old ghost town of Hancock can be reached by passenger car; 4WD is needed from Hancock to the pass. It is a steep, rocky, and rough road in places. The pass itself is above timberline, with good views all directions. It is a half-mile southeast of Mount Chapman.

The pass is on the Continental Divide Trail. The residents of the Chalk Creek Valley and nearby Buena Vista use this area for snowmobiling in the winter.

HANDCART PASS

Elevation: 12,260 feet
Location: T6S R76W, Map 6
County: Park/Summit
Topo: Montezuma

National forest: Arapaho/Pike
On the Continental Divide

Handcart Pass is accessible by foot, although gated private land on the south side makes bushwhacking necessary. The pass divides the waters of the Snake River to the north and the North Fork of the South Platte River to the south.

The pass was named in honor of the handcarts used by early settlers who moved West toting their goods. The first explorers in this region also used these carts. An 1872 map of Colorado shows the site as Hand Cart Pass.

The pass is at the head of Hall Valley, which is next to Handcart Gulch. Handcart Gulch was prospected by two Norwegians in the early 1860s, who served as human mules to cart their own mining supplies into the gulch.

The trail to the pass was an old pack trail that was used before another route, about a mile to the northeast, was constructed.

Ore was discovered here in 1866 when three miners found the Leftwick lode area. They sold the claim to Colonel Hall from Georgetown. Some of the Reynolds Gang gold is supposed to be buried on the south side of this pass. (The Reynolds Gang was a group of eight Southern Confederate sympathizers who, in 1864, committed robberies in Colorado to help support their cause.)

The pass is on the Continental Divide Trail west of Handcart Peak

and above the Whale Mine on the south side. It is not named on forest service or topo maps. It is identified by historical research.

HANKINS PASS

Elevation: 10,010 feet
Location: T10S R72W, Map 6
County: Park
Topo: McCurdy Mountain
National forest: Pike

Hankins Pass is accessible by foot on forest service trail #630 (the Hankins Trail) in the Lost Creek Wilderness Area. It divides the waters of Tarryall Creek to the west and Hankins Gulch to the east.

This is an interesting hike in an interesting area that is not well known. Do not follow the 1980 Pike National Forest Service map, which shows a road through private land. The landowner does NOT allow access to the forest.

The pass is located on the north side of South Tarryall Peak.

HARDSCRABBLE PASS

Elevation: 9,300 feet
Location: T22S R71W, Map 9
County: Custer
Topo: Rosita
Public access through private land

Hardscrabble Pass is passenger-car-accessible. It divides the waters of North Hardscrabble Creek to the east and Poverty Gulch to the west.

The pass is named for the "hard scramble" some settlers had when they fled from Indian attacks here in the 1840s.

Utes used this old crossing to move in and out of the Wet Mountain Valley. About 1835, as white settlers reached this region, conflicts with the Utes erupted. The Arapaho and Sioux became active in the region in 1838, and the settlers then moved into forts. The Utes fought on the side of the settlers because they were also in conflict with Arapaho and Sioux warriors.

By 1870 a wagon road had been opened over the pass. In the winter of 1872–1873, settlers from Rosita and Pueblo contributed funds to improve the road.

The pass is honored by a poem, "Report of My Strange Encounter with Lilly Bull-Domingo," by Thomas Hornsby Ferril. Part of this interesting poem runs, "I stopped my car on the hump of Hardscrabble Pass up Hardscrabble Creek to stare across the blue Wet Mountain Valley . . . ."

Hardscrabble Pass is not named on forest service or topo maps. Ormes identified it in one of his *Colorado Skylines* books, and much historical data exists about the Hardscrabble settlement.

HARDSCRABBLE SADDLE

Elevation: 8,859 feet
Location: T5S R85W, Map 5
County: Eagle
Topo: Suicide Mountain
On BLM land

Hardscrabble Saddle is accessible by 4WD from the east. It divides the waters of Hardscrabble Gulch to the west and Abrams Creek to the east.

The pass is located behind ranch property. Power lines run up the gully behind the ranch and cross the saddle. Bureau of Land Management roads lead to the saddle. The pass is a couple of miles west of The Seven Hermits. It is named on forest service and BLM maps.

HARTMAN DIVIDE

Elevation: 7,940 feet
Location: T1S R81W, Map 2
County: Grand
Topo: Radium
On private land

There is no access to Hartman Divide. It divides the waters of the Colorado River to the north and Sheephorn Creek to the south.

The 4WD road that used to reach the pass is now fenced and locked at the Sheephorn Ranch. About three-quarters of a mile from the gate to the east is a good view of the divide. This is not a major crossing, but it is a nice saddle. The state land here is called the Hartman Unit.

HAYDEN PASS

Elevation: 10,709 feet
Location: T47N R10E, Map 9

County: Fremont/Saguache
Topo: Coaldale
National forest: Rio Grande/
    San Isabel

Hayden Pass is 4WD-accessible on forest routes #970 on the west side and #6 on the east side. It divides the waters of Hayden Pass Creek to the west and the Middle Prong Hayden Creek to the east.

Some believe the pass is named for the explorer Ferdinand Hayden, who crossed here while surveying in 1875. The forest service maintains, though, that the pass is really named for an early settler of the Wet Mountain Valley, Lewis Hayden. Others believe the name refers to the state geologist who surveyed the Sangre de Cristo Grant for Governor Gilpin. The official designation is for Lewis Hayden.

The pass was used by Utes to move between the San Luis Valley and the Arkansas River to the north. In 1874 the Cañon City and San Luis Valley Wagon Road Company planned a route over the pass. By 1879 this was a well-used pass and better known than many others near here. Hayden Pass provided a good shortcut route, some twelve miles shorter than another pass farther west.

Hayden Pass is a little-used crossing at the northern end of the Sangre de Cristo mountain range. It makes for a good summer drive over a back road that is easy (if you have a 4WD) to traverse.

The pass is shown and named in the 1877 *Atlas of Colorado* and current forest service maps.

HAYSTACK GATE

Elevation: 9,756 feet
Location: T9S R90W, Map 5
County: Mesa/Pitkin
Topo: Quaker Mesa
National forest: White River

Haystack Gate is accessible by 4WD on forest route #302. It divides the waters of West Divide Creek to the west and North Thompson Creek to the east.

This minor crossing is located south of Glenwood Springs, two miles west of Twin Peaks and past the Sunlight Ski Area, where a backcountry road winds through the forest. The pass is named on forest service and BLM maps.

HECKERT PASS

Elevation: 12,700 feet
Location: T11S R86W, Map 5
County: Pitkin
Topo: Capitol Peak
National forest: White River

Heckert Pass is accessible by foot in the Maroon Bells–Snowmass Wilderness Area. It divides the waters of Bear Creek to the north and Snowmass Creek to the south.

The USGS Board on Geographic Names officially named the pass in 1959 in honor of John Heckert, who lost his life on Capitol Peak in July 1957.

The pass is between Snowmass Lake and Pierre Basin in the Elk mountain range. It is about a mile north of the west side of Snowmass Lake. The pass isn't visible from the lake, and it is a hard climb to reach it.

HEIGHT DIVIDE

Elevation: 7,583 feet
Location: T5N R87W, Map 2
County: Routt
Topo: Dunckley
Public access through private land
Other name: Hite

Height Divide is accessible by passenger car on county road #37. It divides the waters of Sage Creek to the north and Fish Creek to the south.

The original name, and the one still used by locals, is Hite Divide. It was named in honor of George Hite, who homesteaded in the area. A mapmaker changed "Hite" to "Height" some time ago.

The divide road provides a backroad drive through interesting countryside with few long-range views. The pass is three miles south of Sage Creek Reservoir.

HELL CREEK DIVIDE

Elevation: 11,180 feet
Location: T2N R74W, Map 3
County: Grand
Topo: Isolation Peak
National forest: Arapaho

Hell Creek Divide is accessible by foot on forest service trail #3 (Roaring Fork Trail) in the Indian Peaks Wilderness Area. It divides the waters of Roaring Fork Creek to the west and Hell Canyon to the east.

The pass is between Mount Irving Hale on the south and Hiamovi Mountain on the north. It is located above Monarch Lake and Lake Granby on the west, Stone Lake and Upper Lake on the east, and is about a mile south of the southern end of Rocky Mountain National Park.

Hell Creek Divide is not named on forest service, topo, or other maps. It is identified by hiking guides.

This is an easy hike that was favored by members of the Colorado Mountain Club during the 1960s.

HEPBURN'S PASS

Elevation: 10,750 feet
Location: T6S R75W, Map 6
County: Park
Topo: Jefferson
National forest: Pike

Hepburn's Pass is accessible by foot on forest service trail #601. It divides the waters of the North Fork of the South Platte River to the west and Bear Creek to the east.

The pass is named for Charles Hepburn, who had a ranch nearby. His place served as a stage terminus beginning about 1869. At one time a road over the pass was considered; it would have run from Hall Valley to Georgetown.

The pass is on the Geneva Creek Hiking Trail. It is not named on forest service or topo maps but has much historic value.

HERMIT PASS

Elevation: 12,990 feet
Location: T44N R12E, Map 9
County: Custer/Saguache
Topo: Rito Alto Peak
National forest: Rio Grande/
  San Isabel
Other name: Eureka

Hermit Pass is accessible by 4WD from the east side via forest route #160. The west side is accessible by foot on forest service trail #747. The pass divides the waters of Rito Alto Creek to the west and Middle Taylor Creek to the east.

A movie, *Continental Divide,* was filmed in this vicinity several years ago. To get the film crews into the movie location more easily, the road was upgraded.

This pass is in the Sangre de Cristo mountain range, between Eureka Mountain and Rito Alto Peak. It makes a good place for cross-country skiing in years of heavy snowfall.

Even 4WD roads can be above timberline. This part of the east side of Hermit Pass is closed by snow in many years until midsummer.

HESPERUS PASS

Elevation: 8,019 feet
Location: T35N R11W, Map 7
County: La Plata
Topo: Hesperus
Public access through private land

Hesperus Pass is passenger-car-accessible via county road #125. It divides the waters of La Plata River to the west and Wildcat Canyon to the east.

The pass was named by the Hayden survey party, who said, "we have given the name Hesperus on account of its being located farther west than any other mountain in Colorado." They named it for Longfellow's poem, "The Wreck of the Hesperus."

Locals remember when the road over the pass was the highway route of US160. The name Hesperus Hill was used to describe the pass. Now US160 follows a new path across the divide north of this older pass.

The Denver and Rio Grande Railroad crossed this divide a little farther north than did either the new or old US160 routes. The railroad has since been abandoned. The north side of the pass is Ute Mountain tribal property.

HOODOO GAP

Elevation: 10,260 feet
Location: T14S R90W, Map 5
County: Gunnison
Topo: Minnesota Pass
National forest: Gunnison

Hoodoo Gap is accessible by foot, but no established trail currently goes over the pass, which is in the West Elk Wilderness Area. It divides the waters of Hoodoo Creek to the north and Spruce Creek to the south.

A cowboy who worked the area remarked over a campfire one evening about the beauty of the spot and how it could "hoodoo you." The name stuck, and the USGS Board on Geographic Names officially named the pass in 1962. This may prove that even the government has a sense of humor.

The pass is about one and a half miles southwest of Mount Gunnison.

HOOSIER PASS

Elevation: 11,539 feet
Location: T8S R78W, Map 6
County: Park/Summit
Topo: Alma
National forest: Arapaho/Pike
On the Continental Divide
Other names: Montgomery, Ute

Hoosier Pass is passenger-car-accessible on CO9. It divides the waters of the Blue River to the north and the Middle Fork of the South Platte River to the south.

The pass was named for Hoosier Gulch, which was worked by prospectors from Indiana in the early 1860s.

Utes used the pass to follow the buffalo. Zebulon Pike in 1806 saw the pass and identified it as the headwaters of the South Platte. He presumed the headwaters to the north were of the Yellowstone River.

In 1812 a party of trappers crossed the pass, looking for beaver in the streams of this region. Then in 1839 the Thomas Farnham exploration party crossed through South Park, noted the large herds of buffalo, and used the pass. Just three years later, in 1842, the Rufus Sage party crossed just ahead of a major winter storm in December. Captain John Fremont traversed the pass in 1844. Kit Carson was the guide on that trip.

The South Park Rail Line considered a route over the pass. The company sent surveyor Francis Case out in the summer of 1864 to evaluate it. He favored putting a rail line over the pass.

In 1860, this pass was the site of the first water diversion project from the West Slope to the East Slope in Colorado.

A charter was given out by the Colorado Territory in November of 1861 to the Breckenridge, Buckskin Joe and Hamilton Wagon Road Company for a toll road from South Park to Breckenridge. In August 1862 the Empire City, New Pass and Montgomery City Road Company planned to go over the pass to Montgomery from Summit County. In 1866 the Union Pacific received a recommendation that the rail route should go over Hoosier Pass rather than the proposed alternate route, through Wyoming.

By 1918 a good road, passable by automobile, had been built over the pass. In the 1930s, a small ski area existed on the pass. Difficulties in reaching it caused it to close in just a few years. Also in the 1930s, the area saw a robbery getaway. Robbers held up the bank at Alma and escaped over the pass.

A cross and a granite boulder were placed atop the pass in 1947 by the Veterans of Foreign Wars as a memorial to men of Park and Summit counties who lost their lives during all wars.

In 1962 the top was still gravel. Hoosier Pass is on the Continental Divide Trail.

HOOSIER PASS

Elevation: 10,313 feet
Location: T15S R69W, Map 6
County: Teller
Topo: Cripple Creek North
Public access through private land

Hoosier Pass is passenger-car-accessible via a dirt road just off CO67. It divides the waters of Poverty Gulch to the west and Grassy Creek to the east.

This pass was named for the nearby Hoosier Mine.

The pass was on the Short Line Railroad that ran between Colorado Springs and Cripple Creek. The rail line was opened March 23, 1901.

HOPE PASS

Elevation: 12,529 feet
Location: T12S R81W, Map 5

County: Chaffee
Topo: Mount Elbert
National forest: San Isabel

Hope Pass is accessible by foot on forest service trail #1470. It divides the waters of Little Willis Gulch to the north and Sheep Gulch to the south.

The pass is named for the mountain aside it. This route was not regularly used until the early 1980s, when the Leadville 100 footrace decided to place its route up and over this high pass. The runners have to cross the pass twice, once from each direction. Also in the 1980s, the pass was "discovered" by Colorado Trail planners.

The pass is located between Quail Mountain and Mount Hope and is on the Colorado Trail. Hope Pass also will be on the new Continental Divide trail when it is completed here. The pass is not named on forest service or topo maps. It is named on Trails Illustrated maps.

HORN FORK PASS

Elevation: 12,780 feet
Location: T13S R80W, Map 5
County: Chaffee/Gunnison
Topo: Mount Harvard
National forest: Gunnison/
   San Isabel
On the Continental Divide

Horn Fork Pass is accessible by foot, but no established trail currently goes over the pass. In the Collegiate Peaks Wilderness Area, Horn Fork Pass divides the waters of Texas Creek to the west and Horn Fork Creek to the east. The pass is named for Horn Fork Creek.

Horn Fork Pass is one and a half miles west of Mount Columbia and one and a half miles north of Birthday Peak. The pass is on the west flank of Mount Columbia.

This pass is not named on forest service or topo maps. James Grafton Rogers located and named it in his listing of Colorado's geographic features. Older locals tell of surveying in the high country near the pass.

HORSE RANCH PASS

Elevation: 8,580 feet
Location: T11N R76W, Map 3
County: Larimer
Topo: Crazy Mountain
On private and BLM land

There is no access to Horse Ranch Pass. It divides the waters of the Laramie River to the west and Shell Creek to the east.

The pass is located just south of the Wyoming border off CO103. Careful study of map and land features will locate it. Roads shown on some maps no longer exist and gated fences on private property block access. The pass is a half-mile south of Dempsey Dome.

Horse Ranch Pass is named on forest service and BLM maps.

HORSESHOE PASS

Elevation: 13,180 feet
Location: T10S R79W, Map 6
County: Lake/Park
Topo: Mount Sherman
National forest: Pike/San Isabel

Horseshoe Pass is in an area of private mining properties: access roads may have gates. A 4WD forest route (#603) provides access from the east. No established trail access is available on the west side. Horseshoe Pass divides the waters of Empire Gulch to the west and Horseshoe Gulch to the east. The pass is named for the horseshoe-shaped mountain just to the south.

In the late 1870s, prospectors lured by silver crossed the pass from Leadville into Four Mile Gulch, which was also sometimes called Horseshoe Gulch. Father Dyer used the pass to cross the mountain range to deliver mail and preach his sermons. By 1875, miners were using the pass to cross between Fairplay and Twin Lakes. The distance between the towns is only twenty-seven miles when Horseshoe Pass is used.

About 1884, the Colorado Midland Railroad proposed running a route line up and over the pass and into Leadville. When James Hagerman was elected president of the railroad in 1885, he favored the route and an 8,200-foot tunnel, to run under the high part of the pass. This route had been suggested by the Colorado Short Line Railroad,

The Colorado Midland Railroad originally planned to cross from the South Platte River Valley to the Upper Arkansas River Valley via Horseshoe Pass. *(Photograph courtesy Mel McFarland collection)*

which merged with the Midland. Emblems praising the route as "The Horse Shoe Pass Route" were printed and pasted on railroad property long before a line was built. But no line was ever built.

The pass top is about eight miles from and above Leadville. The area is dotted with mines and well worth a visit for the historic interest alone. The pass is located between Horseshoe Mountain on the south and Mount Sheridan on the north.

HORSETHIEF PASS

Elevation: 5,830 feet
Location: T9N R69W, Map 3
County: Larimer
Topo: Livermore
On private land

There is no access to Horsethief Pass. It divides the waters of Owl

Creek to the west and Park Creek to the east.

This pass would make unnecessary three miles of travel around a butte area and crossing a small stream. The property owner knows the pass is marked on various maps, but has "no idea why anyone would want to use it when all that's needed is to go around the end of a hill."

The pass is not named on the Roosevelt National Forest Service map. It is named on the topo and Larimer County maps.

HUNCHBACK PASS

Elevation: 12,493 feet
Location: T40N R6W, Map 8
County: San Juan
Topo: Storm King Peak
National forest: Rio Grande/
  San Juan
On the Continental Divide

Hunchback Pass is accessible by foot on forest service trail #529 on the northern edge of the Weminuche Wilderness Area. It divides the waters of Bear Creek to the north and Vallecito Creek to the south. The pass is named for nearby Hunchback Mountain.

Rhoda's division of the Hayden survey party used the pass in 1874. Many sheep grazed on the hillsides when Franklin Rhoda was there, as they still do today.

The pass is just south of and above Kite Lake; there is an easy hike to the top and pretty views all around. An old cabin at Kite Lake provides overnight shelter; it is heavily used, so don't count on sleeping there.

Hunchback Pass is on the Continental Divide Trail and east of Hunchback Mountain.

HURRICANE PASS

Elevation: 12,850 feet
Location: T42N R7W, Map 8
County: San Juan
Topo: Handies Peak
Public access through private land

Hurricane Pass is accessible by 4WD. It divides the waters of the Uncompahgre River to the west and the West Fork of the Animas River to the east.

The pass route is a very steep road that is open for a very short time in very dry summers. The best route is to drive up California Gulch, over the pass, and down to Lake Como in Poughkeepsie Gulch.

The pass is on the northeast flank of Hurricane Peak. The Mountain Queen mine is near the top on the east side. This pass is not named on forest service or topo maps. It is identified by Gregory and Smith in *Mountain Mysteries*.   □

I

ICEBERG PASS

Elevation: 11,827 feet
Location: T5N R75W, Map 3
County: Larimer
Topo: Trail Ridge
In Rocky Mountain National Park

Iceberg Pass is accessible by passenger car on US34, Trail Ridge Road. It divides the waters of Fall River to the north and the Big Thompson River to the south.

The pass was named in 1924 by Roger Toll, then superintendent of Rocky Mountain National Park.

The road at the pass follows the ridge line, so travelers do not go from drainage to drainage, as is usual.

Iceberg Pass is mistakenly named "Keberg" Pass on the Arapaho National Forest maps of 1932 and 1939, where the first two letters of the pass name, "I" and "c," were printed close together and someone thought it looked like a "K."

This pass is near Iceberg Lake.

ICEFIELD PASS

Elevation: 11,850 feet
Location: T6N R74W, Map 3
County: Larimer
Topo: Comanche Peak
In Rocky Mountain National Park

Icefield Pass is accessible by foot, but there are no distinct trails to the pass. It divides the waters of the South Fork of the Cache la Poudre River to the west and the North Fork of the Big Thompson River to the east.

The pass was named in 1924 by Roger Toll, then Rocky Mountain National Park superintendent.

Lake Louise, near the pass, is a popular destination. The pass is north of Rowe Mountain. From the top, the view to the east is spectacular: a steep valley with a snowbank right at your feet. Reaching the top, though, requires bushwhacking and some rock scrambling.

ILLINOIS PASS

Elevation: 10,020 feet
Location: T5N R77W, Map 3
County: Grand/Jackson
Topo: Radial Mountain
National forest: Arapaho/Routt
On the Continental Divide

Illinois Pass is accessible by foot via forest service trail #25 on its south side. It divides the waters of the Illinois River to the north and Trout Creek to the south.

A popular snowmobiling route in the winter crosses from Gould to Granby. The trail is almost hidden in willows during the summer. Look for moose here. The top is not well defined, not marked, and is buried in trees. There are no good views. There are now many logging roads in the area to confuse the hiker, so it can be difficult to stay on the correct route to the pass.

Illinois Pass is on the Continental Divide Trail and three miles east of Radial Mountain.

IMOGENE PASS

Elevation: 13,114 feet
Location: T42N R8W, Map 7
County: Ouray/San Miguel
Topo: Ironton
National forest: Uncompahgre

Imogene Pass is accessible by 4WD on forest route #869. It divides the waters of Savage Creek to the west and Imogene Creek to the east.

Imogene Pass is named for the wife of Andy Richardson, partner with Tom Walsh in the operation of the Camp Bird Mine, which is down the north side of the pass. The pass is sometimes pronounced *em-o-jean,* but correct pronunciation is *eye-mo-gene.* Locals seem to use either pronunciation.

A road over the pass was built in the 1870s to carry ore from the Tomboy Mine to Ouray. The Tomboy is one and a half miles below the summit of the pass, on the south side.

Power transmission lines crossed the pass in the 1890s, taking power from the San Miguel River at Ames (near Telluride) to Ouray. This was the first commercial transmission of alternating-current electrical power.

The top of the pass is marked with remnants of Fort Peabody, a tiny rock hut built in 1903 by the state militia when they were called out to keep peace in the mining area. Fort Peabody was named for the then-incumbent governor of Colorado.

The road over the pass fell into disrepair in the early 1900s when mining activity dried up. This historic spot was made available to the public again in 1966 when, thanks in large part to various 4WD clubs, the road was made passable again. This is a good 4WD route, very popular in the summer when thrill-seeking tourists make a round trip from Ouray by going over Black Bear Pass, lunching in Telluride, and returning via Imogene Pass. The trip can be more thoroughly enjoyed by taking an excursion rather than driving it oneself. The road is open a short time in the late summer, and then only if the previous winter was not a heavy snowfall season.

The Tomboy Mine provides an opportunity for buffs to tramp around looking at the size of the buildings. Read the Backus book, *Tomboy Bride,* for a firsthand account of life at this mine on the south side of the pass.

The pass is located between Chicago Peak and Telluride Peak. Look for tee shirts in Telluride tourist shops that read, "I survived Imogene Pass 13,114 feet."

INDEPENDENCE PASS

Elevation: 12,095 feet
Location: T11S R82W, Map 5
County: Lake/Pitkin
Topo: Independence Pass
National forest: San Isabel/
  White River
On the Continental Divide
Other names: Hunter's, Ute

Independence Pass is passenger-car-accessible (no units over total length of thirty-five feet are allowed) whenever the road is open, on CO82. It divides the waters of the Roaring Fork River to the west and North Fork Lake Creek to the east.

The pass is named for the town and the mine of Independence, just to the west of the pass. The mine was discovered on July 4, 1879, hence the name.

Ute Spring and then Ute City were early names for the town of Aspen, which is on the west side of the pass. Because it was in Ute territory, the town's original names were meant to honor the Indians. For many years the rugged peaks of the Continental Divide near here were considered the border between white and Indian territory.

Zebulon Pike noted the pass as an opening in the Sawatch Mountains when his party went through in 1806. Crossings in the late 1870s and early 1880s, when the trail over

The ghost town of Independence is under restoration on the west side of Independence Pass.

the pass was first used by settlers, were difficult. A toll road was started by the Twin Lakes and Roaring Fork Company. They tried to keep the road cleaned off in the wintertime for seventeen miles above Twin Lakes. The road beyond Twin Lakes, if not blown dry by the wind, was likely drifted shut.

By June 1881, miners were streaming over the pass for the riches they'd heard about in the Aspen silver mining district. The toll was a quarter for each pack animal. That summer saw the first wagon try to cross the pass. It was more carried across than driven across and took almost a month to make the trip. But soon stagecoaches were crossing the range regularly. The fare from Leadville to Aspen was eight dollars. A trip required from ten to twenty-five hours, changing the horse teams five times, and passing through three toll gates. When the railroad reached Aspen (from Leadville via the Hagerman Tunnel in 1887), the trail over the pass was not used as much and the regular stage business plummeted.

Some road improvements were made almost annually to keep the route open. By 1920 a fair roadway was available. In the 1930s, the eastern part of the road was greatly enhanced by the work done for the Twin Lakes Diversion Tunnel. There is some current interest in keeping the pass road open all year.

Independence Pass is on the Continental Divide Trail; it is the middle point between the New Mexico and Wyoming borders. Several campgrounds are close to the pass.

The partially restored community of Independence is worth a visit. For Sunday-afternoon drivers or for those not accustomed to drives with steep drop-offs, the trip across Independence Pass should be made from the east to the west. This keeps the traveler on the mountain side of the road at the narrowest spots and will minimize uneasiness.

INDIAN PASS

Elevation: 8,290 feet
Location: T4N R81W, Map 2
County: Grand
Topo: Whiteley Peak
On Colorado state land

Indian Pass is 4WD-accessible and is just off forest route #103. It divides the waters of Badger Creek to the north and Muddy Creek to the south.

The pass is named on the Arapaho National Forest Service map. It is located in ranching country. The top is open, with good views toward the Rabbit Ears mountain range.

INDIAN CAMP PASS

Elevation: 9,724 feet
Location: T3S R88W, Map 2
County: Garfield
Topo: Deep Lake
National forest: White River

Indian Camp Pass is passenger-car-accessible on the south side via forest route #600, with foot access on the north side. The pass divides the waters of Buck Creek to the west and Dry Sweetwater Creek to the east.

This is an old Indian crossing. The area is heavily used in late fall for hunting, and is reached by a road that runs along the south edge of the Flat Tops Wilderness Area. Be sure to look into the deep canyon from the Deep Creek Overlook.

Theodore Roosevelt camped near Deep Lake when he was hunting in the Flat Tops area in 1905. The pass is one mile northwest of Triangle Mountain and four miles north of Deep Lake.

INDIAN CREEK PASS

Elevation: 9,600 feet
Location: T30S R69W, Map 9
County: Costilla/Huerfano
Topo: McCarty Park
National forest: San Isabel and private land
Other name: Indian

Indian Creek Pass is 4WD-accessible via forest route #410. It divides the waters of the North Fork of Indian Creek to the west and South Middle Creek to the east.

The pass was used as a military crossing when forts dotted the southern portion of our state. In 1819, Governor Melgare's survey party noted an old game trail over the pass.

Captain John Gunnison's explorers noted the pass when they scouted nearby.

Indian Creek Pass is the low, somewhat flat and indistinct crossing that was much used in the last portion of the nineteenth century to go west from Aguilar and Trinidad. It has been forgotten in the last half-century.

The immense Forbes Ranch holdings in the San Luis Valley creep up the west side of the pass. Access from the west side is through this private development. The pass is four miles north of Harrison Peak. It is not named on forest service or topo maps.

INTER OCEAN PASS

Elevation: 9,770 feet
Location: T14S R91W, Map 5
County: Delta
Topo: Paonia
National forest: Gunnison

Inter Ocean Pass is accessible by foot on forest service trail #890. It divides the waters of Minnesota Creek to the north and Little Cole Creek to the south.

This pass's name is misleading— it is not on the Continental Divide, as may be inferred from the name.

The pass is one mile east of Mount Lamborn and is shown on forest service and topo maps. The hike over Inter Ocean Pass could be made as a through-trip with arrangements for a second vehicle to be waiting at the opposite end of the trail.

IRON MINE GAP

Elevation: 7,634 feet
Location: T7N R101W, Map 1
County: Moffat
Topo: Greystone
On BLM land
Other name: The Gap

Iron Mine Gap is 4WD-accessible. It divides the waters of Grass Draw to the north and the Yampa River to the south.

Locals use the name Iron Mine Gap, but some maps show the alternate name of The Gap. An old mine shaft is still open at the top. There are good views to the south and west, into Dinosaur National Monument. Lots of sagebrush and open country mark this back-road route.

Good maps are needed to locate this pass. The pass is named Iron Mine Gap in the BLM maps book and The Gap on the topo map. □

J

JACK SPRINGS PASS

Elevation: 7,232 feet
Location: T5N R101W, Map 1
County: Moffat
Topo: Skull Creek
Public access through private land
Other name: Skull Creek

Jack Springs Pass is 4WD-accessible. It divides the waters of Wolf Creek to the north and Miller Creek to the south.

The pass is named for the nearby town of Jack Springs. The alternate name of Skull Creek derived from a human skull found in a nearby creek.

The road climbs gradually to the top of the pass, which is not visible until just before it is reached. The top is open, with lots of grazing for animals. Sagebrush, junipers, and rabbits share the countryside.

The pass is a narrow saddle between canyon rim areas and located close to the Dinosaur National Monument area. It is named in the BLM maps book and on the topo map.

JACK'S CABIN PASS

Elevation: 8,760 feet
Location: T15S R84W, Map 5
County: Gunnison
Topo: Almont
Public access through private land

Jack's Cabin Pass is passenger-car-accessible on forest route #813. It divides the waters of East River to the west and Taylor River to the east.

The pass is named for the small community of Jack's Cabin, first called Howeville. Howeville was a stage stop on the route between Gunnison and Crested Butte. An old cemetery is still seen close to the old town. The road over the pass was developed in the 1880s to connect the Almont Valley and the Taylor River areas. The road is usually called Jack's Cabin Cutoff by locals; it's a good shortcut road between Taylor Park and Crested Butte but has few interesting views.

Jack's Cabin Pass is not named on forest service or topo maps.

JONES PASS

Elevation: 12,451 feet
Location: T3S R76W, Map 3
County: Clear Creek/Grand
Topo: Byers Peak
National forest: Arapaho
On the Continental Divide
Other names: New, Packard

Jones Pass is 4WD-accessible from the east only; there is no access from the west. The pass can be reached by a passenger car with high clearance in a good year if carefully driven. The pass divides the waters of Jones Creek to the west and the West Fork of Clear Creek to the east.

The pass is named for John Jones, an early miner and road-builder. He owned property near Hot Sulphur Springs and lived at Empire. He wanted to go back and forth between these two points with a minimum of distance, so he built the first wagon road over Jones Pass. It was never a good road.

The pass was first called Packard after George Packard, who claimed to have discovered it sometime before 1860. It was used by trappers seeking new locales for their beaver collection points.

In August 1862, Colorado Territory issued a charter for a toll road to the Empire City, New Pass, Breckenridge and Montgomery City Road Company for a toll road from Empire to Georgetown over Jones Pass. The Colorado and California Wagon Road Company was issued a charter by Colorado Territory in January 1867 to construct a toll road from Empire over Jones Pass to the Williams Fork and beyond. The pass was visited by the Hayden survey party in 1873. A wagon road crossed the pass into Middle Park from the takeoff on the eastern side, above the small mining camp of Empire.

By 1909, work had begun on the two-mile tunnel under Jones Pass that would divert water from the Williams Fork River to Clear Creek. To provide access to both ends of the tunnel from the east, the Denver parks and improvements department in 1938 opened a road over the pass. In 1965 the tunnel under the pass was named the August P. Gumlick Tunnel. Mr. Gumlick had been a member of the Denver Water Board.

Today's road runs up through a mining valley, then goes past the American Metals Climax-Henderson Mine. The dirt road is easily traveled with only a few rough spots. The summit is open and has spectacular views in all directions. This route is well used by mountain bikers because it is a good shelf road.

With 4WD, visitors can descend partway down the west side until stopped by a locked gate at land controlled by the Denver Water Board.

The pass serves as an access point on the Continental Divide Trail.

JONES SUMMIT

Elevation: 8,266 feet
Location: T50N R7W, Map 5
County: Montrose
Topo: Grizzly Ridge
Public access through private land

Jones Summit is passenger-car-accessible on CO347 at the southern edge of the Black Canyon of the Gunnison National Monument. It divides the waters of the Gunnison River to the north and Piñon Springs Draw to the south.

Ute Indians lived here when the first explorers reached this area in the 1700s. The national monument was established in 1933 by President Herbert Hoover and encloses twenty-one square miles of rim and canyon. The south rim drive starts at Jones Summit. This part of the road is kept open all year.

The pass is located at the end of CO347. From the top there are many good views to the west and south, but none into the canyon itself.

Jones Summit is named on the forest service's Gunnison National Forest map.

JUNIPER PASS

Elevation: 11,030 feet
Location: T4S R73W, Map 6
County: Clear Creek
Topo: Idaho Springs
National forest: Arapaho

Juniper Pass is passenger-car-accessible on CO103. It divides the waters of Devils Canyon to the north and Beaver Dam Creek to the south.

The pass is located about a quarter-mile west of Warrior Mountain and one and a half miles northeast of Echo Lake. The Juniper Pass Picnic Ground marks the pass summit.

The pass is not named on forest service maps. It is named on topo and Trails Illustrated maps.   □

K

KEBLER PASS

Elevation: 9,980 feet
Location: T14S R87W, Map 5
County: Gunnison
Topo: Mount Axtell
National forest: Gunnison

Kebler Pass is passenger-car-accessible on county road #12. It divides the waters of Ruby Anthracite Creek to the west and Coal Creek to the east.

The pass is named for John Kebler, president of the Colorado Fuel and Iron Corporation, which owned many coal properties in Colorado. The pass was originally used as an Indian trail through the mountains.

Today's road follows the old grade of the Crested Butte Branch of the Denver and Rio Grande Railroad. This route opened in September 1893 and provided access for the mines around the old town of Irwin, allowing them to get ore to the smelter at Crested Butte. The town of Kebler Pass was located atop the pass and served as a rail station.

The old Irwin or Ruby Camp cemetery is at the top of the pass, which is tree-covered and lacks really good views. In the late 1930s, the dirt road over the pass was improved.

The road connects Crested Butte and the Paonia Reservoir. Many old mining towns are close. Views to the Ruby Range (north) and of the surrounding West Elk Mountains are better from the road than from the pass itself.

KELLY PASS

Elevation: 11,220 feet
Location: T8N R76W, Map 3
County: Jackson
Topo: Clark Peak
In the Colorado State Forest

Kelly Pass is accessible by foot. It divides the waters of Kelly Creek to the north and the North Fork of the Canadian River to the south.

Hikers use this pass as a route to the pretty fishing hole of Kelly Lake, which is about a quarter-mile north of the pass. Watch for the hermit who may still be living in these hills!

The pass is not named on forest service or topo maps. It is named on the Trails Illustrated maps.

KENNEBEC PASS

Elevation: 11,740 feet
Location: T37N R10W, Map 7
County: La Plata
Topo: La Plata
National forest: San Juan

Kennebec Pass is accessible by foot on forest service trail #520. It divides the waters of the South Fork of Hermosa Creek to the north and Junction Creek to the south.

The USGS Board on Geographic Names officially named the pass in 1949 in honor of the nearby Kennebec Mine.

Kennebec is an unusual and outstanding pass on a high ridge overlooking a pretty tree-lined valley. Interesting mines are near. Close to the pass, to the southeast and on a deadend trail, is a well-preserved mine.

The pass is on the saddle north of Cumberland Mountain. The south access is via forest route #171 out of Durango. Many hikers reach Kennebec Pass via the Colorado Trail each year.

KENOSHA PASS

Elevation: 10,000 feet
Location: T7S R75W, Map 6
County: Park
Topo: Jefferson
National forest: Pike
Other name: Ute

Kenosha Pass is passenger-car-accessible on US285. It divides the waters of Kenosha Gulch to the north and Snyder Creek to the south.

Originally called Kenosha Hill or Kenosha Summit, the pass name honors Kenosha, Wisconsin, the home of an early stage driver who crossed the pass regularly.

White men who first looked into South Park from the curve on the southwest side of Kenosha Hill were just as awed by the view as are today's modern highway visitors. Utes used the pass as their main crossing from the South Platte to South Park.

Zebulon Pike visited this region in 1806. Fur traders used the Indian route in the 1820s and 1830s, finding it the easiest way west from the eastern plains of Colorado. Captain John Fremont crossed here in 1844.

In June 1859, Indians killed five prospectors at the pass. By 1862, Concord stagecoaches had regular routes over the pass. Mail, parcels, and larger freight items were also carried. Kenosha House, on the west side of the pass, was an established stage stop by 1864.

The Denver, South Park and Pacific Railroad reached the pass in 1879, where travelers could board stages to head into South Park. A station house, water tank, and siding were located at the open pass top from 1891 to 1893.

The poet Walt Whitman was spellbound by the views from the station house when his train stopped there for water in 1879. He called the mountains visible across the park "the back-bone of our hemisphere" and marveled at the expanse laid out before him.

In 1858, prospectors began going over the pass to look for gold in South Park. South Park was home to many large herds of buffalo, and the last stand of those animals (early in the 1900s) was in the southwest corner of the park.

Oxen crossed the pass, too. In the 1870s, the Spotswood Express Stage Line used teams of these sturdy beasts to pull their stages, hoping they would prove reliable for high-country travel. The line was derisively called "The Oxpress," and the project did not last long. These animals were no better equipped to deal with the scarcity of oxygen at high altitude than were horses.

The highway was much improved in 1938–1939. The present highway crosses the pass at a higher point than the lowest part of the pass saddle.

The Colorado Trail crosses the pass, which is an excellent point for food caches or trail access.

THE KEYHOLE

Elevation: 13,140 feet
Location: T4N R74W, Map 3
County: Larimer
Topo: Longs Peak
In Rocky Mountain National Park

The Keyhole is reached by foot on Longs Peak Trail. It divides the waters of Glacier Creek to the west and Boulder Brook to the east.

The USGS Board on Geographic Names officially named the pass in 1911, using the name suggested by early peak hikers.

When Isabella Bird climbed Longs Peak in 1873, she called The

Keyhole "The Notch." That, too, is an appropriate name. This oval opening in the rock, which resembles a keyhole, stands out on the northern ridge of Longs Peak. The Agnes Vaille Shelter House is at The Keyhole. This shelter honors the young mountaineer who lost her life after reaching the top of Longs Peak in winter, and a young member of the rescue party, Herbert Sortland, who lost his own life attempting to save her.

The pass is a saddle between Longs and Storm peaks, with a view to the west of the upper part of Glacier Gorge. The best access to The Keyhole is via the Longs Peak Trail; the west access is difficult and long.

From the east, The Keyhole is where the final ascent to the top of Longs Peak begins for those hikers without technical equipment.

KNIFE POINT PASS

Elevation: 12,860 feet
Location: T39N R7W, Map 8
County: San Juan
Topo: Storm King Peak
National forest: San Juan

Knife Point Pass is accessible by foot in the Weminuche Wilderness Area, but no established trail currently goes over the pass. It divides the waters of No Name Creek to the west and Sunlight Creek to the east.

This is a steep crossing between Peak 10 and Knife Point. The hike is long, across a grassy hill on the Vallecito side, with a fearful view down into the scree on the other side of the pass. Most hikers descend this side by sliding down the scree. Don't attempt to climb up the scree.

Watch for a spring along the Sunlight Trail lower in the valley basin. The pass is in the rugged Needles mountain range. It is not named on forest service or topo maps. It was identified by Ormes in his *Guide to the Colorado Mountains.*

KOKOMO PASS

Elevation: 12,022 feet
Location: T7S R79W, Map 6
County: Eagle/Summit
Topo: Copper Mountain
National forest: Arapaho/
** White River**

Kokomo Pass is accessible by foot via a good trail from the west (forest service trail #2108) or the north (forest service trail #41). Access from the east is blocked off by the Climax mine. It divides the waters of Cata-ract Creek to the west and Kokomo Gulch to the east.

An old wagon road connected the mining town of Kokomo (now buried under the mining tailings of the modern molybdenum mine at Climax) with the Eagle River mining communities. The town of Kokomo began in 1878, when a group of Indiana prospectors found large silver deposits in the vicinity. Fire destroyed the town in 1881 when its population was near ten thousand; it was rebuilt.

Kokomo Pass is on both the Colorado Trail and the Continental Divide Trail. However, as of the summer of 1993, only Colorado Trail signs existed on the pass.

The pass is a narrow saddle between an unnamed 12,374-foot point and North Sheep Mountain. The top is open with good views southeasterly to Clinton Reservoir and CO91. Tailings are not visible below, but the scars of mining activity on Bartlett Mountain show clearly across the valley.   ☐

L

LA MANGA PASS

Elevation: 10,230 feet
Location: T33N R5E, Map 8
County: Conejos
Topo: Cumbres
National forest: Rio Grande

La Manga Pass is passenger-car-accessible on CO17. It divides the waters of La Manga Creek to the north and the North Fork of the Rio de los Piños to the south.

The Spanish word for "sleeve" is *manga.* Perhaps to some early visitors in this southern part of the state the pass looked like a sleeve.

Unfortunately, La Manga Pass is rarely recognized in its own right. It is nearly always mentioned with Cumbres Pass. Early commuters, though, did not necessarily use both passes together to move through these ridges and valleys.

La Manga Pass is northwest of Piño Peak.

LA POUDRE PASS

Elevation: 10,192 feet
Location: T6N R75W, Map 3
County: Grand/Larimer
Topo: Fall River Pass
National forest: Roosevelt/Rocky
  Mountain National Park
On the Continental Divide
Other names: Long Draw,
  Mountain Meadows

La Poudre Pass is passenger-car-accessible from the north almost to the top via forest route #156, and by foot from the south. The pass divides Long Draw Creek to the north and the Colorado River to the south.

The USGS Board on Geographic Names officially named the pass in 1932 in honor of the nearby La Poudre River. This river, which Long Draw drains into, was first named by French trappers who worked for the American Fur Company. They hid their powder kegs near Laporte, on the river now called Cache la Poudre.

Stages used the pass as early as the late 1870s. In 1881 a mail route ran into the mining town of Lulu. An

1883 map shows the pass as "Poudre Pass."

The pass was called Mountain Meadows Pass in the late 1800s, when the present access was opened in order for the Grand Ditch to cross the Continental Divide. This diversion began moving water in 1892. A 1918 listing names the pass as "Poudre Lakes." Long Draw is the name of the reservoir located below the pass, where the water from the Grand Ditch is released into the Cache la Poudre River.

La Poudre Ranger Station is at the pass, which is less than a quarter-mile from the parking lot at the park boundary. The pass is an indefinite section of a flat area. It is one mile east of Mount Neota and next to the Neota Wilderness Area. La Poudre Pass is on the Continental Divide Trail.

LA SALLE PASS

Elevation: 9,733 feet
Location: T11S R73W, Map 6
County: Park
Topo: Glentivar
National forest: Pike

La Salle Pass is 4WD-accessible. It divides the waters of the South Platte River to the west and Marksbury Gulch to the east.

The pass is named for Samuel La Salle, who lived at Tarryall Creek and held an early claim that bears his name. He, with help from others, built a wagon trail over the pass.

This was once a well-used crossing through the Puma Hills into South Park. The Sulphur Spring stage station was located where the road from La Salle Pass rejoined the main route west of Colorado Springs.

The road over the pass provides a good backcountry drive through some pretty scenery. Somewhere along the roadway you may see a deer peeking out through the trees. The top is tree-covered and lacks vistas. It is marked with a sign.

The road that begins to climb southward at the pass summit leads to the top of Badger Mountain and the communications equipment installed there. Look for the good views from this side road, not from the pass itself.

The pass is on the saddle between Martland and Badger peaks. Current forest service signs lead the traveler to La Salle Pass from the west side of Badger Mountain, although access from the east side of Badger is also possible. Roads here do not follow the 1985 Pike National Forest map. Stay under the powerline, along which the correct road runs.

LA VETA PASS

Elevation: 9,382 feet
Location: T28S R70W, Map 9
County: Costilla/Huerfano
Topo: La Veta Pass
Public access through private land
Other names: Abaja, Abajo, Abeyta

La Veta Pass is passenger-car-accessible on a side road that leaves and then returns to US160. It divides the waters of Sangre de Cristo Creek to the west and South Abeyta Creek to the east.

The USGS Board on Geographic Names officially named the pass in 1965. Denver and Rio Grande Railway incorporators were responsible for choosing the name La Veta, which means "the vein" in Spanish. They christened the railroad town at the east terminus of the pass with this name, which was then also applied to the pass. The pass was known as Abeyta Pass in 1870, when it was opened as a toll road by the Cucharas and Sangre de Cristo Road Company.

In 1779, Governor Juan Bautista de Anza crossed near here and noted the trail running over La Veta Pass while traveling to New Mexico. In 1858, Antoine Leroux guided Captain Marcy's troops over the pass into the central Rockies. The first toll road over the pass was constructed by H. T. Sefton, Sr., in the early 1870s. This route became known as the Baldy Scott Toll Road.

By late 1872, rumors were abounding in Denver that the railroad would be going over Abaja, the "low" pass. Sure enough, the Denver and Rio Grande Railroad began construction of a narrow-gauge line over the pass in the mid-1870s to serve the coal mining camps of La Veta and Walsenburg. The Muleshoe Curve on the east side of the pass was one of the most-photographed features on any Colorado rail line. The narrow gauge ran from 1877 to 1899, with an interruption from 1890 to 1892. The tracks were removed in 1902.

In 1875, the Barlow and Sanderson Company was regularly running six-horse stagecoaches on a road that paralleled the railroad route.

In 1913 and 1914, the old wagon road was improved for regular use, and by 1916 a good auto road went over the pass. The Spanish Trail auto route crossed the pass. (During this period, highways were known by trail names, rather than numbers.)

A new road was built to the pass in the late 1950s. The road is still extant but deteriorating. The top is now deserted, with some buildings remaining from when it was on the main road between the San Luis Valley and Walsenburg.

LAKE PASS

Elevation: 12,226 feet
Location: T12S R82W, Map 5
County: Chaffee/Gunnison
Topo: Pieplant
National forest: Gunnison/
   San Isabel
On the Continental Divide
Other names: Lake Creek, Lake
   Fork, Ute

Lake Pass is accessible by foot via forest service trail #543 (on the south side) in the Collegiate Peaks Wilderness Area. It divides the waters of Red Mountain Creek to the south and South Fork Lake Creek to the north.

The USGS Board on Geographic Names officially named the pass in 1970 for the two lakes at its top. Neither lake is visible until the top is in easy view. One lake is on the southeast side of the top of the pass, the other is on the west side.

An 1882 map of Colorado shows the pass as "Lake Creek Pass."

This is one of the oldest crossings in the upper Arkansas River Valley region. Prospectors were using the route in the late 1850s, following an already established trail. In 1867, the route was called the "old Ute Pass," and the crossing was used to go from the Arkansas Valley to the Gunnison River Valley. Once called Ute Pass, it was the crossing used by the Ute Indians to move between Taylor Park and the Twin Lakes region.

Hayden's survey party crossed the pass in 1873. Also in 1873, horses and men were using the pass, but no road existed over it then. A wagon road crossed the pass from about 1882 through the end of that century. That road is no longer visible on the north side of the pass, although some maps still show its trail.

The pass can be reached from the south at the northern end of Taylor Park, or from the north at the border of the wilderness area.

The Continental Divide Trail crosses the pass, but not by an established route. Bushwhacking is required to reach the pass from the north, off a trail through the low valley. Crossing the stream is easier than facing the willows that border it. Look for and follow game trails when it is necessary to go through the willows. The remains of an old building may be seen at the north foot of the pass if your bushwhacking serendipitously takes you to the right spot.

The pass is open, which leaves it exposed to all weather conditions, which change fast in this high country.

LAST DOLLAR PASS

Elevation: 10,663 feet
Location: T43N R10W, Map 7
County: San Miguel
Topo: Sams
National forest: Uncompahgre

Last Dollar Pass is 4WD-accessible on forest route #638. It divides the waters of Alder Creek to the north and Summit Creek to the south.

The top is tree-covered, but just to the southeast are many open views of the Summit Creek Valley. The road over the pass continues to Telluride Road and is a good backcountry drive. The pass road crosses the Hastings Mesa. The south ascent is on a slippery clay shelf. And there are many early snows here to create conditions difficult for driving. The north access takeoff point is close to Dallas Divide. The Last Dollar Pass route was developed to provide a shortcut from the Dallas Divide area

to Telluride. It is still a shortcut, though in miles, not time. The pass is not named on forest service or topo maps.

LIZARD HEAD PASS

Elevation: 10,250 feet
Location: T41N R9W, Map 7
County: Dolores/San Miguel
Topo: Mount Wilson
National forest: San Juan/
  Uncompahgre

Lizard Head Pass is passenger-car-accessible on CO145. It divides the waters of the South Fork of the San Miguel River to the north and the Dolores River to the south.

This was a heavily traveled route used by Indians first, then by Spanish explorers, and later by trappers and prospectors. It is considered one of the best places in the state to see fall colors.

A trail crossed here by the mid-1830s. In the 1870s, a wagon road was developed, and the Rio Grande Southern Railroad crossed the pass in 1891. Otto Mears developed the rail line over the pass. He started building it in 1888 and it was completed within three years. A mining camp existed at the pass during the peak of the mining boom.

Snowsheds about a quarter of a mile long covered the track at the top of the pass because of the heavy snows. The Galloping Goose, a famous train engine, was used on the route. In March of 1944, ten people were stranded in the Galloping Goose; they were rescued by dog-sled.

Hardly anyone notices this pass because it is overshadowed by the striking Lizard Head rock formation nearby. The pass, though, has its share of interest. It is named for the rock formation, which is acknowl-edged a tough technical climb be-cause the rock is so loose.

LONE CONE PASS

Elevation: 11,029 feet
Location: T41N R12W, Map 7
County: Dolores/San Miguel
Topo: Groundhog Mountain
National forest: San Juan/
** Uncompahgre**

Lone Cone Pass is passenger-car-accessible on forest route #611. It di-vides the waters of Beaver Creek to the north and Little Fish Creek to the south.

The south side of the pass has dif-ficult switchbacks. It is between Dunn Peak and Groundhog Moun-tain, just southeast of Groundhog Mountain. It is not named on forest service or topo maps. It was identi-fied by Koch in *The Colorado Pass Book.*

LONE PINE PASS

Elevation: 10,140 feet
Location: T15S R90W, Map 5
County: Gunnison

Topo: Mount Guero
National forest: Gunnison

Lone Pine Pass is accessible by foot on forest service trail #862 in the West Elk Wilderness Area. It di-vides the waters of Lone Pine Creek to the north and Sink Creek to the south.

The area is well used in the fall by hunters who work the high coun-try. The pass is about a mile west of Mount Guero. It is not named on forest service or topo maps. It is identified by local usage.

LONG SADDLE

Elevation: 6,371 feet
Location: T27S R67W, Map 10
County: Huerfano
Topo: Walsenburg North
Public access through private land

Long Saddle is passenger-car-ac-cessible on CO69. It divides the waters of Butte Creek to the north and Sandy Arroyo to the south.

The pass is between I25 and Gardner. The top is open and has a good overview of the surrounding mining operations. To the north is a great view of the south face of Greenhorn Mountain; the tip of Pikes Peak is visible to the northeast. The Spanish Peaks are visible to the south.

Long Saddle is a true pass; how-ever, it is an easy crossing on a minor ridge. The top is open and sagebrush-covered.

The pass is named in the BLM maps book and on the topo map.

LOS PIÑOS PASS

Elevation: 10,514 feet
Location: T45N R1W, Map 8
County: Saguache
Topo: Stewart Peak
National forest: Gunnison

Los Piños Pass is passenger-car-accessible on forest route #788. It divides the waters of Cebolla Creek to the west and Los Piños Creek to the east.

A Ute Indian agency was established here in 1869. The facility has been converted into a forest service work station and is now called the Old Agency Work Center.

In July 1874, Hayden's survey party crossed the pass and explored Cebolla Creek. The old Saguache and San Juan toll road was built over the pass by Otto Mears in 1874.

The pass is part of the mountain-bike-detour portion of the Colorado Trail.

The top is tree-covered with some pine, but mostly aspen. The view above the road to the southwest is of open valley. The top does not have signs, but several empty posts stand as a clue that it may have been marked at some previous time.

The road is passable by sturdy 2WD cars with high clearance; it is narrow in spots, but otherwise good. It is well traveled, especially during hunting season. Other visitors appre-

ciate the good fishing in the streams nearby.

LOST MAN PASS

Elevation: 12,810 feet
Location: T10S R82W, Map 5
County: Pitkin
Topo: Mount Champion
National forest: White River

Lost Man Pass is accessible by foot on forest service trail #1996 in the Hunter Fryingpan Wilderness Area. It divides the waters of the Roaring Fork River to the south and Lost Man Creek to the north.

The pass was named by Len Shoemaker, Aspen District Forest Ranger in the 1920s. Billy Koch was lost there in the late 1800s because he took the wrong fork of a creek. After he told about being lost, his friends assigned "Lost Man" to the creek, lake, and pass.

This is a popular hike into a high glacial basin; it is just east of Aspen and the access is on a main highway, CO82. The trail runs past a high-country lake with views that abound in all directions.

The pass is on the east flank of Geissler Mountain. Lost Man Lake is a half-mile north of the pass; Independence Lake is a half-mile south. The pass is not named on forest service or topo maps.

LOU CREEK PASS

Elevation: 10,870 feet
Location: T46N R7W, Map 8

This glacial lake, in an alpine tundra setting, is one view from Lost Man Pass. (*Photograph courtesy Dannels collection*)

County: Gunnison/Ouray
Topo: Courthouse Mountain
National forest: Uncompahgre

Lou Creek Pass is accessible by foot from the east side on forest service trail #222. The west side access requires a lengthy hike. The pass divides the waters of Lou Creek to the west and the Cimarron River to the east.

There is no evidence that anything more than a trail ever crossed here. The route was used to move between the Silver Jack area and Ridgway as early as the 1910s.

Watch for flies, mosquitoes, and gnats. It is worth braving them, though, because the wildflowers are very pretty. Part of the trail follows a logging road. The top is a well-defined ridge line and is tree-covered. This is a good hike in a pretty setting, away from population centers. One east-side access route starts at the dam on Silver Jack Reservoir.

LOVELAND PASS

Elevation: 11,990 feet
Location: T4S R76W, Map 6
County: Clear Creek/Summit
Topo: Loveland Pass
National forest: Arapaho
On the Continental Divide

Loveland Pass is passenger-car-accessible on US6. It divides the waters of the North Fork Snake River to the west and Clear Creek to the east.

The pass is named for W. A. H. Loveland, who founded the city of Golden and developed the wagon road over the pass in 1879. Before Loveland's wagon road was built, this route was not used because other, easier routes across the Divide were available.

Competition existed, even in the mountains, even in the 1870s. Loveland knew where a crossing existed but he lacked plans to develop a road over this crossing until he heard that Stephen Decatur had men building a route up Grizzly Gulch over another route. Then Loveland got busy and pushed his road over his yet-unnamed saddle. His High Line Wagon Road was begun in February 1879, and the sixty-mile route took less than four months to complete. This road was called the Post Road #13. In the first month of its toll operation, an average of fifty teams a day used it.

When Loveland finished his road, stage lines began running between Georgetown and the Snake River Valley mining communities. Even though the road was available and used, its desirability decreased after about three years because it was rougher than other crossings already in use. And at about this time, rail access to the central Rockies was available. Loveland thought his route could be used for his Colorado Central Railway over the Divide. But that was not destined to happen.

In 1881, a tunnel under the pass was started but not finished. The intent was that the tunnel would be paid for with the ore that would be removed during its construction. But it kept falling in. In the 1940s, another tunnel attempt was made; it was not successful, either.

In 1879, telephone lines were built over the pass. These lines were purchased in 1889 by the Colorado Telephone Company. By 1899, weather conditions had convinced the telephone company to bury these lines rather than try to keep them up in the winter months. That didn't work, because the ground shifted when it froze each winter. So stouter poles were erected and the lines were remounted. These telephone lines were removed for good in 1967.

The first automobile to drive over the pass crossed in 1929. In the mid-1930s, Charles Vail, the state highway engineer, developed the old wagon route over the pass into a modern highway. In the late 1930s, the grade was reduced from an average of eight percent to six percent and rebuilt into a two-lane gravel-surfaced road. The route was not paved until 1950.

Now that I70 uses the Eisenhower and Johnson (Straight Creek) tunnels under the Continental Divide near Loveland Pass, very few locals use the "old" route over the pass, US6. Each summer, though, visitors drive to the top of this historic pass to look for miles in every direction at the beautiful scenery. And truckers, denied access to the tunnel if they are carrying hazardous materials, regularly take the US6 route year-round. The pass road, although high and snow-prone, is kept open, closing only as needed for clearing.

The tunnels are named for President Eisenhower, who was a regular visitor of Colorado, and former governor Johnson. On days of heavy traffic the tunnels can be converted away from the normal configuration, in which both tunnels offer two lanes heading east and two west. One tunnel is left in the original pattern, and the other is divided, providing three lanes of traffic in one direction, with the remaining lane traveling the other way.

Loveland Pass is on the Continental Divide Trail.

LUCAS PASS

Elevation: 12,408 feet
Location: T7S R78W, Map 6
County: Summit
Topo: Breckenridge
National forest: Arapaho

Lucas Pass is accessible by foot on forest service trail #39 through the Breckenridge Ski Area. It divides

the waters of Tenmile Creek to the west and Sawmill Gulch to the east.

The pass is named for the parents of Bill Lucas, the regional forester who envisioned the Colorado Trail.

The pass runs over the divide of the Tenmile Mountain Range, crossing between Peaks 8 and 9, then goes down into the Tenmile Valley. It is on the Colorado Trail.

LYNX PASS

Elevation: 9,020 feet
Location: T2N R83W, Map 2
County: Routt
Topo: Lynx Pass
National forest: Routt

Lynx Pass is passenger-car-accessible on forest route #270. It divides the waters of Morrison Creek to the north and Little Rock Creek to the south.

The pass is named for the bobcats that used to be seen here.

This is a dirt road, easily passable when dry, not so easily managed in bad conditions. It has a nondescript top—a tree-covered area with no views. But it makes for a good backcountry drive.

A campground and a forest service station are located near the pass. ☐

M

MACGREGOR PASS

Elevation: 8,780 feet
Location: T5N R73W, Map 3
County: Larimer
Topo: Estes Park
In Rocky Mountain National Park

There is no access from the south to MacGregor Pass, due to private land holdings, and no established trail leads to the pass from any other direction. It divides the waters of Black Canyon Creek to the north and Fall River to the south.

A late-nineteenth-century home-steader in the hills west of Estes Park was one Esther Burnell. She built a cabin, "Keewaydin," on her 120 acres near the pass.

The pass is not named on forest service, topo, or other maps. It was identified by Enos Mills, a naturalist of the Rocky Mountain National Park region, and Esther's husband.

MAGGIE GULCH PASS

Elevation: 12,540 feet
Location: T41N R6W, Map 8
County: San Juan
Topo: Howardsville
National forest: Rio Grande/
  BLM land
On the Continental Divide

Maggie Gulch Pass is accessible by foot on forest service trail #918. It divides the waters of Maggie Gulch to the west and West Fork Pole Creek to the east.

An old mining camp crossing above the little town of Middleton, the pass was used only about ten years, from the early 1890s to the early 1900s. The crossing was used mostly by locals; others preferred passes located farther south.

The pass is northeast of Canby Mountain. It is not named on forest service or topo maps.

MANDALL PASS

Elevation: 11,940 feet
Location: T1N R87W, Map 2
County: Garfield
Topo: Devils Causeway
National forest: Routt

Mandall Pass is accessible by foot on forest service trail #1121. It divides the waters of East Fork Williams Fork to the north and Mandall Creek to the south.

The pass is two miles west of Orno Peak. It is named on the forest service's White River map.

MANZANARES PASS

Elevation: 9,460 feet
Location: T28S R71W, Map 9
County: Costilla/Huerfano

Topo: Red Wing
National forest: San Isabel and
private land

Manzanares Pass is 4WD-accessible but requires permission to cross private land areas. It divides the waters of Manzanares Creek to the north and Placer Creek to the south.

The pass is named for Señor Manzanares of Walsenburg, an early Huerfano Valley resident. Sometimes the pass name has been incorrectly spelled "Manzaneres."

An 1880s wagon road crossed the pass and connected the mining camps around Russell on the west side of the Sangre de Cristos with Malachite on the east side. The pass is now used mostly to move cattle and sheep during the summer. Access to the pass is via the Stanley Creek (forest service trail #412) route. It is not named on forest service or topo maps.

MARCELLINA PASS

Elevation: 10,325 feet
Location: T13S R87W, Map 5
County: Gunnison
Topo: Oh-be-joyful
National forest: Gunnison
Other name: Ruby

Marcellina Pass is passenger-car-accessible on forest route #826. It divides the waters of Ruby Anthracite Creek to the west and Coal Creek to the east.

A 1900 reprint of the Anthracite 15-minute quad map shows the pass located near the little lake (Lake Irwin, earlier called Lake Brennan) by the ghost town of Irwin. Present highway maps do not show this pass, although during the 1940s the pass was named regularly on maps. However, it was shown on county road #12 rather than in its proper location. An 1897 map shows the pass as Ruby Pass. It is southwest of Scarp Ridge.

MARSHALL PASS

Elevation: 10,846 feet
Location: T48N R6E, Map 6
County: Saguache
Topo: Mount Ouray
National forest: Gunnison/
San Isabel
On the Continental Divide

Marshall Pass is passenger-car-accessible via forest routes #243.2 (on the west) and #200 (on the east) in good weather conditions. It divides the waters of Marshall Creek to the west and Poncha Creek to the east.

The pass is named for Lieutenant William Marshall, a member of the Wheeler survey party who developed a toothache and looked for a quicker route through the mountains to get back to Denver and a dentist in 1873.

Captain John Gunnison saw but did not use the pass in 1853.

In 1877, Otto Mears built a wagon road over the pass. He later sold his

This 1968 photograph shows the remains of some of the buildings that once stood atop Marshall Pass.

route to the railroad for thirteen thousand dollars. President Grant crossed the pass in a stagecoach in July 1880.

In 1891, Marion Muir Richardson wrote a poem to honor Marshall Pass. She noted the coming together of the East and the West and ended with the line, "And night winds wake the pines on Marshall Pass."

The pass was crossed by the Denver & Rio Grande Railway. A total of twenty-three snowsheds were built over the top. The first train went over in 1881, running between Salida and Gunnison. The route was used to move ore from the Gunnison Valley and beyond to the Eastern Slope. The railroad station

atop the pass was named Marshall Pass Station and had a post office until 1952. In 1890 a fire destroyed the station, telegraph office, some snowsheds, and the agent's residence atop the pass. The station house burned again on the Fourth of July in 1923. President Taft rode across the pass on the railroad.

The only recorded holdup of the train occurred in 1902, when masked bandits commandeered the train and took passengers' cash. The bandits had anticipated a payroll box to be on the train, but it wasn't, so they left almost empty-handed. They were one day too early for the payroll box.

In 1902, Thomas Gist crossed the

pass and claimed the first crossing by automobile. In the 1930s, the state highway department had to decide whether to route US50 over Marshall or Monarch Pass. Much debate ensued, and Monarch won out.

In 1951 a forest fire burned many acres near the pass. The railroad narrow gauge ceased operation in 1953, and the track was pulled up in 1955. In 1962 a gas pipeline was laid across the pass.

This is a good drive on an old but easy railroad grade past a pretty mountain lake (O'Haver). Easy access from two major highways (US285 and US50) makes Marshall one of the most-traveled passes in central Colorado. Look for the good views of Mount Ouray along the road and from the open top. The area is a favorite of winter snowmobile and cross-country enthusiasts because of the easy grade and the well-marked route.

The Colorado Trail crosses the pass, as does the Continental Divide Trail.

McCLURE PASS

Elevation: 8,763 feet
Location: T11S R89W, Map 5
County: Gunnison/Pitkin
Topo: Placita
National forest: Gunnison/
**   White River**

McClure Pass is passenger-car-accessible on CO133. It divides the waters of Lee Creek to the west and

the Crystal River to the east.

The pass is named for Thomas "Mack" McClure, who built a large house in about 1884 close to the road over the pass. The house was used as a stage stop and was known as McClure House.

A wagon road was built in the 1890s; in the 1940s a better road, though still only one-lane, was built across the pass. In 1966 the road was further improved and paved.

The current road is a good route but subject to mud slides. The top is wooded with beautiful views peeking between the trees. This is an uncrowded area, a good get-away-from-it-all location.

McCORD PASS

Elevation: 10,825 feet
Location: T3S R81W, Map 2
County: Eagle
Topo: Lava Creek
National forest: White River

McCord Pass is accessible by 4WD on forest route #784. It divides the waters of Piney River to the west and Sheephorn Creek to the east.

The pass is reached by a narrow shelf road that crosses an avalanche run above Walters Lake. This route provides an excellent view of the valley and the mountains to the east. Snow on the shelf road can keep this area closed until late in the summer each year.

This remote pass is located between Lost Lake and Walters Lake, about a mile northwest of Piney Peak. It is named on the topo map.

McHENRYS NOTCH

Elevation: 12,820 feet
Location: T4N R74W, Map 3
County: Grand/Larimer
Topo: McHenrys Peak
In Rocky Mountain National Park
On the Continental Divide

McHenrys Notch is accessible by foot, but no established trail currently goes over the pass. It divides the waters of North Inlet to the west and Shelf Creek to the east.

The USGS Board on Geographic Names officially named McHenrys Notch in 1961. The pass is not named on forest service maps. It is named on the topo map.

MEADOW PASS

Elevation: 10,210 feet
Location: T38N R3E, Map 8
County: Rio Grande
Topo: Beaver Creek Reservoir
National forest: Rio Grande
Other name: Meadows

Meadow Pass is accessible by foot on forest service trail #842. It divides the waters of Tewksberry Creek to the north and Park Creek to the south.

The pass has also been called Meadows Pass. It is a tree-covered saddle, an indistinct area between Cattle Mountain and an unnamed

cone-shaped peak on the east. The pass is two miles southwest of Beaver Creek Reservoir.

MEDANO PASS

Elevation: 10,030 feet
Location: T25S R72W, Map 9
County: Huerfano/Saguache
Topo: Medano Pass
National forest: Rio Grande/
**   San Isabel**
Other names: Madenos, Pike's Gap,
**   Sandhill, Sand Hill, Williams**

Medano Pass is accessible by 4WD via forest routes #235 (on the west side) and #559 (on the east side). It divides the waters of Medano Creek to the west and South Muddy Creek to the east.

Locals pronounce the name *med-eh-know*, not *ma-don-o*, which would be the more pure Spanish pronunciation. The word *medano* means "sand hill" in Spanish.

A continual wind blows across the San Luis Valley from west to east, moving grains of sand from the dunes in Great Sand Dunes National Monument up the pass, hence its name.

An 1892 map shows this as Madenos Pass. An 1897 map locates and names the pass as Sand Hill Pass.

By 1850 this route was used regularly by fur traders and trappers who moved through from the east looking for riches in the southwest part of the state. In 1866 a band of Utes killed settlers near the little town of

Great Sand Dunes National Monument is in the northeast corner of the San Luis Valley and at the west foot of Medano and Mosca passes.

La Veta. The warriors fled through the pass, where Kit Carson and Chief Ouray caught up with and captured the transgressors.

Captain John Fremont considered the pass a worthy candidate for a railroad crossing, although he noted it would not work for a stage road because the sand would "choke" the western end. Captain John Gunnison crossed the pass in 1853 while looking for a railroad route. In 1873, Lieutenant E. H. Ruffner and his exploration group noted the small stream coming down the gulch and marked a pass near today's Medano Pass. The route was rarely used for wagons because it was never in

much better shape than it is today. Most of the explorers who crossed the pass called it Williams Pass after Bill Williams, who led many of their parties over the range.

One reason given for not developing the road over Medano any more than what now exists is that some day the sand may completely cover the west access to the pass.

This is a definite 4WD road: the top is rough, rutty, and has some big holes to catch wheels. The east side of the pass is frequented by courteous drivers who post paper-plate signs about road conditions on the west side, which can be even worse than the east access. It may be wiser to do the west side by hiking, but if an attempt is made to cross by 4WD, do it late in the year.

The most interesting feature here is the Great Sand Dunes National Monument on the west side of the pass. The trip is well worth the effort to visit this unusual location.

MERIDIAN PASS

Elevation: 10,710 feet
Location: T6S R73W, Map 6
County: Park
Topo: Harris Park
National forest: Arapaho/Pike

Meridian Pass is accessible by foot via forest service trails #604 on the south side (in Pike National Forest) and #41 on the north side (in Arapaho National Forest), at the edge of the Mount Evans Wilderness Area. It divides the waters of Indian Creek to the north and Elk Creek to the south.

This is part of the extensive Mount Evans hiking trails system; it makes a good hike on an easy pathway. This is an easy hike with little elevation gain. At the top is an outhouse (at times only the hole is there), a small spring, and a camping spot. The top is wooded, covered with gnarled aspen trees and pines in a sandy soil. Walk over to the east side of the saddle to get good views to the southwest of Bandit Peak and the above-timberline ridge running south from it. Look for eagles soaring around the top of Rosedale Peak,

just to the west of the pass. Rocky outcroppings make good nesting spots for the forest birds.

The pass is not named on forest service or topo maps. It is identified in Mount Evans hiking guides.

MIDWAY PASS

Elevation: 11,841 feet
Location: T10S R83W, Map 5
County: Pitkin
Topo: Thimble Rock
National forest: White River

Midway Pass is accessible by foot on forest service trail #1993 in the Hunter Fryingpan Wilderness Area. It divides the waters of Midway Creek to the north and Coleman Creek to the south.

Midway can be hiked from the town of Aspen via the west ascent. Lots of lakes are nearby, and the hike can be combined with hikes to other passes. The east ascent is unusual in that the hike involves going down to the pass rather than climbing up to it.

From the pass, look across to the Maroon Peaks. Watch for deer and elk in the upper valleys. Midway Lake is a mile north of the pass.

MILK COW PASS

Elevation: 10,980 feet
Location: T42N R4E, Map 8
County: Saguache
Topo: Pine Cone Knob
National forest: Rio Grande

Milk Cow Pass is passenger-car-accessible on forest route #650. It divides the waters of Groundhog Creek to the north and Lone Rock Creek to the south.

The USGS Board on Geographic Names officially named the pass in 1981. The name comes from local usage.

This is a backcountry road through rolling hills and pretty scenery. The saddle is open, a pleasant change after driving through trees to reach the top. The pass is wide; the road runs along the south edge of the saddle, giving the best views to the south. Cattle browse on the grass here every summer. Views to the north are of the hills beyond La Garita Park. A small knoll beside the road has old cabin timbers at its top, with views to the south of the Rio Grande Valley.

The high point of the road is about one-quarter mile before the saddle. The road is bumpy with a few long climbs; otherwise a passenger car can manage quite well. Pine Cone Knob is three miles south of the pass.

MILNER PASS

Elevation: 10,758 feet
Location: T5N R75W, Map 3
County: Grand/Larimer
Topo: Fall River Pass
In Rocky Mountain National Park
On the Continental Divide
Other names: Bihhle-Thoson,
  Deer, Miner

Milner Pass is passenger-car-accessible on US34. It divides the waters of the Colorado River to the west and the Cache la Poudre River to the east.

The USGS Board on Geographic Names officially named the pass in 1932. It honors T. J. Milner, a railroad engineer who surveyed a route between Denver and Salt Lake City over the pass. The USGS recognized also a variant name of "Miner."

The Arapahos called this "Deer Pass." Their word for deer was *Ba ha thoson,* which anglicized is "Bihhle-Thoson," still used as an alternate name.

An old Indian trail, the pass runs by Poudre Lake. The top is open and marked. A road of sorts was started in 1913, when the route was declared a highway, and finished in 1920 although it had been discussed since 1895. Improvements were made in 1932.

Milner Pass is on the Continental Divide Trail. It is the Continental Divide crossing on Trail Ridge Road.

MINNESOTA PASS

Elevation: 9,992 feet
Location: T14S R90W, Map 5
County: Gunnison
Topo: Minnesota Pass
National forest: Gunnison

Minnesota Pass is accessible by foot on forest service trail #870, on the western edge of the West Elk Wilderness Area. It divides the waters of East Fork Minnesota Creek to the west and Browning Creek to the east.

The USGS Board on Geographic Names officially named the pass in 1962. It, and one of the creeks the pass heads, honor a family from Minnesota who homesteaded here.

This is prime hunting country.

MINNIE GULCH PASS

Elevation: 12,740 feet
Location: T41N R6W, Map 8
County: San Juan
Topo: Howardsville
National forest: Rio Grande/
** BLM land**
On the Continental Divide
Other name: Presto

Minnie Gulch Pass is accessible by foot. It divides the waters of Minnie Gulch to the west and Middle Fork Pole Creek to the east.

The original name of the pass was Presto Pass; later it was called Minnie Gulch, for the gulch it heads.

In 1874, John Ufford proposed a road over the pass; he called it Presto Pass. His name for the Middle Fork Pole Creek was Urbana Creek. A rough wagon road was built over the pass, but it did not survive. This route was used to cross between Animas Forks Basin and San Juan Basin.

This pass was probably not used much except by locals. Others would have preferred the easier crossings farther south. This old crossing is south of the Cuba survey point and

above the mining area of Middleton. Minnie Gulch Pass is not named on forest service or topo maps.

MISSOURI PASS

Elevation: 11,986 feet
Location: T7S R82W, Map 5
County: Eagle
Topo: Mount Jackson
National forest: White River

Missouri Pass is accessible by foot on forest service trail #2003 in the Holy Cross Wilderness Area. It divides the waters of Cross Creek to the north and Missouri Creek to the south.

The high-country Missouri lakes (there are fourteen) make a trip into Missouri Pass a worthwhile destination. The pass is north and above the highest lake, up the wall of the basin. Making a loop trip with other passes would provide a good outing. Be sure to visit the old Holy Cross City site.

Missouri Pass is not named on forest service or topo maps. It is named on the Trails Illustrated maps.

MOCCASIN SADDLE

Elevation: 7,730 feet
Location: T5N R73W, Map 3
County: Larimer
Topo: Longs Peak
Public access through private land

Moccasin Saddle is passenger-car-accessible. It divides the waters of

A prospector leads his pack animals over Missouri Pass in this historical photograph. *(Photograph courtesy Denver Public Library, Western History Department)*

Big Thompson River to the west and Fish Creek to the east.

The pass is shown and named in local Estes Park promotional material. The pass is on a road used as a bypass around the congested downtown area.

This is a minor pass, but it does separate watersheds and is a definite saddle between two mountains. The road over it is new.

The pass is not named on forest service or topo maps. It is identified on local maps.

MOLAS PASS

Elevation: 10,899 feet
Location: T40N R8W, Map 7
County: San Juan
Topo: Snowden Peak
National forest: San Juan
Other names: Molas Divide,
  Molas Lake

Molas Pass is passenger-car-accessible via US550. It divides the waters of Molas Creek to the north and East Lime Creek to the south.

This is a pretty area with rugged steep walls to jagged above-timberline views of the West Needle mountain range. Geologists particularly like the rock strata exposed near the pass.

Until the highway was built, this area was marshy and full of willows. In the late 1930s, a massive tree-planting program was begun to replace lodgepole pines lost to an old burn at the pass top.

A 1988 study found the clearest, cleanest view (meaning the one with the fewest number of particulates in the air) of the state at Molas Pass. Monitors studied air pollution and visibility. Clear air at the pass allows visibility of over 140 miles in any direction.

Molas Pass is on the Colorado Trail. It is three miles south of Sultan Mountain. Fishing enthusiasts stop at Little Molas Lake near the pass summit.

MONARCH PASS

Elevation: 11,312 feet
Location: T49N R6E, Map 5
County: Chaffee/Gunnison
Topo: Pahlone Peak
National forest: Gunnison/
  San Isabel
On the Continental Divide
Other name: Agate

Monarch Pass is passenger-car-accessible on US50. It divides the waters of North Fork Agate Creek to the west and the South Arkansas River to the east.

The USGS Board on Geographic Names officially named the pass in 1945. The name recognizes the mining community of Monarch, which was located on the east side of the pass. The Board had first named this crossing Agate Pass in 1941.

This route over Monarch Pass was built in 1939 and replaced a previous Monarch roadway (called Monarch-Old elsewhere in this text).

Advertisements such as this were used to entice the horseless-carriage traveler to visit Colorado's high country. (*Photograph courtesy Donna Nevens*)

There is no record that even a wagon road existed over the pass before this road was built.

Much controversy surrounded the choice of this route. It was debated whether the highway should cross the old railroad grade of Marshall Pass—many nearby residents favored that route. In the end, though, Charles Vail, the state highway engineer, prevailed, and this road was constructed. The construction cost was one and a quarter million dollars.

Controversy continued. Mr. Vail wanted to name the pass after himself, and when the road opened, signs at the top read "Vail Pass." Locals and vandals painted the signs black. Mr. Vail eventually got his own pass many years later and many miles away.

Because the new pass road crossed what had been occasionally called Agate Pass, signs with that name were next erected. Locals continued to call the pass Monarch, and in order to eliminate the confusion that was resulting, the highway department finally gave in, and the name Monarch Pass was assigned to the new route.

Many visitors to this mountain region know Monarch as a ski area rather than for the history of the road. The ski area opened in 1939 and has recently become known as a ski area with excellent snow conditions.

Each summer thousands of visitors ride the tram (built in 1966) atop the pass on the highest gondola ride in the U.S. A fire in 1988 destroyed a tourist shop here. It was rebuilt and is now considered one of the best roadside stops in the mountains.

Monarch Pass is on the Continental Divide Trail. Maurice Browning Cramer expressed his views in a poem, "Monarch Pass," where he claims visibility into Arizona, New Mexico, Wyoming, and Utah from the pass.

MONARCH PASS-OLD

Elevation: 11,375 feet
Location: T49N R6E, Map 5
County: Chaffee/Gunnison
Topo: Pahlone Peak
**National forest: Gunnison/
    San Isabel**
On the Continental Divide

Monarch Pass-Old is passenger-car-accessible on forest route #237.

It divides the waters of Porphyry Creek to the west and the South Arkansas River to the east.

The USGS Board on Geographic Names officially named the pass Old Monarch Pass in 1945.

This road was built across the Continental Divide in 1922 and served until the modern highway (see Monarch Pass) was constructed in 1939. This road was part of the "Rainbow Route" across the country, back in the days when roads had names rather than numbers. The cost of construction for this road in 1922 was only $200,000.

This second crossing named Monarch replaced the 1880s-vintage road used by the miners. The newer road was designed for automobile traffic, although it was never paved. Today the route is still open each summer and makes a fine detour off the highway. The road quickly enters a forest and follows power lines. Either enter or exit this back road one mile east of the present pass top.

In the winter many snowmobilers and cross-country skiers try their skills on this road.

Monarch Pass-Old is on the Continental Divide Trail.

MONARCH PASS-ORIGINAL

Elevation: 11,525 feet
Location: T49N R6E, Map 5
County: Chaffee/Gunnison
Topo: Garfield

National forest: Gunnison/
San Isabel
On the Continental Divide

Monarch Pass-Original is accessible by foot from the west side only. It divides the waters of Major Creek to the west and the South Arkansas River to the east.

The road over this first of the three Monarch passes was built by the Boon brothers in 1880. A stage line then ran over the pass. The route carried a lot of traffic because it supplied mining camps in the eastern end of the Gunnison Valley. The original route was replaced in 1922 when the state highway department built a road over what is today known as Old Monarch Pass.

To reach the pass, follow the old roadbed up from the west side to the top, which overlooks the very back and top side of the ski area below to the east. The top is tree-covered, with views. Monarch Ski Area has posted a large snow fence at the top (for snow control on the slopes) and many "No Trespassing" signs to deny access on the east side. Obey them. Future expansion of the ski area may close the upper side of the west access.

The Continental Divide Trail crosses the pass saddle. Original Monarch Pass is not named on forest service or topo maps.

MONTGOMERY PASS

Elevation: 11,005 feet
Location: T7N R76W, Map 3

County: Jackson/Larimer
Topo: Clark Peak
In the Colorado State Forest

Montgomery Pass is accessible by foot via forest service trail #977 from the east side. It divides the waters of the North Fork Michigan River to the west and Montgomery Creek to the east.

The top of the pass is marked by a sign but is not named. The top is open, a typical saddle pass with beautiful scenery. Views to the west are super, but it can be very windy at the top. It is a short but scenic hike. The trail follows the old jeep road access to the top.

The west-side access nears the pass via a 4WD road, and a short hike leads to the top. The pass is named on the forest service's Routt map.

MONUMENT PASS

Elevation: 11,006 feet
Location: T46N R7W, Map 8
County: Gunnison/Ouray
Topo: Washboard Rock
National forest: Uncompahgre

Monument Pass is accessible by foot. It divides the waters of North Fork Lou Creek to the west and the Cimarron River to the east.

No trail runs over the pass; to hike it involves bushwhacking and orienteering. It's in an obscure location and probably used now only to move animals from one feeding area to another.

MONUMENT HILL DIVIDE

Elevation: 7,352 feet
Location: T11S R67W, Map 10
County: Douglas/El Paso
Topo: Greenland
Public access through private land
Other names: Arkansas Divide, Black Forest Divide, Colorado Divide, Lake Pass, Palmer Divide

Monument Hill Divide is passenger-car-accessible on I25. It divides the waters of the South Platte River to the north and the Arkansas River to the south.

The many alternate names for the pass reflect the various geographical features of the area. The name "Lake Pass" is for the little lake at Palmer Lake.

This easily accessible and usually unrecognized pass is a historic location. Trappers, prospectors, and traders used the crossing. In 1820, Stephen Long led his expedition across the Black Forest Divide; then, in the 1830s, the large Bean-Sinclair party followed the easy trail from Colorado Springs to Denver. Captain John Fremont used the pass when he left Denver in 1843 and went to Pueblo to buy mules.

Many early visitors from the eastern U.S. rode on the narrow gauge line from Denver to Colorado Springs and then farther south. Some of these visitors were intimidated by the mountains to the west and would not consider venturing up into the wild lands but enjoyed the scenery the Front Range trip would give them.

Pioneers began settling along "the divide" in the 1850s. Some of them experienced Indian attacks, so they began to cluster together for protection and little towns were formed.

The Denver and Rio Grande Railway began the route from Denver to Colorado Springs in 1871; the first train reached Colorado Springs that same year. Palmer Lake, at the top of the pass, is named in honor of the founder of the D&RG, William Jackson Palmer. The little lake at Palmer Lake (which is entirely fed by springs and drains out both ends) sitting atop the divide was originally called Divide Lake. Stages ran regularly between Santa Fe and Denver; the most difficult part of the route was crossing the divide.

Today's weather forecasters usually refer to the pass area as the Palmer Divide when discussing the weather conditions. The terrain slopes upward from both sides to create harsher storms than those the large cities on the Front Range might experience.

Before the divide area became a sea of housing to provide bedroom communities for Colorado Springs and Denver, farmers raised potatoes, hay, and sheep there. Much timber-cutting was done east of Palmer Lake, near the community of Black Forest.

MOON PASS

Elevation: 10,580 feet
Location: T43N R4E, Map 8

County: Saguache
Topo: Bowers Peak
National forest: Rio Grande

Moon Pass is passenger-car-accessible on forest route #675. It divides the waters of Moon Creek to the north and South Fork Carnero Creek to the south.

An old Indian trail crossed the pass. Some modern historians claim the pass was on the route that Captain John Fremont was following on his disastrous trip in the San Juans in 1854.

The road over the pass is a fair dirt road and makes an interesting drive to a nice tree-covered summit. The pass is three miles west of Lookout Mountain.

MOSCA PASS

Elevation: 9,750 feet
Location: T27S R72W, Map 9
County: Alamosa/Huerfano
Topo: Mosca Pass
National forest: Rio Grande/
  San Isabel
Other names: Fly, Musco,
  Robideau's, Robidoux

Mosca Pass is accessible by foot on the west side via forest service trail #883. The east side is accessible by passenger car via forest route #583. It divides the waters of Mosca Creek to the west and May Creek to the east.

The Indians called the pass *mosca,* the Spanish word for "fly." In 1864, an elderly resident of Costilla claimed an old name for the pass was Paso de Arena, and that Mosca came from his father, an early Spanish guide. Others believe the name comes from Alverdo Moscoso, an explorer with DeSoto, who may or may not have reached Colorado. Because many early journal writers noted the abundance of pesky mosquitoes and flies here, it is most reasonable to believe the "fly" connection.

Robidoux Pass is named at this location on an 1863 map of Colorado.

Zebulon Pike crossed the pass in 1807 (although some writers claim Pike used the Medano Pass route), then Gunnison crossed in 1853. Gunnison deemed the pass as unacceptable for a railroad route and of very little value as a wagon road.

The earliest known regular use by whites began with the crossings made by Antoine Robideau in the late 1820s. He used the old Indian crossing to move goods to his camp near today's Delta. A small supply town, also named Mosca, grew up at the foot of the pass on the west side.

In 1871, Frank Hastings got a charter from the Colorado Territory to construct a toll road over the pass. When the Hayden survey party reached the pass area in the mid-1870s, they found a toll road had already been built. By the early 1880s, stages were running across the pass between Mosca and Silver Cliff.

In 1880 the mail contract for the forty-mile route from Malachite to Alamosa via Mosca Pass was awarded to Antonio Archuleta. He usually had to carry the mail by horseback because the road washed out regularly. Homesteaders used the pass to move into the newly available lands in the San Luis Valley.

Floods destroyed the road in 1880, 1906, and 1911. The road was sold to the state in the late 1880s, then the state sold the road in the 1890s to Will and Coley King. The toll road was finally abandoned in 1901.

In the 1930s, state road maps showed a dirt road over the pass. In fact, the route was considered for some time as a possible highway between Pueblo and the San Luis Valley. In 1939, San Luis Valley and southern Colorado businessmen approached the state, requesting a highway across the old route. Some road improvements were made in 1954. And in 1964 the state highway department again considered an all-year road over the pass, but this has not come to pass.

MOSQUITO PASS

Elevation: 13,186 feet
Location: T9S R79W, Map 6
County: Lake/Park
Topo: Climax
On BLM land

Mosquito Pass is 4WD-accessible on forest route #12. The west side of the pass is on BLM land; the east side is in Pike National Forest. The pass divides the waters of Birdseye Gulch to the west and South Mosquito Creek to the east.

The story about how the mining district and pass got their names is interesting but believable. When several residents of the region met, sometime before August 1861, they made suggestions for a name but could not arrive at a consensus; the names were recorded in a book and the book was closed. When they met again to review their ideas, a dry mosquito was smashed on the page where the names had been recorded. A unanimous vote followed

and the name has been "Mosquito" ever since.

Thomas Farnham and his exploration group crossed the pass in 1839, led by a local blacksmith named Kelly. Kelly knew that Indians used the crossing regularly, and he also knew how to avoid them.

The mining camp of Mosquito opened in 1861 on the east side of the pass. Augusta Tabor crossed Mosquito with her husband, H.A.W. Tabor, in 1870 on horseback. She noted there was no road at all and that the way was very steep.

A wagon road went across the pass in the early 1870s to accommodate the silver rush. When Hayden's

A narrow and bumpy road leads to the summit of Mosquito Pass, a favorite 4WD weekend trip. (*Photograph courtesy Dannels collection*)

surveyors visited in 1873 they found the pass already named and well used, although the route was still difficult: it was rough and designed mainly for pack animals and pedestrians.

A telegraph line was built across the pass in 1878. This proved to be helpful during severe snowstorms, because travelers could follow the line of poles to stay on the road. Storms kept knocking down the telegraph lines, however.

Mosquito Pass had very heavy traffic during the Leadville mining boom days, which began in the spring of 1878. Pack outfits, ore wagons, and regularly scheduled stage runs all used the road. The pass was called "a highway of frozen death" because many poorly prepared miners died while crossing the pass on foot in order to save the stage fare on the trip between Fairplay and Leadville.

Construction of an improved wagon road was begun on the Leadville side in November of 1878 and on the Fairplay side in December of 1878. The Mosquito Pass Wagon Road Company helped each county build the toll road and toll gates were placed on the private road's portion. When trains reached Leadville in 1882, coming up the Arkansas River Valley from Buena Vista, the pass fell into disuse.

About this same time, talk began about a railroad going over the pass. The Denver and South Park Railroad looked at the pass but rejected it as too high to surmount. In 1882, rail lines were run to the London Mine on the east side to carry ore into the valley. A tunnel was also proposed, but it never materialized. A telephone line was built across the pass in 1889.

As the mines played out, the pass fell into disuse and the road was not kept up. The route was abandoned by 1910. In the 1930s some interest was again expressed in a tunnel under the pass.

At the pass top is a small memorial marker honoring Father Dyer, who is buried in the Cedar Cemetery in Castle Rock. Father Dyer, known as the "Snowshoe Itinerant," was a circuit preacher in the mining camps. He also carried the mail, beginning in early 1864, crossing the pass on skis and snowshoes in the wintertime. Usually he crossed the pass at night because the snow was harder then and he would stay atop the crust. His pay for carrying the mail was eighteen dollars per week.

Today the annual "Get Your Ass Over the Pass" world championship burro race is held in July or August. It was started in 1949 and is sponsored by the communities of Fairplay and Leadville.

MOUNTAIN SHADOWS PASS

Elevation: 6,817 feet
Location: T13S R67W, Map 10
County: El Paso
Topo: Cascade
Public access through private land

Even big cities have passes. This one is located on the west side of Colorado Springs.

Mountain Shadows Pass is passenger-car-accessible. It divides the waters of two branches of Douglas Creek.

This pretty little spot in Colorado Springs is just across the road from the entrance to the Flying W Ranch in the Mountain Shadows Community.

The pass top is marked and has good views south and east into the downtown section of Colorado Springs. The pass is not named on the Pike forest service or topo maps. It is identified by a street sign.

MUDDY GAP

Elevation: 4,540 feet
Location: T28S R53W, Map 10

County: Las Animas
Topo: Rock Canyon
Public access through private land

Muddy Gap is passenger-car-accessible on county road #90.0. It divides the waters of Muddy Creek to the west and Johnny Creek to the east.

This pass is in a wide open, mostly flat area in the plains of southeast Colorado. Take a dusty, narrow road to reach the top, which is located on a high point where the road bends around a protruding mesa.

The pass is not named on forest service or BLM maps. It is named on the topo map.

MUDDY PASS

Elevation: 8,710 feet
Location: T5N R82W, Map 2
County: Grand/Jackson
Topo: Rabbit Ears Peak
National forest: Arapaho/Routt and
   public access through private land
On the Continental Divide

Muddy Pass is passenger-car-accessible on US40. It divides the waters of Grizzly Creek to the north and Little Muddy Creek to the south.

The pass is named for a tributary of the Colorado River, Muddy Creek. The creek does get muddy, especially after a good rainfall.

Rufus Sage crossed into Middle Park over Muddy Pass in December of 1842. He called the crossing a "large opening." Captain John Fremont crossed in 1844 and remarked that the pass offered one of the most beautiful views he had ever seen. He wrote, "We fell into a broad and excellent trail, made by buffalo, where a wagon would pass with ease." He met an Arapaho war party that was going after the Utes. Kit Carson was Fremont's guide on this trip.

The pass is named on a map of Middle Park dated 1859. The area got national publicity in 1879, when George Bird Grinnell wrote two articles for *Forest & Stream* magazine about North Park and the crossings into it.

The pass was used as a regular crossing from Middle Park to North Park. Early surveyors considered the pass an ideal rail route. In 1881, the Denver, Utah and Pacific surveyed for a rail line, but no track was ever laid.

Muddy Pass is on the Continental Divide Trail.

MUDDY PASS

Elevation: 8,625 feet
Location: T3S R82W, Map 2
County: Eagle
Topo: Lava Creek
National forest: White River
Other name: Muddy Creek

Muddy Pass is passenger-car-accessible via county road #6 and forest route #405. It divides the waters of Muddy Creek to the west and Piney River to the east.

A dirt road runs through a sagebrush valley to reach the top, which is identified on a sign as Muddy Divide. Sheep graze here in the summertime. Good views can be had from the top: east to the west side of the Gore Creek Wilderness Area, and west toward Castle Peak.

MUMMY PASS

Elevation: 11,260 feet
Location: T6N R74W, Map 3
County: Larimer
Topo: Comanche Peak
In Rocky Mountain National Park

Mummy Pass is accessible by foot in Rocky Mountain National Park. It

This view is west off the top of Mummy Pass in Rocky Mountain National Park.

divides the waters of Mummy Creek to the west and South Fork Cache la Poudre River to the east.

The USGS Board on Geographic Names officially named the pass in 1932 for the mummy shape of the mountain range.

This is a favored hiking trip on a remote, quiet trail leading into a large valley. Mirror Lake and other passes are close and worth the effort as side trips. The pass is not on the main trail.

MUSIC PASS

Elevation: 11,380 feet
Location: T24S R73W, Map 9
County: Custer/Saguache
Topo: Crestone Peak

National forest: Rio Grande/
**   San Isabel**
Other name: Sand Creek

Music Pass is accessible by foot via forest service trail #1337 on the east side. It divides the waters of Sand Creek to the west and Music Pass Creek to the east.

The USGS Board on Geographic Names officially named the pass in 1969. It is named for the quiet singing sounds reputedly heard atop the pass. Three miners who camped at the pass in the 1860s claimed to have heard violin music and promptly named it "Music Pass." Other people claim the name comes from when a band of Utes was frightened away because they heard music on the pass in the very early 1800s. They refused to use the crossing again.

The pass was not as well used as were others in the same region during the settling of the West, but it served as an alternate route into the corner of the San Luis Valley north and east of the Sand Dunes.

On the east side, about one and a half miles of trail lead from a parking area to this beautiful pass. Because the trail was a 4WD road until recently, it is an easy hike. A longer and harder access can be made from the west side.

Look down into the Sand Creek Basin from the top. Bighorn sheep gather at the natural mineral spring in the valley below. Just off the top is an old lean-to, hidden in trees. A note inside the shelter explains that it has already saved three lives, and requests that hikers not destroy it.

The pass is at timberline with bristlecone and gnarled pines near. The view to the east is into the south end of the Wet Mountain Valley. The pass is about a mile northwest of Snowslide Mountain. The Sand Creek Lakes on the west side of the pass are desirable fishing destinations. □

N

NAPOLEON PASS

Elevation: 12,020 feet
Location: T15S R81W, Map 5
County: Gunnison
Topo: Cumberland Pass
National forest: Gunnison

Napoleon Pass is accessible by foot. It divides the waters of Middle Willow Creek to the north and Quartz Creek to the south.

The pass is named for "Frenchy" Address Napoleon Perault, the owner of a couple of saloons in Tincup from around 1879 to 1896.

The pass is west of Fitzpatrick Peak, and the area is not well used by hikers. Mountain goats live here, but they are hard to spot, particularly if snow is still on the mountainsides. On the approach from the south, the trail is indistinct; it looks like a game trail. The hike is a gentle but continual upward climb to the wide saddle. The view to the north is into Taylor Park and across to the Elk mountain range.

Old maps show the pass trail as Virginia City Trail. Virginia City is an old name for nearby Tincup.

THE NARROWS

Elevation: 6,635 feet
Location: T33S R56W, Map 10
County: Las Animas

Topo: Pine Canyon
On private land

There is no access to The Narrows. It divides the waters of Chacuaco Creek to the north and Cow Canyon to the south.

No record exists of any strong historical interest in this area.

Locals now use the pass as a cattle-drive route. The trail stays atop a mesa and provides access to grazing areas.

The pass is not named on BLM maps. It is named on the topo map.

THE NARROWS

Elevation: 5,700 feet
Location: T51N R12W, Map 4
County: Montrose
Topo: Roubideau
On BLM land

The Narrows is passenger-car-accessible on forest route #503, the 25 Mesa Road. It divides the waters of Cottonwood Creek to the west and Roubideau Creek to the east.

The Narrows is a historic sheep drive way. The actual pass is on a narrow point where the Roubideau and Cottonwood canyons come close together and is shown on BLM and topo maps.

NEBO PASS

Elevation: 12,460 feet
Location: T39N R6W, Map 8
County: San Juan

Topo: Rio Grande Pyramid/
    Storm King Peak
National forest: Rio Grande/
    San Juan
On the Continental Divide

Nebo Pass is accessible by foot on forest service trail #815 in the Weminuche Wilderness Area. It divides the waters of Vallecito Creek to the west and West Ute Creek to the east.

The pass is named for the mountain to its southwest, Mount Nebo.

Franklin Rhoda, a member of the Hayden survey party, was at the pass in 1874. Although it was noted in exploration diaries, there is not much record of the pass being used for anything more than what it is today, a trail.

The pass is on the Continental Divide Trail, and a pretty little lake lies near the top. Nebo Pass is not named on forest service or topo maps.

NEW YORK PASS

Elevation: 12,265 feet
Location: T11S R83W, Map 5
County: Gunnison/Pitkin
Topo: New York Peak
National forest: Gunnison/
    White River

New York Pass is accessible by foot on forest service trail #761.1A in the Collegiate Peaks Wilderness Area. It divides the waters of New York Creek to the north and Bowman Creek to the south.

The pass is named for the New York Mine.

This is a rarely used crossing between Taylor Park and Lincoln Gulch, on the Elk mountain divide. New York Peak is two miles to the north. The pass is not named on forest service or topo maps. It was identified by Len Shoemaker, Aspen-area forest ranger.

NINEMILE GAP

Elevation: 7,476 feet
Location: T2N R93W, Map 1
County: Rio Blanco
Topo: Ninemile Gap
Public access through private land

Ninemile Gap is passenger-car-accessible on CO13 and CO789. It divides the waters of Good Spring Creek to the north and Curtis Creek to the south.

The top is open, with lots of deer and antelope in the vicinity. The Jensen State Wildlife Area is at the top of the pass. Building remnants of an old railroad work station are still extant. The pass is three miles west of Yellow Jacket Peak.

NORTH PASS

Elevation: 10,149 feet
Location: T46N R4E, Map 8
County: Saguache
Topo: North Pass
**National forest: Gunnison/
  Rio Grande**
On the Continental Divide

Other names: Cochetopa, North Cochetopa, Saguache, West Pass Creek

North Pass is passenger-car-accessible on CO114. It divides the waters of Lujan Creek to the west and East Pass Creek to the east.

The USGS Board on Geographic Names officially named the pass in 1963.

Old Indian trails (mostly Ute) went over the pass. Then the route was used by trappers to reach the rich waters in the western part of the state, where beaver and other fur-bearing animals were to be found. Antoine Robideau took wheeled wagons over the pass in the early 1830s.

In 1853, John Gunnison mapped the area and noted in his journal, "Elevation of the pass is not enough to give an extensive view, but the numerous small, grassy valleys, and pine and aspen groves . . . afforded us a pleasant prospect."

The Colorado Territory issued a charter to the Saguache, Los Piños, Lake Fork and Upper Rio Las Animas Toll Road Company in 1873 to construct a wagon road over this pass. The Hayden survey party mapped it in 1877; they observed the area was laced with possible crossing routes.

By 1916 a highway existed over this pass; the road was paved in 1962. This road connects the upper western end of the San Luis Valley with the Gunnison Valley.

The Continental Divide Trail and the Colorado Trail cross CO114 about a mile west of the top of the pass, along Lujan Creek.

NORTH LA VETA PASS

Elevation: 9,413 feet
Location: T28S R70W, Map 9
County: Costilla/Huerfano
Topo: La Veta Pass
Public access through private land
Other name: Muleshoe Saddle

North La Veta Pass is passenger-car-accessible on US160. It divides the waters of Sangre de Cristo Creek to the west and South Abeyta Creek to the east.

The USGS Board on Geographic Names officially named North La Veta Pass in 1965.

In 1803, James Purcell crossed the pass, the first recorded use by whites of this mountain opening. Zebulon Pike's exploration party tried to investigate the area in February of 1807, but it was turned back by heavy snows.

Locals called this saddle, before the highway over it was built, "Muleshoe Saddle," for the small railroad settlement on the east side named Muleshoe.

A new road was built in 1961 to 1962 and opened to the public in 1963. It is a straighter, more direct, higher, and, some feel, less-interesting route than the earlier crossing over nearby La Veta Pass. A good view of Mount Maestas is southeast of the pass.

The scenic pull-out atop the pass is said to be haunted by a disgruntled headless woman. Single men, be alert!

NORTH PAWNEE PASS

Elevation: 4,425 feet
Location: T8N R55W, Map 10
County: Logan
Topo: Wild Horse Lake
Public access through private land

North Pawnee Pass is passenger-car-accessible on county road #11. It divides the waters of Pawnee Creek to the north and Sand Creek to the south.

The pass is located just outside Pawnee National Grasslands and is one of the few northeastern Colorado "named" passes.

North Pawnee Pass is named on the topo map.

THE NOTCH

Elevation: 10,140 feet
Location: T37N R5W, Map 8
County: Hinsdale
Topo: Granite Peak
National forest: San Juan

The Notch is accessible by foot, but no established trail currently goes over the pass, which is in the Weminuche Wilderness Area. It divides the waters of two canyons of the Los Piños River.

The pass is one and a half miles northeast of Coyote Basin Spring. It is a shallow saddle below timberline. The pass is between two unnamed peaks of 10,722 feet and 10,383 feet, and is named on the forest service map.

THE NOTCH

Elevation: 9,490 feet
Location: T38N R3W, Map 8
County: Hinsdale
Topo: Oakbrush Ridge
National forest: San Juan

The Notch is accessible by foot, but no established trail currently goes over the pass. It divides the waters of Middle Fork Piedra River to the west and East Fork Piedra River to the east.

The pass is just northeast of and adjacent to 10,182-foot Rock Mountain. It is named on the forest service map.

THE NOTCH

Elevation: 11,795 feet
Location: T7S R83W, Map 5
County: Eagle
Topo: Mount Jackson
National forest: White River

The Notch is accessible by foot in the Holy Cross Wilderness Area. It divides the waters of East Brush Creek to the north and Lime Creek to the south.

This is a poor timberline ascent; it is north above Woods Lake about two miles and on the west shoulder of Fool's Peak. Lake Charles is a mile north of the pass. The Notch is not named on the forest service or topo maps. James Grafton Rogers located and named it in his listing of Colorado's geographic features.   □

O

OH-BE-JOYFUL PASS

Elevation: 11,740 feet
Location: T13S R87W, Map 5
County: Gunnison
Topo: Oh-be-joyful
National forest: Gunnison
Other name: Hancock

Oh-be-joyful Pass is accessible by foot via forest service trail #835 on the west side; the trail is unnumbered on the east side, on the eastern edge of the Raggeds Wilderness Area. It divides the waters of Buck Creek to the west and Oh-be-joyful Creek to the east.

The pass is named for one of the creeks it heads and the mountain nearby. Oh-be-joyful Mountain and Creek are, in turn, named for a hymn. A Scotsman, Jim Brennan, prospected here in 1879 and chose names from various hymns for many nearby geographic features.

The alternate name, Hancock Pass, is for one of the mountains touched by the pass and is sometimes used by locals.

The pass is located in the Ruby mountain range, north of Hancock Peak and south of Richmond Mountain. This area is popular with mountain bikers and hikers in late summer but is subject to heavy snowmelt runoff and flooded creeks before late summer.

OHIO PASS

Elevation: 10,074 feet
Location: T14S R87W, Map 5
County: Gunnison
Topo: Mount Axtell
National forest: Gunnison

Ohio Pass is passenger-car-accessible on forest route #730. It divides the waters of Ruby Anthracite Creek to the north and Ohio Creek to the south.

The pass was first crossed by Utes. A wagon road opened in the 1880s.

The Denver, South Park and Pacific Railroad ran a line called the Ohio Creek Extension and laid track from Gunnison heading into the coal-mining district in 1882. The track never got beyond the top of Ohio Pass, though, because the ore ran out before the trains got to it.

The Ohio Creek Extension section was bought by the Denver and

Rio Grande Western Railway in 1937. Tracks were removed in the mid-1940s. Part of today's car route follows the old railroad grade. The top is tree-covered, with no great views. At the pass, the road runs adjacent to the West Elk Wilderness Area.

OPHIR PASS

Elevation: 11,789 feet
Location: T42N R8W, Map 7
County: San Juan/San Miguel
Topo: Ophir
National forest: San Juan/
**   Uncompahgre**
Other name: Howard

Ophir Pass is 4WD-accessible. It divides the waters of the South Fork of the San Miguel River to the west and Middle Fork Mineral Creek to the east.

Ophir is the biblical name for the location of King Solomon's mines. The area in Colorado was originally called Howard's Fork to honor Lieutenant George Howard, a prospector in the 1870s, hence the alternate name of Howard Pass, which was also the original name of the pass. Maps from the 1860s show the pass as Howard Pass.

The route was first known as the Navajo Trail. Indians moved across the pass between the San Miguel Valley and the Animas Valley on hunting trips. An Indian fortress was still visible near the top of the pass in the 1880s.

A scree pile marks the top of Ophir Pass, high in the San Juan mountain range north of Durango.

Fur trappers were probably the first white men over the pass. They discovered it while looking for a shortcut route into the high country. Other explorers followed in the early 1860s, and a regular route began to develop. A toll road ran over the pass by 1881. In 1891 the Rio Grande Southern built through the area, and the Ophir Loop, an engineering marvel, brought in considerable traffic.

The current road over the pass was opened in 1953 for backcountry enthusiasts. The road is now also popular with mountain bikers. This route serves as a summer shortcut between Silverton and Telluride. It is a steep shelf road on the west side

of the pass.

The unmarked top is a very narrow V with loose slide rock all around. Before beginning up the west side of the pass, check to see that no traffic is near.

OWL CREEK PASS

Elevation: 10,114 feet
Location: T45N R6W, Map 8
County: Gunnison/Ouray
Topo: Courthouse Mountain
National forest: Uncompahgre
Other name: Courthouse

Owl Creek Pass is passenger-car-accessible in dry weather on forest route #858. It divides the waters of

Owl Creek to the west and the West Fork Cimarron River to the east.

This road used to be called the Cimarron Cutoff Trail and parts of it were used by Otto Mears for one of his toll roads. It provided a route between Ridgway and the Silver Jack area.

The access road to the pass (from the west) climbs up and up through a wooded section. Keep the jagged peaks of the Turret Ridge in mind and head generally toward them. Chimney Peak and Courthouse Mountain are just two of the outstanding rock formations worth studying. Various mountains here are used for technical climbing.

Winter-sports fans use the area for snowmobiling, cross-country skiing, and snowshoeing. There is some coal mining in the area. ☐

P

PACKERS GAP

Elevation: 4,705 feet
Location: T26S R56W, Map 10
County: Otero
Topo: Packers Gap
Public access through private land

Packers Gap is accessible by passenger car on county road #GR-G, a backcountry route. It divides the waters of Crooked Arroyo to the west and Jack Canyon to the east.

The pass is well defined on topo and BLM maps. The top is a gentle and indistinct slope. The area is now used for grazing cattle.

PAHLONE PASS

Elevation: 11,505 feet
Location: T48N R6E, Map 6
County: Chaffee/Gunnison

Topo: Pahlone Peak
National forest: Gunnison/ San Isabel
On the Continental Divide

Pahlone Pass is accessible by foot via forest service trails #531 from the northwest, #1412 on the east side, and #1776 across the ridge of the pass. It divides the waters of Green Creek to the north and Agate Creek to the south.

The pass is a half-mile west of Chipeta Mountain, three miles south of Pahlone Peak, and is on the Colorado Trail and the Continental Divide Trail. However, the pass is not named on forest service or topo maps.

PAMENA GAP

Elevation: 4,630 feet
Location: T29S R56W, Map 10

County: Las Animas
Topo: O V Mesa
On private land

There is no access to Pamena Gap. It divides the waters of the Purgatoire River to the west and Chacuaco Creek to the east.

This is a minor pass in southeast Colorado that can be located via the Eight Mile Canyon, but a local rancher denies access across and beyond his property.

The pass is just above the Purgatoire River canyon. Use the BLM or topo maps to pinpoint it.

PARADISE DIVIDE

Elevation: 11,250 feet
Location: T12S R87W, Map 5
County: Gunnison
Topo: Oh-be-joyful
National forest: Gunnison/
  White River

Paradise Divide is 4WD-accessible on forest routes #734 on the south side and #317 on the north side. It divides the waters of Rock Creek to the north and the Slate River to the south.

The divide is sometimes also called Paradise Pass. The road follows part of the old grade of the Colorado Marble Company's railroad. The railroad was reaching for the marble quarries beyond the pass, on the north side.

This route leads up an easy ascent through a river valley, then becomes more difficult, with switchbacks near the top. Look for the great view to the north; to the south high mountains are very close. Spring rains can mean lots of heavy runoff early in some years. This is a very popular tourist area, particularly on weekends.

The pass is southeast of Cinnamon Mountain. It is not named on forest service or topo maps, but there are signs at the top.

PASS CREEK PASS

Elevation: 9,380 feet
Location: T28S R70W, Map 9
County: Costilla/Huerfano
Topo: La Veta Pass
Public access through private land

Pass Creek Pass is passenger-car-accessible. It divides the waters of Pass Creek to the north and Sangre de Cristo Creek to the south.

Following Indian use, Spanish explorers crossed here to move up the mountains and into the valleys just west of the Front Range. Traders and trappers traveled from Taos or Santa Fe to sell their goods to early settlers near Hardscrabble. They would then trap beaver in the streams of the high country before heading south again.

The pass was regularly used in the early years as an access to the forts built in the eastern end of the San Luis Valley: Fort Massachusetts and Fort Garland. By the 1850s, these military posts were attracting many visitors. The army used the pass to bring supplies to the forts.

American explorers also noted or used the pass. The low crossing was especially well suited for the wagon road that eventually was built over the pass. Governor Melgare, Captain John Gunnison, Lieutenant E. H. Ruffner, and others mentioned the pass in their journals.

Pass Creek Pass crosses between the Wet Mountain Valley and the San Luis Valley. Today, it is just a pleasant drive through a pretty countryside. The north approach to the pass runs along the west side of Sheep Mountain. This pass is located near several other passes, all of which are worth investigating.

PAWNEE PASS

Elevation: 12,541 feet
Location: T1N R74W, Map 3
County: Boulder/Grand
Topo: Monarch Lake
National forest: Arapaho/Roosevelt
On the Continental Divide
Other name: Breadline Trail

Pawnee Pass is accessible by foot via forest service trails #1 on the west side (Arapaho National Forest) and #907 on the east side (Roosevelt National Forest), in the Indian Peaks Wilderness Area. It divides the waters of Cascade Creek to the west and South St. Vrain Creek to the east.

The alternate name "Breadline Trail" originated in 1882, when the area was surveyed for a possible railroad crossing. Indians were hired by the railroad to carry supplies to the surveyors; they carried bread (and other items) over a saddle close to this pass. No indication exists that the pass might have been used regularly by earlier visitors except for local access. The proposed railroad involved a tunnel under the pass, but it didn't get beyond the discussion stage.

Most of the elevation gain in hiking over the pass is in the last two miles, above Lake Isabelle. The trail is well defined and easy to follow. Be sure to check out the Isabelle Glacier in the high reaches just on the east side of the pass.

The best time to hike the pass from the east side is late in the year and on a weekday: on weekends the trailhead area near Brainard Lake is like a big-city parking lot.

The pass is open, wide, and flat. Several mountains nearby are popular destinations during the summer months. During winter months, cross-country skiers like the lower part of the trail to Pawnee Pass both on the east and west sides of the Continental Divide.

PAWNEE PASS

Elevation: 4,424 feet
Location: T8N R55W, Map 10
County: Logan
Topo: Willard
Public access through private land

Pawnee Pass is passenger-car-accessible on CO14. It divides the waters of Sand Creek to the south and Pawnee Creek to the north.

This pass is just east of Pawnee National Grasslands. It is located on the edge of the same mesa as North Pawnee Pass. The pass is not named on BLM or highway maps. It is named on the topo map.

PEARL PASS

Elevation: 12,705 feet
Location: T12S R85W, Map 5
County: Gunnison/Pitkin
Topo: Pearl Pass
National forest: Gunnison/
  White River

Pearl Pass is 4WD-accessible via forest routes #128 on the north and #738 on the south, adjacent to the Maroon Bells–Snowmass Wilderness Area. It divides the waters of Copper Creek to the north and East Brush Creek to the south.

The pass is named for the nearby Pearl Mine.

Prospectors from the Crested Butte mining area crossed over the pass in mid-1879 and found gold above the Ashcroft mining location. A road over the pass was opened in September 1882 to enable wagons to take the ore from the upper mines on the north side down to mills near Crested Butte. The road operated only about three years because other routes provided lower and, often, better access.

The roadbed was abandoned for many years in the first part of this century and then reopened, with help from 4WD clubs. An awesome top in remote country makes Pearl Pass one of the most spectacular 4WD roads in the state. It is located on a ridgeline of Elk Mountain. The pass is not a typical pass saddle but rather a short, sharp crossing over a steep point on that ridge. Pearl Mountain is west of the pass, Star Peak is east, and Carbonate Hill is south.

The pass top is marked with a sign and does not have much room in which to park or turn around. Copper Basin, on the north side, is a big, open high-mountain cirque that deserves viewing. Waterfalls abound on the north side of the pass. The south side skirts a shoulder of Pearl Mountain. Crossing the pass from north to south, which provides better traction on the larger rocks of the north side, is better.

On the south side of the pass a landowner has built four gates in a mile of private land, making public access very difficult. The road is open only for a short period each summer, even in low-snowfall years. Some 4WD clubs consider Pearl Pass one of the three most difficult pass roads in the state. One reason is the potential for damage to tires on the sidehill sections of the pass.

The Pearl Pass Klunker Tour is a mountain bike challenge between Crested Butte and Aspen that is held each year. This event started in 1976 and has grown steadily since, but it is definitely for experienced riders only.

PENNOCK PASS

Elevation: 9,143 feet
Location: T7N R72W, Map 3
County: Larimer
Topo: Pingree Park
National forest: Roosevelt

Pennock Pass is accessible by passenger car on county road #44H. It divides the waters of the Cache la Poudre River to the west and Box Prairie Creek to the east.

The pass is believed to be named for an early settler, Taylor Pennock.

This is a backcountry road that makes a good off-the-main-road trip in the Poudre Canyon region. Watch for the good views to the southwest.

PEON PASS

Elevation: 10,336 feet
Location: T46N R4E, Map 8
County: Saguache
Topo: North Pass
National forest: Gunnison/
**   Rio Grande**
On the Continental Divide

Peon Pass is accessible by 4WD via forest routes #784 on the east and #785 on the west. It divides the waters of Lujan Creek to the west and Spanish Creek to the east.

This almost unknown crossing is about two miles north of North Pass.

It was and still is used as an alternate crossing of the Cochetopa Hills. Although it is somewhat higher than North Pass, it runs up an easy grade and is in a pleasant wooded area. A wide saddle marks the top.

The pass is on the Colorado Trail and serves as an access point for hikers. It is also on the Continental Divide Trail. Look for the Colorado Trail and Continental Divide Trail signs to identify the top of the pass; the logging roads can confuse hikers and backcountry drivers.

Peon Pass is shown and named on county maps from the 1960s. It is not named on current forest service or topo maps.

PIEDRA PASS

Elevation: 11,410 feet
Location: T38N R1W, Map 8
County: Mineral
Topo: Palomino Mountain
National forest: Rio Grande/
**   San Juan**
On the Continental Divide
Other name: Red Mountain

Piedra Pass is accessible by foot on forest service trail #580 on the northern border of the Weminuche Wilderness Area. It divides the waters of Mountain Creek to the north and the East Fork of the Piedra River to the south.

The original name of the pass was Red Mountain, but newer forest service maps use "Piedra Pass."

An old wagon road reached the

top of the pass many years ago, but now the entire route is trails only. Some mining was done here in the late nineteenth and early twentieth centuries.

The pass is just at timberline and dotted with ponds. The Continental Divide Trail (#813 in this area) goes by the pass.

An Anasazi settlement has been discovered close to the pass. Using modern techniques to date the site, archaeologists estimate that some of the artifacts may be from about 5900 B.C., leading some historians to believe these mountains have been used extensively for many centuries.

POMEROY PASS

Elevation: 12,740 feet
Location: T51N R6E, Map 6
County: Chaffee
Topo: St. Elmo
National forest: San Isabel

Pomeroy Pass is accessible by foot. It divides the waters of Pomeroy Gulch to the north and the North Fork of the South Arkansas River to the south.

Some forest service maps from the 1940s and 1950s show this as "Pomroy" Pass; modern maps include the "e" for various features, but the current forest service and topo maps do not name the pass.

The pass is located between Pomeroy Mountain and an unnamed 13,070-foot peak. Forest service trail #1437 takes the hiker to the Pome-

roy Lakes; bushwhacking is necessary above the lakes to reach the pass.

PONCHA PASS

Elevation: 9,019 feet
Location: T48N R8E, Map 6
County: Chaffee/Saguache
Topo: Poncha Pass
Public access through private land
Other names: Gunnison's, Puncho

Poncha Pass is passenger-car-accessible on US285. It divides the waters of San Luis Creek to the south and Poncha Creek to the north.

The origins of the name "Poncha" are unclear. The name could be from the Spanish for "a low gap in the mountains," meaning "paunch"; it could be a corruption of the word "Ponca," an Indian tribe; or it could be from "Puncho," a name given to the pass by Franklin Rhoda when he crossed in 1874. The most believable origin derives from Governor Juan Bautista de Anza. He crossed the pass in 1779 and called it "Poncha," after the Spanish word for mild. And it is a mild crossing.

James Pattie, a trapper, is believed to be the first white to cross the pass. In 1825, he moved through looking for beaver streams. By the 1830s, the trail was recognized as "the route to follow." The Bean-Sinclair expedition followed buffalo tracks across the pass from South Park to the Rio Grande in 1830.

Lieutenant Edward G. Beckwith tried to change the name of the pass to "Gunnison's," after the leader of an 1853 mapping expedition, Captain John Gunnison, who was killed a short time later in Utah. That name didn't stick and Poncha it was, again. Another member of the Gunnison party, Sheppard Homans, did see his name applied to an open park near the pass. That name is still used today, Homans Park.

In 1855, Colonel Thomas T. Fauntleroy led a cavalry charge up from Fort Massachusetts, in eastern San Luis Valley, and chased a band of Indians back across the pass, killing about forty of them near Salida. His troops continued to monitor the movement of Indians through the pass until the forts were closed. The military called the route through the pass Old Government Road.

Chief Ouray told of taking his Ute warriors over the pass in 1867 or 1868, chasing some horse-stealing Yampa Indians led by Chief Colorow. Hot mineral springs on both sides of the pass made it a favorite camping spot for the Indians.

The *Rocky Mountain News* reported in 1868 that gold had been discovered at the pass. Interest in the area quickly picked up.

Otto Mears built the first road over the pass in 1869, a toll road, with the help of John Lawrence of Saguache. This route, called the Poncha Pass Wagon Road, was officially chartered in November 1870. Mears sold the road to the Denver & Rio Grande railroad in 1880. However, two other charters had been issued before his; in 1861 and 1865, Colorado Territory had issued permission for roads to other companies. Either the companies did not operate long enough for roads to be constructed, they started and did not complete a road, or traffic did not warrant a road. Perhaps when Mears built, the time was right. By 1870, regular stages were running over Mears's road.

The Colorado Springs and South Park Railroad Company looked at the route as early as 1867. They wanted to cross "Pauncha" Pass into the rich farmland of the San Luis Valley. By 1881, a railroad was over the pass. This Denver & Rio Grande route was converted to standard gauge in 1930 and abandoned in 1950. Tracks were removed in 1951.

In 1914 the Poncha Pass road was rebuilt to provide a hard-gravel automobile route. In the 1920s, before route numbers were assigned to roads, the route was called The Tenderfoot Trail.

About three miles south of the pass, at Round Hill, is a cache of buried gold, or so an old story says.

POUGHKEEPSIE PASS

Elevation: 12,740 feet
Location: T42N R7W, Map 8
County: San Juan
Topo: Ironton
Public access through private land

Poughkeepsie Pass is accessible by 4WD. It divides the waters of the

A view of Poughkeepsie Pass from the top of Corkscrew Pass.

Uncompahgre River to the north and Cement Creek to the south.

The pass was used to provide access to mining districts. An old pack trail, built in 1879, runs from Silverton up Cement Creek to the pass. The route is a very narrow shelf road on the east side; it is extremely rugged and steep and has sheer drop-offs.

Two mines, the Adelpheh and the Alpha, are located at the pass summit. These mines were owned by H. A. W. Tabor. The mining camps here were nearly deserted by the late 1880s.

The pass is not named on forest service or topo maps. It was identified in the 1880 book *Colorado,* by Frank Fossett.

PRAIRIE DIVIDE

Elevation: 7,936 feet
Location: T10N R72W, Map 3
County: Larimer
Topo: Haystack Gulch
National forest: Roosevelt

Prairie Divide is passenger-car-accessible on county road #179. It divides the waters of Bull Creek to the west and the North Fork of Rabbit Creek to the east.

The top is open, grassy, and resembles a high mesa, with a broad, fairly flat expanse of land running north to south and another broad, flat expanse running east to west.

The actual pass is about a half-mile off the top of Prairie Divide

Ridge. Look for nice views to the northeast.

PROMONTORY DIVIDE

Elevation: 8,579 feet
Location: T24S R71W, Map 9
County: Custer/Huerfano
Topo: Devils Gulch
Public access through private land
Other names: Muddy Creek, Sheep Tick Canyon

Promontory Divide is passenger-car-accessible on CO69. It divides the waters of Antelope Creek to the north and Muddy Creek to the south.

This area was crossed by Zebulon Pike on his exploration west in 1806. In 1846, Alexander Barclay crossed "Sheep Tick Canyon Pass." Fremont's 1848 expedition crossed this "bleak, bald ridge."

Lieutenant E. H. Ruffner on his trip in 1873 noticed the easy grade of this pass, which he called the Muddy Creek Pass. Maps from 1873 show the crossing as "Muddy Creek Pass."

The pass is on a long ridge running northeast about fifteen miles from the base of the Sangre de Cristo mountain range.

PTARMIGAN PASS

Elevation: 12,180 feet
Location: T4N R74W, Map 3

In some national forests, routes open to motor vehicles are marked with white arrows. This road is off Promontory Divide, in the Wet Mountain range.

County: Grand/Larimer
Topo: McHenrys Peak
In Rocky Mountain National Park
On the Continental Divide
Other name: Flat Top

Ptarmigan Pass is accessible by foot. It divides the waters of Ptarmigan Creek to the west and Fern Creek to the east.

The pass was named by Roger Toll in 1924 for the ptarmigan, a high-country bird that changes color: it is white in winter and brown during the summer months.

A 1905 Grand County map names the pass "Flat Top," for the nearby mountain.

The pass is a low point between Ptarmigan Point and Flattop Mountain, and it may be reached by hiking along the ridge.

PTARMIGAN PASS

Elevation: 11,777 feet
Location: T4S R77W, Map 6
County: Grand/Summit
Topo: Dillon
National forest: Arapaho

Ptarmigan Pass is accessible by foot via forest service trail #69 on the west side and an unnumbered trail on the east side. It divides the waters of the South Fork Williams Fork to the north and Laskey Gulch to the south.

The pass is named for nearby Ptarmigan Mountain and was an Indian crossing above the Blue River.

The young man for whom the town of Dillon is named, Tom Dillon, is said to have wandered over the pass after becoming lost in the high country while prospecting. He had encountered Indians and was extremely relieved to reach the confluence of the rivers below the pass (at today's Silverthorne-Dillon area), where he found shelter.

. The pass is on an open tundra ridge in the Williams Fork mountain range. The trail becomes obscure just before the top.

PTARMIGAN PASS

Elevation: 11,765 feet
Location: T6S R79W, Map 6
County: Eagle/Summit
Topo: Pando
National forest: Arapaho/
White River

Ptarmigan Pass is passenger-car-accessible from the south via forest route #702, and by 4WD from the north side. It divides the waters of Resolution Creek on the west and Wilder Gulch on the east.

The road is steep near the top of the pass but can be driven with a car. The area is inhabited by lots of sheep in the summer and one lonely sheepherder. The north side of the pass is a very rough and narrow road with muddy spots.

The view from the open top is expansive: the Gore Range is to the north and the Collegiate Range is to the south. The pass is on the east flank of Ptarmigan Hill. This area was well used in the training days of the Tenth Mountain Army Division at Camp Hale, below in the valley to the south.

Winter cross-country skiers and summer hikers use the Wilder Gulch on the north side of the pass. Access to it is off the Vail Pass bike path.

PUERTO BLANCA PASS

Elevation: 11,900 feet
Location: T38N R2W, Map 8
County: Mineral
Topo: Palomino Mountain
National forest: San Juan

Puerto Blanca Pass is accessible by foot via forest service trail #580 in the Weminuche Wilderness Area. It divides the waters of Puerto Blanca Creek to the west and Rainbow Creek to the east.

Puerto blanca is Spanish for "white door." The pass is southwest of Red Mountain.

PUZZLE PASS

Elevation: 11,160 feet
Location: T36N R11W, Map 7
County: La Plata
Topo: La Plata
National forest: San Juan

Puzzle Pass is accessible by foot, but no established trail currently goes over the pass. It divides the waters of the La Plata River to the west and Lightner Creek to the east.

The USGS Board on Geographic Names officially named the pass in 1949, after the Puzzle vein of mineral ore.

Puzzle Pass is located east of the Golden King Mill and just to the north of Baker Peak, the highest, double-coned peak in the area. The top (visible from the forest service road below) is tree-covered and only a slight dip between Baker Peak and the next ridge. The pass is not named on the forest service map. It is named on the topo map.   □

R

RABBIT EARS PASS

Elevation: 9,426 feet
Location: T5N R82W, Map 2
County: Grand/Jackson
Topo: Rabbit Ears Peak
National forest: Routt
On the Continental Divide

Other name: South Rabbit Ears

Rabbit Ears Pass is passenger-car-accessible on US40. It divides the waters of Muddy Creek to the west and Grizzly Creek to the east.

The USGS Board on Geographic Names officially named the pass in

1969 for Rabbit Ears Peak, located about two miles north. The twin rocks are an old volcanic plug and can be seen from near Walden to Kremmling.

Construction of the paved highway route over the pass was begun in 1957, and the road opened in August 1959. While the road-building was in progress, US40 traffic was re-routed over Gore Pass. This route replaces the historic crossing at Old Rabbit Ears Pass, which is a little north of the newer pass.

There are many beautiful views in this section of the state, which is less well visited than other parts of the mountains. The pass is in the Park mountain range. Dumont Lake and Summit Lake are desirable destinations here.

Rabbit Ears Pass is on the Continental Divide Trail. The area is heavily used in the wintertime for cross-country skiing.

RABBIT EARS PASS-OLD

Elevation: 9,610 feet
Location: T5N R82W, Map 2
County: Grand/Jackson
Topo: Rabbit Ears Peak
National forest: Routt
On the Continental Divide

Rabbit Ears Pass-Old is passenger-car-accessible. It divides the waters of Muddy Creek to the west and Grizzly Creek to the east.

The first Rabbit Ears Pass road was built in 1876 and followed pros-

pector trails. This area was first investigated by Coues and his section of Hayden's survey party in September 1876. The pass was used to drive horses out of North Park in the late 1880s. A more modern road was built in 1915, and it was used by automobiles, although it was only dirt. It was called the Moffat Highway and was part of the Victory Highway before route numbers were assigned. Later, this route was paved. In the late 1930s, highway crews began struggling with the effort to keep the pass road open all winter long.

This is the older crossing; it is located about a mile north from the newer and present crossing of US40. It is still paved but is not well maintained. A bronze tablet, erected in 1929 to mark the pass, is still visible.

The top is tree-covered; a trail heading north is clearly marked. The pass is named on the forest service's Arapaho map.

The area receives a lot of winter precipitation. In some years, Rabbit Ears Pass-Old has greater snow depth than any other place in the state.

RAILROAD PASS

Elevation: 10,700 feet
Location: T37N R2E, Map 8
County: Mineral
Topo: Wolf Creek Pass
National forest: Rio Grande/
** San Juan**
On the Continental Divide

Railroad Pass is accessible by foot on forest service trail #813. It divides the waters of Pass Creek to the north and Silver Creek to the south.

Hayden's survey party noted the pass. The 1928 and 1942 San Juan National Forest Service maps name the pass. The pass is also named on the current San Juan National Forest Service map, but it is shown in the wrong location.

Railroad Pass is on the Continental Divide Trail (#813 in this area). Alberta Park Reservoir is below the pass to the north.

RATON PASS

Elevation: 7,881 feet
Location: T35S R63W, Map 10
County: Las Animas
Topo: Fishers Peak
Public access through private land
Other name: Cimarron

Raton Pass is passenger-car-accessible on I25. It divides the waters of Raton Creek to the north and Railroad Canyon, in New Mexico, to the south.

Raton is the Spanish word for "mouse" or "pack rat." Cimarron Pass was the name assigned to the crossing by William Palmer in 1867 when he was developing his Denver & Rio Grande railroad route through the pass.

Raton Pass began as an old Indian trail. In 1719, the governor of New Mexico, Antonio Valverde y Cosio, crossed the pass, but he described it as a very difficult trail. Pedro Villasur crossed the pass in 1720. The Mallet brothers laid out a route through the pass between Trinidad and Santa Fe in 1739.

Military groups crossed the pass in the early 1800s; Raton Pass was on the mountain branch of the famous Santa Fe Trail and saw thousands of footsteps long before wagons ever moved across it. This old route was a hard climb for even the sturdiest men or animals. It was said to be filled with cliffs and rocks, precipices, overhanging tree branches, and lots of mud holes.

At times, various travelers used the creek bed to ascend the pass rather than attempting to stay on the rough trail. Until the army began using the route regularly in the mid-1840s it remained difficult, and many travelers opted for the easier crossing of Sangre de Cristo Pass. In 1845, Captain John Fremont sent Lieutenant Abert and a small company of thirty-five men to assess the pass while the remainder of his survey group remained at Bent's Fort. In 1847, Kit Carson camped at the pass.

Richens "Uncle Dick" Wootton built a toll road over the pass in 1865 that operated until 1878, when he sold it to the railroad. His selling price was fifty dollars per month for the rest of his life—the West's first pension plan. Wootton never charged Indians a toll to cross his road. The Arapahos called him "Cut Hand" because he was missing two fingers on his left hand.

One story of the pass is about the fight between the Atchison, Topeka and Santa Fe railroad and the Denver & Rio Grande over the first passage through the mountains. The Atchison, Topeka and Santa Fe won. Other stories from this time are about the skeleton in Wootton's mine and how he discouraged the Goodnight cattle drivers from using his pass road by the high toll rates he charged.

The railroad put a tunnel through the mountain to the west of the pass. A helper engine was required to make the uphill climb. To improve time on the crossing, a second set of tracks was laid (except through the tunnel) during the six-year period of 1900 to 1906. Then in 1908 the railroad built a second tunnel. In 1949 the older tunnel was abandoned; it was blocked off in 1953 and both directions of rail traffic began use of the newer 1908 tunnel.

By 1916 a good auto road was in place over the pass; at this time the route was called the National Old Trails Road. Later, when numbers were assigned to highways, it became US85/US87. Major improvements were made to the highway in the early 1940s.

In 1960 the modern I25 route was begun and dedication services for the interstate completion were held in August 1965 atop the pass. Colorado and New Mexico held a joint celebration. The pass is named on most highway maps.

RED BUFFALO PASS

Elevation: 11,540 feet
Location: T5S R79W, Map 6
County: Eagle/Summit
Topo: Vail Pass
National forest: Arapaho/
  White River
Other names: Gore-Willow Creek,
Wilkerson

Red Buffalo Pass is accessible by foot via forest service trails #60 (the Gore Range Trail) on the east side and #2015 on the west side, in the Eagles Nest Wilderness Area. It divides the waters of Gore Creek to the west and South Willow Creek to the east.

The USGS Board on Geographic Names officially named the pass in 1963, during the development of the I70 highway. The name Red Buffalo was coined from two peaks nearby: Red Peak and Buffalo Mountain. The alternate name of "Wilkerson" was bypassed by the board because another pass (on US24 west of Colorado Springs) already uses that name. The name Wilkerson honored a local miner. The other alternate name, Gore-Willow Creek, appears on some forest service signs and designates the creek drainage on either side of the pass.

This route was used by prospectors to move between mining districts. Before the road farther south was built in 1940, Red Buffalo Pass took all the traffic through this area.

This pass was much discussed in

A rest break on a long hike provides the opportunity to take in the view. This one is looking northeast from the top of Red Buffalo Pass.

the early 1960s, when the I70 route through the main range of the Rockies was in the planning stages. Before the final route was chosen, this more-direct crossing was heavily favored by many people. It is a much shorter route than the long swing south from Silverthorne to Copper Mountain, west over Vail Pass, then north again and into Vail. One reason Vail was ultimately chosen for I70, instead of this route over Red Buffalo, was the impact to wildlife. It was felt the migration routes of deer, elk, and bighorn sheep would be greatly disrupted by a road through this otherwise pristine high country.

Two unnamed lakes, christened on a hiking trip by the authors as Edward's Lake and Lake Gloria, dot the scene just below the top of Red Buffalo Pass on the east side.

From the top, good views can be had of the Gore mountain range to the north and the Tenmile mountain range to the east. This is a remote hiking area that is nonetheless close to a major highway.

The eastern lower part of the trail gets much use in the summer, particularly on weekends; most hikers retrace their steps back down long before the pass is reached.

On the west side of the pass look for the gravesite of the prospecting Recen brothers, which serves as a trail landmark.

RED DIRT PASS

Elevation: 11,560 feet
Location: T10N R82W, Map 2
County: Jackson/Routt
Topo: Mount Zirkel
National forest: Routt
On the Continental Divide

Red Dirt Pass is accessible by foot on forest service trail #1127 in the Mount Zirkel Wilderness Area. It divides the waters of Gold Creek to the west and Shafer Creek to the east.

The pass is in the Sierra Madre (also called Park) mountain range, and is a mile southeast of Mount Zirkel. Gold Creek Lake and Gilpin Lake are favorite destination points here.

Forest service maps show the trail passing through a valley meadow just before the final ascent, but trail rerouting now takes it across the hillside, and the boggy, marshy areas below are thus bypassed. The top is a defined saddle with no signs. Views probably would be very good on a clear day. (The authors didn't see anything when they were there!) The last half-mile is up very steep switchbacks.

The Wyoming Trail (#1101) goes over the pass. The Continental Divide Trail is also shown to cross the pass, but this section of the trail is not clearly defined. Future improvement of the section of trail around Red Dirt Pass is planned.

RED DOG PASS

Elevation: 11,700 feet
Location: T5N R76W, Map 3
County: Jackson
Topo: Mount Richthofen
National forest: Routt

Red Dog Pass is accessible by foot on forest service trail #1141 in the Never Summer Wilderness Area. It divides the waters of Silver Creek to the north and the South Fork Michigan River to the south.

The pass is a high saddle above a large meadow. A good view of Mount Richthofen and Tepee Mountain can be seen from the top. The actual crossing is approximately fifty feet higher than the lowest part of the saddle. Snowfields in the low saddle make crossing there impossible even in late July. The pass is at the far west end of the saddle and very near a sharp cut (to the west) into the next drainage, which adds character to this area.

The trail is difficult to find and follow—keep watching for peaks to indicate direction. There are many streams to cross.

The pass is located in the Never Summer mountain range, which is aptly named. Many summer days are more rainy than dry here.

The Continental Divide Trail crosses the pass. The pass is not named on forest service or topo maps. It is identified from trail hiking guides.

RED HILL PASS

Elevation: 10,051 feet
Location: T9S R77W, Map 6
County: Park
Topo: Como
Public access through private land

Red Hill Pass is passenger-car-accessible on US285. It divides the waters of Crooked Creek to the west and Trout Creek to the east.

The pass is believed to be named for the reddish colored mountain nearby.

In 1944, a University of Denver study group discovered a Folsom point at Red Hill. Although this does not prove Folsom man was ever here (the point might have been carried here by other prehistoric people), it does indicate early usage of the area.

The pass was used as early as the 1850s as a crossing into mining camps. In 1859, prospectors moved over the pass to reach the South Platte River. Father Dyer mentions the pass in his book *The Snowshoe Itinerant*, which was written in the 1860s.

In October 1879, the Red Hill, Fairplay and Leadville Railroad Company was incorporated to construct a railroad from a point on the Denver, South Park and Pacific Railroad near Red Hill to Leadville via Fairplay. The railroad reached Red Hill early in 1879. The area boomed immediately.

Red Hill was a major station for the railroad. Before the rails continued over the Tenmile mountain range on the west side of South Park, Red Hill was the point where travelers boarded stages for points beyond. The railroad station was on the west shoulder of the ridge and about a mile or so south of the present highway.

In August of 1880 a major fire destroyed the depot at Red Hill, producing an explosion of over a half-ton of gunpowder. One man was killed, three were severely injured, and it took several months to rebuild the station house.

The population of the little station community was never more than about twenty-five and there was no post office; even so, the station house operated until the early 1900s.

Many nineteenth-century writers tell of their experiences taking the railroad to Red Hill and boarding stages for other locations: Fairplay, Breckenridge, Leadville, Buena Vista, and points in between. Wall and Witter, a stage company, ran a stage line from Red Hill to Leadville in 1879. McLaughlin ran four-horse stages from Red Hill to Leadville, beginning in June 1880.

The abandoned railroad grade can be seen, in places, above the modern highway today. The actual crossing of the historic pass is in a little dip due north about a third of a mile from the current US285 crossing. Its elevation is 9,986 feet. Topo maps show the historic crossing rather than that of the highway.

This pass is on a low ridge entirely within South Park.

RED MOUNTAIN PASS

Elevation: 11,100 feet
Location: T42N R8W, Map 7
County: Ouray/San Juan
Topo: Ironton
National forest: San Juan/
Uncompahgre
Other names: Mineral Creek,
Sheridan

Red Mountain Pass is passenger-car-accessible on US550, the Million Dollar Highway. It divides the waters of Mineral Creek to the south and Red Mountain Creek to the north.

The pass is named for the nearby red mountains, as is the creek draining from the pass on the north side.

The Franklin Rhoda exploration party crossed the pass, which they didn't think was too bad, in 1874, but the canyon below terrified them.

Otto Mears built a toll road in 1882 and 1883 (after gold was discovered at the Yankee Girl Mine) over the pass (he called it the Rainbow Route), then he brought the railroad up as far as Ironton in 1888, running it alongside his wagon road. He called his railroad crossing "Sheridan."

A severe rock slide in 1888 wiped out part of the road, and a tunnel was constructed through it for wagon traffic. Today, snowsheds along the route provide summer and winter

protection against rockfalls and avalanches. The slide area on the pass is called the East River Slide; it is the location of many avalanche-caused highway deaths in Colorado.

From 1921–1924, much reconstruction work was done on the road. It was covered with gravel and widened to one lane with turnouts. The name Million Dollar Highway was applied to the route then. Some say the name was given because the road work cost a million dollars, others say it is for the gold-laden dirt with which the road is made. Still others claim the name is for the "million dollar view." One claim is made that a visitor named the route with, "I wouldn't go over that road again for a million dollars."

By 1939 the highway department was keeping the road open all winter. Today's highway is slightly higher on the mountainside than is the old original Mears toll road. The snowshed was constructed in 1985.

The highway is now a National Forest Scenic Byway and is part of the San Juan Skyway. If you drive the pass in the summer, be sure to look across the gorge at the cabin with laundry hung out to dry. Then ask the locals in Ouray about the antique store there and how to get to it.

RED MOUNTAIN PASS

Elevation: 12,860 feet
Location: T12S R82W, Map 5
County: Chaffee/Pitkin

Topo: Independence Pass/Pieplant
National forest: San Isabel/
  White River
On the Continental Divide
Other name: Red Rock

Red Mountain Pass is accessible by foot from the east via forest service trail #1466, on the edge of the Collegiate Peaks Wilderness Area. It divides the waters of Lincoln Creek to the west and South Fork Lake Creek to the east.

The trail was well used by miners crossing between Twin Lakes and the upper reaches of the Elk mountain range. Ferdinand Hayden crossed the pass in 1873 – he called it Red Rock Pass for the red stones of the nearby mountain. This crossing was used before other, more northerly, routes were discovered.

A wagon road went over the pass, and the east side is still cribbed in spots. From the top, looking into the west side, it is hard to believe any wagon ever went down the scree-covered slope. Most of the mineral ore was taken out of the old Ruby mining area, then over the pass to a town called Everett, and then to Leadville and the smelter.

The pass is a keyhole type: a cut between rocks on the ridge. The cut may have been made by human design, because it doesn't appear natural.

The pass was and still is often confused with Lake Pass, because Red Mountain is visible on the access to both passes. Another point of confusion is that Lake Pass drains south via Red Mountain Creek.

This pass is named on several 1870s and 1880s maps.

RED MOUNTAIN PASS

Elevation: 8,220 feet
Location: T12N R76W, Map 3
County: Larimer
Topo: Crazy Mountain
On BLM land

There is no access to Red Mountain Pass. It divides the waters of Pfister Draw to the west and Stink Creek to the east.

Map study will point out Red Mountain and the old wagon tracks leading to a low pass just north of Dempsey Dome. Roads shown on older maps no longer exist, and gates and fences on private property prevent access to the pass, which is barely within Colorado.

The pass is a mile south of Red Mountain. It is named on the Roosevelt forest service map.

RENO DIVIDE

Elevation: 11,146 feet
Location: T13S R84W, Map 5
County: Gunnison
Topo: Pearl Pass
National forest: Gunnison

Reno Divide is 4WD-accessible on forest route #759. It divides the waters of Cement Creek to the west and Flag Creek to the east.

Look for Reno Divide southeast, across the Cement Creek Valley, from Hunters Hill. The pass is not named on forest service or topo maps. It is named on a map of the Gunnison area.

RICHMOND PASS

Elevation: 12,657 feet
Location: T43N R8W, Map 7
County: Ouray
Topo: Ironton
National forest: Uncompahgre

Richmond Pass is accessible by foot on forest service trail #205. It divides the waters of Richmond Creek to the west and Red Mountain Creek to the east.

The old hiking trail is almost gone and it is difficult to find the trailhead, but the hike is well worth the search. The view to the west from the top is awesome – the whole Yankee Boy Basin is below. And the ring of mountains around the basin looks so close that you feel you can reach out and touch them.

The pass is above the Greyhound Mine (on the south) and the upper Camp Bird property (on the west). Hayden Mountain is a quarter-mile north.

RIFLE SIGHT NOTCH

Elevation: 11,070 feet
Location: T2S R75W, Map 3
County: Grand
Topo: East Portal
National forest: Arapaho

Rifle Sight Notch is passenger-car-accessible on forest route #149. It divides the waters of Middle Fork Ranch Creek to the north and South Fork Ranch Creek to the south. Ranch Creek was called Fawn Creek in the mid- to late 1800s.

The Notch is on the old Corona railroad line. Snow would accumulate at this location because of the way the winds whipped it. The Notch is crossed by an abandoned (and very unsafe) railroad trestle. A good view of the trestle is from the roadway.

The pass is not named on forest service maps. It is named on the topo map.

RIPPLE CREEK PASS

Elevation: 10,343 feet
Location: T2N R88W, Map 2
County: Rio Blanco
Topo: Ripple Creek
National forest: Routt/White River
Other names: Simpson Park,
 Simpson's

Ripple Creek Pass is passenger-car-accessible via forest routes #16 on the north side (Routt National Forest) and #8 on the south side (White River National Forest). It divides the waters of Poose Creek to the north and Snell Creek to the south.

The pass is an old Indian crossing that was used for travel between the White River and the Williams River.

In 1866 the Colorado Territory legislature issued a toll road charter

This old railroad trestle spans the opening known as Rifle Sight Notch, on forest route #149 in Grand County.

to the Overland Wagon Road Company for a road over Simpson's Pass.

The pass is three miles southeast of Pagoda Peak. Vaughn Lake (about three miles northeast) is reason enough to look for this pass. It's a pretty lake in a lush meadowed valley, with a pretty mountain scene behind it. The top of the pass is signed and tree-covered but has views to the west and south.

RIVER HILL

Elevation: 9,590 feet
Location: T40N R3W, Map 8
County: Hinsdale
Topo: Little Squaw Creek
National forest: Rio Grande

River Hill is accessible by passenger car on forest route #520. It divides the waters of Sawmill Canyon to the north and the Rio Grande River to the south.

This pass is the low point on a mountain ridge between Road Canyon Reservoir and Rio Grande Reservoir, in the San Juan mountain range.

River Hill is named on the forest service and topo maps.

ROCK CREEK TRAIL PASS

Elevation: 10,670 feet
Location: T8S R73W, Map 6
County: Park
Topo: Topaz Mountain

National forest: Pike
Other name: Lost Park Divide

Rock Creek Trail Pass is passenger-car-accessible on forest route #56. It divides the waters of Long Gulch to the west and South Fork Lost Creek to the east. Long Gulch was previously called East Fork Rock Creek.

This very old crossing, used for centuries by Indians to move through South Park, then used by prospectors, is almost unknown to today's visitors.

The *New Map of Colorado 1882* shows the pass as Rock Creek Pass and marks the trail over it. Maps from 1898 and 1908 also show the pass and a wagon road over it. The pass had been called Lost Park Divide in recent years.

The top is wooded with pines and marked with a cattle guard; it is a mile and a half northeast of North Tarryall Peak. It is not named on current forest service or topo maps.

ROGERS PASS

Elevation: 11,860 feet
Location: T2S R74W, Map 3
County: Gilpin/Grand
Topo: Empire
National forest: Arapaho/Roosevelt
On the Continental Divide
Other name: South Boulder

Rogers Pass is accessible by foot via forest service trail #900 on the east side (Roosevelt National Forest), and by an unnumbered trail on the west side (Arapaho National Forest). It divides the waters of Jim Creek to the west and South Boulder Creek to the east.

The USGS Board on Geographic Names officially named the pass in 1916 for an early mayor of Central City, Andrew Rogers. The original name of South Boulder Pass comes from the creek on the east side of the pass.

An old Ute trail crossed the pass. The route seems to have been used as a trail crossing; the few recorded attempts to take wagons or cattle across had disastrous results.

The eponym of the pass, Andrew Rogers, proposed a tunnel under the saddle in 1867. It finally happened in the 1920s – under a neighboring pass. In 1889 the state legislature considered building a canal over the pass to bring water from the western side of the Front Range into the population centers on the east side.

An old rough road heads partway to the pass from the west side (until recently the pass could be reached by 4WD from the west), but it is now closed to vehicular traffic. The pass is above timberline and visible for some time before you reach it. Early-day locals called the saddle a "hogback," a term now applied to a different geographic feature.

On the east side, Heart, Iceberg, and Crater lakes are popular destinations. A great vista awaits the hiker at the pass summit, and the ski runs above Winter Park are visible and well defined. Because the trail is not well known, this is a prime hiking area. The pass is north of James Peak.

ROLLING MOUNTAIN PASS

Elevation: 12,490 feet
Location: T40N R9W, Map 7
County: San Juan
Topo: Engineer Mountain
National forest: San Juan

Rolling Mountain Pass is accessible by foot on forest service trail #507. It divides the waters of South Fork Mineral Creek to the north and Cascade Creek to the south.

The pass is named for the adjacent Rolling Mountain, a mile and a half to the north.

This is one of the "new" passes, named by users (and writers) of the Colorado Trail. Although the route has been used as a trail for many years, the name was only recently assigned to the spot. The pass is on the Colorado Trail. It is not named on forest service or topo maps.

ROLLINS PASS

Elevation: 11,660 feet
Location: T1S R74W, Map 3
County: Boulder/Grand
Topo: East Portal
National forest: Arapaho/Roosevelt
On the Continental Divide
Other names: Boulder, Corona

Rollins Pass is passenger-car-accessible from the west via forest route #149, and by foot from the east when the Needles Eye Tunnel is closed. It divides the waters of Ranch Creek on the west and South Fork Middle Boulder Creek on the east. Ranch Creek was originally named Fawn Creek.

The pass was originally called Boulder Pass, for the creek on its east side.

The pass has often been called Corona (Spanish for "crown") Pass for the station atop the pass. It was called Rollins Pass in 1886 for John Q. A. Rollins, who developed the road over it. It was officially named by the USGS Board on Geographic Names in 1907.

Ute Indians crossed the pass as they headed into the plains to look for buffalo. Plains Indians, such as the Arapaho, also used the crossing to move into the high country to find elk and lodgepole pines for their tepees. In the first part of the 1900s, earthwork fortifications, believed built by Indians for shelter and as lookouts, were discovered atop the pass. Skirmishes were common here in the early 1800s.

Captain John Fremont and his party crossed the pass in 1844. Two of his party are said to be buried on the east side of the summit. In the mid-1860s the Union Pacific Railroad looked at the crossing, seeking a route west for the rail line. A blizzard convinced them not to consider seriously the Boulder Pass crossing.

The army used the pass, bringing wagons across as early as 1863, as it returned from an Indian uprising in Utah Territory. The Mormons, in their move west from Illinois to Utah, may have used the pass, taking their wagons apart and carrying the pieces over the worst stretches. John Rollins is believed to have led them through the mountain range over his pass.

Rollins, operating as the Rollinsville and Middle Park Toll Road Company, got a charter in 1866 from the Colorado Territory to build a road over the pass. This road was completed in 1873.

A mail contract for the area between Rollinsville and Hot Sulphur Springs was awarded in 1875. About this time, traffic was beginning to use the new Berthoud Pass road to the south, and heavy use of Rollins's road declined. It served as a cattle trail and for other local usage. Then David Moffat came into the picture. He wanted to build a rail route to the West Coast and chose the Rollins route for his train. He envisioned a tunnel under the pass, but until it could be constructed, temporary track would be laid over the top.

The first train to travel to the top of the pass ran in September 1904. The route was advertised as running over "the top of the world." Many accidents happened while the trains ran over this exposed high-altitude line. Fumes built up in the snowsheds, trains became stranded on the line even with snow-catchers attached, avalanches or rock slides pushed cars off the tracks, and wind made work on the line very uncomfortable. The top was wide, barren, and windswept in summer and winter. Snowsheds were used at the very top to offer protection from winter snowstorms, drifts, and wind. Covered walkways took people from the snowsheds on the tracks to the station house.

This "temporary track" was finally no longer needed when the Moffat Tunnel, which runs under the pass for 6.4 miles, was built in 1927. The old tracks over the top were abandoned in 1935, although they had not been used since 1928. The pass route lay dormant for many years.

In 1925 a silent movie was filmed atop the pass. *White Desert* tells about the construction of a railroad tunnel, shows many trains in action, and premiered in Denver.

In 1956 the forest service reworked the old railroad route into a passable auto road, which they dubbed Corona Pass, although that is not the official name. This was a one-lane gravel road with some pullouts.

The Needles Eye Tunnel, on the east side of the pass just above Jenny Lake, collapsed in 1979 and was reopened with the help of the Rollins Pass Restoration Association in 1988. It collapsed again in July 1990. When the Needles Eye Tunnel is closed (it's a mile east off the top) there is no direct passenger-car access to the pass from the east side

(4WD vehicles can go over a rough neighboring pass road).

Many good views may be had from the top of this pass west into the Fraser River Valley and across to the Winter Park Ski Area. Look for the many lakes near the top.

The top is adjacent to the Indian Peaks Wilderness Area and serves as an access point to various trails. The pass is on the Continental Divide Trail and is a favorite of mountain bikers because of the easy railroad grades.

Rollins Pass is usually early to close (it can be closed by early September) and late to open (it might be open in early July) due to heavy snow accumulations.

ROSALIE PASS

Elevation: 11,660 feet
Location: T6S R74W, Map 6
County: Park
Topo: Mount Evans
National forest: Pike

Rosalie Pass is accessible by foot on forest service trail #603 in the Mount Evans Wilderness Area. It divides the waters of Scott Gomer Creek to the west and Deer Creek to the east.

The pass and the neighboring mountain of the same name honor Rosalie Osbourne, a friend of the artist Albert Bierstadt.

This is a pretty hike, with lots of wildflowers during July and early August. The view from the pass top is open with high peaks in the distance. The pass is on the saddle between Tahana Mountain and Kataka Mountain.

The area is easy to reach from population centers on the Front Range. The pass is not named on forest service or topo maps. It is identified from hiking guides.

RUBY PASS

Elevation: 12,900 feet
Location: T39N R7W, Map 8
County: La Plata
Topo: Storm King Peak
National forest: San Juan

Ruby Pass is accessible by foot, but no established trail currently goes over the pass, which is in the Weminuche Wilderness Area. It divides the waters of No Name Creek to the north and Ruby Creek to the south.

This is a high pass in the Needles mountain range between Monitor Mountain and Peak 12. This is a very rough area.

The view to the south is of North Eolus Peak. The pass is not named on forest service or topo maps. It is identified from hiking guides. □

S

THE SADDLE

Elevation: 12,398 feet
Location: T6N R74W, Map 3
County: Larimer
Topo: Trail Ridge
In Rocky Mountain National Park

The Saddle is accessible by foot. It divides the waters of Hague Creek to the north and the Roaring River to the south.

The USGS Board on Geographic Names officially named The Saddle as a mountain pass in 1959. The area was well used, before Rocky Mountain National Park was established, as a resort trail.

The hiking access is via Lawn Lake. The pass is between Hagues Peak and Fairchild Mountain.

The Saddle is named on the 1984 Roosevelt forest service map; it is not named on the newer (1990) Roosevelt-Arapaho map.

THE SADDLE

Elevation: 7,460 feet
Location: T7S R99W, Map 4
County: Garfield
Topo: The Saddle
On BLM land

There is no access to The Saddle. It divides the waters of Kimball Creek to the north and Dry Fork to the south.

A view to the pass is possible from county road #202 (also called the Kimball Creek Road), but access is blocked by private gates on the north and south.

Locals know the area as "the Saddle." There has not been a compelling reason to use the pass, because the end of the ridge is only a mile or so down the road, where most people go. The Saddle is aptly named: It looks like a saddle for a horse's back. It is located on Cow Ridge.

The pass is not named in the BLM maps book. It is named on the topo map.

THE SADDLE

Elevation: 6,700 feet
Location: T49N R12W, Map 4
County: Montrose
Topo: Camel Back
On BLM land

The Saddle is accessible by foot. It divides the waters of Potter Creek to the west and Criswell Creek to the east.

This pass is located southwest of Delta. It is not named in the BLM maps book. It is named on the topo map.

This pass, northeast of Grand Junction, is aptly named The Saddle, for the saddle-shaped dip of the ridge line.

THE SADDLE

Elevation: 9,340 feet
Location: T2S R79W, Map 3
County: Summit
Topo: Squaw Creek
National forest: Arapaho

The Saddle is accessible by foot, but no established trail goes over the pass. It divides the waters of Shane Gulch to the north and Lonesome Gulch to the south.

The pass is named on the 1989 Arapaho National Forest, Dillon Ranger District, map.

SADDLE NOTCH

Elevation: 7,198 feet

Location: T5N R71W, Map 3
County: Larimer
Topo: Drake
Public access through private land

Saddle Notch is accessible by 4WD on forest route #923. It divides the waters of Saddle Notch Gulch to the north and Skinner Gulch to the south.

The pass is a mile south of Sheep Mountain and one and one-half miles west of Stone Mountain.

SALT CREEK PASS

Elevation: 9,716 feet
Location: T13S R77W, Map 6
County: Chaffee/Park

Topo: Marmot Peak
National forest: Pike/San Isabel

Salt Creek Pass is passenger-car-accessible via county road #309 (San Isabel National Forest) and forest route #436 (Pike National Forest). It divides the waters of Salt Creek to the north and Trout Creek to the south.

Because of the easy on and off to US285, this is an interesting pass at the south end of the Mosquito mountain range, but it is rarely used. Marmot Peak is four miles west of the pass.

The pass is not named on the forest service or topo maps. James Grafton Rogers located and named it in his listing of Colorado's geographic features.

SAMS DIVIDE

Elevation: 7,620 feet
Location: T14S R91W, Map 5
County: Delta
Topo: Paonia
National forest: Gunnison

Sams Divide is 4WD-accessible by a spur road off forest route #798. It divides the waters of German Creek to the west and Sams Creek to the east.

The divide and other features in this area are named for Sam Angevine, an early rancher here. Sam must have been some character; a neighboring rancher once said the name Sams Divide is fitting because

"Sam should have been divided from the rest of the world."

The pass is located north of Mount Lamborn, southeast of Elephant Hill, and above Lone Cabin Reservoir. It is not named on the forest service map. It is named on the topo map.

SAN FRANCISCO PASS

Elevation: 8,420 feet
Location: T34S R62W, Map 10
County: Las Animas
Topo: Barela
On private land
Other name: Sugarite

There is no access to this San Francisco Pass. It divides the waters of San Francisco Creek to the north and Chicorica Creek, in New Mexico, to the south.

This old crossing, a low alternative to other nearby crossings, has a lot of history. Spanish conquistadores used the route to move into the west end of the Kansas Territory.

In 1818, Lieutenant Jose Maria de Arce went over the pass when returning to New Mexico after investigating Indian uprisings to the north. In 1849, several hundred sheep drowned in a flood in the pass access; at this time the old name of Ahogadero Creek was changed to San Francisco Creek to erase the bad memories of the loss.

The pass is situated on a private ranch, and both the north and south accesses are blocked by property gates. The pass is still used to move cattle across the open lands for grazing, but public access is now denied.

The pass is shown on an 1897 map of Colorado. It is named in the BLM maps book and on the topo map.

SAN FRANCISCO PASS

Elevation: 9,150 feet
Location: T35S R69W, Map 9
County: Las Animas
Topo: Torres
On private land

There is no access to this San Francisco Pass. It divides the waters of Bonito Canyon to the north and the North Fork of the Vermejo River to the south.

An old wagon road crossed this pass. The route ran between Costilla, New Mexico, and the San Luis Valley in Colorado. At one time there were many brown bears in this area.

The top of the pass is visible from the locked gate at a private-property boundary about three miles from the top.

The pass is named in the BLM maps book and on the topo map.

SAN FRANCISCO PASS

Elevation: 11,929 feet
Location: T35S R70W, Map 9
County: Costilla
Topo: Culebra Peak
On private land

There is no access to this San Francisco Pass. It divides the waters of San Francisco Creek to the west and Ricardo Creek to the east.

The pass can be identified by map search, but access is blocked by private land; visitors cannot even see the pass from a road.

The pass is located on a saddle just south of Purgatoire Peak. A foot trail over the pass still shows on 1950s maps. The pass is about two and a half miles north of the state border.

In the 1920s, the state highway department was urged by southern Colorado residents to build a good road over this pass. The main use of the pass was for driving livestock between grazing areas.

This San Francisco Pass is not named in the BLM maps book or on the topo map.

SAN LUIS PASS

Elevation: 11,960 feet
Location: T43N R1W, Map 8
County: Mineral/Saguache
Topo: San Luis Peak
National forest: Gunnison/
  Rio Grande
On the Continental Divide

San Luis Pass is accessible by foot on forest service trail #467 on the southern edge of the La Garita Wilderness Area. It divides the waters of Cascade Creek to the north and West Willow Creek to the south.

The pass was well used before

A carpet of wildflowers provides access to pretty San Luis Pass, north of Creede.

1870 to cross from the west end of the San Luis Valley into the Cochetopa Hills. There is no evidence it was ever anything more than just a good trail.

The pass is part of the history of the Fremont disaster of 1854: Some historians believe Bill Williams meant to lead the party over San Luis Pass but instead went up the wrong drainage and got lost east of here.

The pass is at the head of a gully and is well marked with trail signs but not named. Mining activity is still heavy above Creede, and homemade signs along the route to the pass alert drivers of the rough road ahead.

Skyline Trail crosses the pass, as

do the Colorado and Continental Divide trails. The area is well known to serious hikers and enjoyed by 4WD enthusiasts – nearby routes to other unnamed saddles in the same area can be reached by 4WD. San Luis Peak is two miles northeast of the pass.

SAND CREEK PASS

Elevation: 8,976 feet
Location: T11N R75W, Map 3
County: Larimer
Topo: Sand Creek Pass
National forest: Roosevelt

Sand Creek Pass is passenger-car-accessible on county road #80C. It divides the waters of Jimmy Creek to the west and Sand Creek to the east.

Look for government soil-erosion projects nearby. A minor crossing in open country, the pass is four miles northwest of Little Bald Mountain.

Sand Creek Pass is named on forest service and topo maps.

SANDY'S FORT PASS

Elevation: 8,323 feet
Location: T43N R14W, Map 7
County: San Miguel
Topo: North Mountain
Public access through private land

Sandy's Fort Pass is passenger-car-accessible on county road #31.U. It divides the waters of Nelson Creek to the west and Naturita Creek to the east.

The pass is located about four miles west of the Miramonte Reservoir. Look for the sign at the top that reads "ORT PASS." A good dirt road runs through open grazing land with scrub oaks.

The pass is not named on the forest service map. It is named in the BLM maps book and on the topo map.

SANGRE DE CRISTO PASS

Elevation: 9,468 feet
Location: T28S R70W, Map 9
County: Costilla/Huerfano
Topo: La Veta Pass
On private land

Other names: Gap of the Sierra Blanca, Taos Trail, Trappers Trail

Sangre de Cristo Pass is no longer accessible to the public. It divides the waters of South Oak Creek to the east and Sangre de Cristo Creek to the west.

The USGS Board on Geographic Names officially named the pass in 1965, using the historic name assigned by Governor Juan Bautista de Anza.

The south access to this most historic Colorado pass is blocked by the Forbes Ranch in the eastern end of the San Luis Valley; the north access is also blocked, by local ranchers.

No other pass in the state had so much to do with the settling of Colorado Territory and the consequent arrival of people from the east into the San Luis Valley as did Sangre de Cristo Pass.

Early in the pass's history, Comanches used it to move between eastern Colorado and New Mexico to trade with the Taos Indians. Utes hunted buffalo on the plains, crossing over the pass from their mountain dwellings. By 1749, French fur traders and trappers reached the area; they hired Indian guides, who showed them this crossing. In 1768, the governor of New Mexico led an army to chase the Comanches and used Sangre de Cristo Pass. Governor Juan Bautista de Anza returned to New Mexico in 1779—he named the pass when his party was camped in the willows near the Huerfano Butte. A brilliant sunset colored the mountain range to the west a bright blood red color; he called it *Sangre de Cristo,* which translates to "blood of Christ."

The pass was the chosen route for the next hundred years, until other passes were developed. Military groups, settlers, and prospectors poured over the pass. A fort was built on the east side in 1819. So many trappers passed over this way that the route became known as "The Trapper's Trail" and "Taos Trail."

A wagon road was built to serve the military settlements farther down in the San Luis Valley in the 1850s. When miners heard about the riches in southwest Colorado, they came from the east and over the pass, across the San Luis Valley, to the San Juan mountain range.

A railroad route was mentioned but never seriously considered, because the road lent itself more to individual traffic than to a rail route. But the west side of the pass was taken by William J. Palmer for his Denver and Rio Grande La Veta rail descent.

The pass is visible from US160, about one-half mile down the west side from the North La Veta Pass summit. Ruts, which run off the pass down to the highway and then below the highway going west, show best when a little snow is on the ground. All these ruts are on private property; they represent a century of travel before the Santa Fe Trail or any other routes were opened.

SANTA MARIA PASS

Elevation: 9,690 feet
Location: T41N R2W, Map 8
County: Mineral
Topo: Bristol Head
National forest: Rio Grande

Santa Maria Pass is accessible by foot from the south side; there is no access from the north side. It divides the waters of Clear Creek to the north and Seepage Creek to the south. The access to the north side of the pass is owned by the Santa Maria Reservoir Association and is blocked to the public. The south side can be reached by 4WD on forest route #509 and then hike a very short distance to the pass.

Bristol Head Mountain is an imposing feature on the skyline for many miles. It's a real thrill to be wandering around in the woods just under the "nose" of this massif.

The top of the pass is about two miles north of Lake #2 and is marked by a sign that reads "Go Back While You Still Can." The old wagon road that crossed the pass is blocked immediately ahead of this. Mounds of dirt, tree branches, and rocks have been piled up to keep vehicles from driving farther.

The adjacent Santa Maria Lake used to be called Mirror Lake. This is a pretty back-road drive off the open valley road.

SCHOFIELD PASS

Elevation: 10,707 feet
Location: T12S R87W, Map 5
County: Gunnison
Topo: Snowmass Mountain
National forest: Gunnison/
White River
Other names: Crystal, East River,
Elk Mountain Divide, Gothic

Schofield Pass is passenger-car-accessible via forest route #317 on the south side and 4WD-accessible via forest route #314 on the north side. It divides the waters of the South Fork of the Crystal River to the north and the East River to the south.

The pass is named for the town of Schofield, which, in turn, was named for Judge B. F. Schofield, who founded the town.

Utes lived near here and they led the first white men over the route. When they were evicted from their homes they placed a curse on the basin on the west side of the pass, which is called "Sonofabitch Basin" by some.

Even when this route was heavily used it was not much better than it is today. Prospectors in the 1860s discovered the crossing and built what was called a road, but it was barely more than a trail.

The Hayden survey party crossed Schofield and named the pass on their map. In the 1930s the pass road

Scenic Emerald Lake sits at the eastern foot of Schofield Pass.

was improved because it had fallen into disuse.

The now summer-only community of Gothic began in the 1880s as a supply point for area prospectors. Gothic is now a biological laboratory site and each summer various residents can be seen counting moths or spiders on little patches of ground.

The pass is above Crested Butte and Gothic, just past pretty Emerald Lake, and often is closed all summer long. Snowdrifts atop the pass may still be higher than vehicles in late July.

The road on the north side is considered one of the most dangerous 4WD routes in the state. In 1970, seven members of one family were killed when their 4WD rolled off the pass road and plunged two hundred feet into the river. Only a year later, another 4WD accident on the road took three more lives. It *is* a bad road. Grades of twenty-seven percent, rocks, stream fordings, and ruts are some of the reasons most people go to Emerald Lake, look at the pass, and return to Crested Butte. It could be said that they have decided to "pass on the pass."

SCOTCH CREEK PASS

Elevation: 10,419 feet
Location: T39N R10W, Map 7
County: Dolores/San Juan
Topo: Hermosa Peak
National forest: San Juan

Scotch Creek Pass is 4WD-accessible on forest route #550. It divides the waters of Scotch Creek to the west and Hermosa Creek to the east.

This pass road is also known as the "Old Scotch Creek Toll Road" or the "Pinkerton Trail." The pass summit is up the old toll road right-of-way. There is considerable logging in this vicinity.

The pass looks south into the Hermosa Creek Basin. The creek that starts at the top of the pass goes in a different direction than does the pass road. After dropping down a way on the road (east side), you will notice a stream coming at you!

Scotch Creek Pass is located above the Purgatory Ski Area. The access is difficult to locate from the east side.

The pass is not named on the forest service or topo maps.

SEARLE PASS

Elevation: 12,020 feet
Location: T7S R79W, Map 6
County: Summit
Topo: Copper Mountain
National forest: Arapaho

Searle Pass is accessible by foot on forest service trail #41. It divides the waters of Searle Gulch to the south and Guller Creek to the north.

This old crossing for miners moving from what we now call Copper Mountain to the Kokomo mining district was not heavily used in the early days. Today the pass *is* well used because it is on the Colorado Trail and has access to a major highway (CO91).

The hike in is a constant climb gaining one thousand feet in two miles. A boulder field just below the pass saddle requires some route-finding. There is no defined trail up to the pass, but it is in sight for most of the hike. Stay above the willows in the creek valley.

Watch for old cabin ruins on the way, including a still-standing outhouse. Old wire, suggesting that perhaps some type of power line was run up to the cabins, still dangles from trees. The pass top is a narrow saddle. Look for the good view north into the back part of the Copper Mountain Ski Area from the top. Some hikers go on to climb Jacque Peak, to the east-southeast and an easy climb from the pass. The pass is east of Sugarloaf Peak.

SERVICEBERRY GAP

Elevation: 8,058 feet
Location: T6N R102W, Map 1
County: Moffat
Topo: Tanks Peak
In Dinosaur National Monument

There is no access to Serviceberry Gap. It divides the waters of the Yampa River to the north and Wolf Creek to the south.

The gap is on Dinosaur National Monument land, but access to it has been blocked by private landowners from both sides.

The pass is not quite visible, but map study shows that it would be directly ahead of the south access point. The old road that leads to the pass is visible.

This pass is not named in the BLM maps book. It is named on the topo map.

SEVEN LAKES PASS

Elevation: 11,050 feet
Location: T14S R68W, Map 6
County: El Paso
Topo: Pikes Peak
On land owned by Colorado
**   Springs Water Department**
Other name: Dead Lake

Seven Lakes Pass is currently not accessible to the public. It divides the waters of Ruxton Creek to the north and Middle Beaver Creek to the south.

The pass is named for the seven natural lakes in its vicinity. The alternate name is for the naturally occurring dead lake atop the pass.

The area was discovered in 1872 by Quincy King, who was looking for "color" on the mountainside. The Seven Lakes were eventually swallowed up by two reservoirs that supply water to Colorado Springs. The first road was built up over the divide in 1880, after the U.S. Army built an observatory above the area. The charter for the road was given to the Cheyenne and Beaver Toll Road Company.

This old pass was well used in the

late 1800s, when Colorado Springs residents took the wagon road up the south side of Pikes Peak to a hotel next to Lake #5 of the seven lakes. Helen Hunt Jackson particularly liked the region; its views were outstanding, and she liked to relax here and think, staring off into the blue skies to the southwest.

A regular wagon route went back and forth between the Broadmoor and the Seven Lakes hotels. In 1902 the City of Colorado Springs acquired the land on which the pass is situated.

The pass is not named on the forest service's Pike map.

SEVEN UTES PASS

Elevation: 10,980 feet
Location: T6N R76W, Map 3
County: Jackson
Topo: Mount Richthofen
In Colorado State Forest

Seven Utes Pass is accessible by foot. It divides the waters of the Michigan River to the north and Silver Creek to the south.

The trailhead for hiking to the pass is at the end of a very rough 4WD road. Because other passes are in the area, this makes a good central spot for a hiking take-off point.

From the top, traffic on CO14 down in the valley can be seen but not heard. The top is tree-covered and indistinct.

When Colorado was considering hosting the 1976 Winter Olympic

Games, the region around Seven Utes Pass was recommended as a ski area for some of the Nordic events. The distance from Denver and other ski venues made it difficult to consider seriously this option. But this is the only fame Seven Utes has had.

The Continental Divide Trail crosses this pass. It is not named on the forest service or topo maps. It is identified by Continental Divide Trail hiking guides.

SHRINE PASS

Elevation: 11,089 feet
Location: T6S R79W, Map 6
County: Eagle/Summit
Topo: Vail Pass
National forest: Arapaho/
  White River

Shrine Pass is passenger-car-accessible via forest routes #16 on the east side and #709 on the west side. It divides the waters of Turkey Creek to the west and West Tenmile Creek to the east.

The pass was unofficially named in 1923 as the "Holy Cross Trail." This route was a favorite project of Orion W. Daggett, publisher of the *Holy Cross Trail,* the newspaper of Redcliff. The Holy Cross Trail highway was the main access to western Colorado before US6 was built across a neighboring pass in 1940. It was the most direct route between Denver and Grand Junction. Then, in 1950, the USGS Board on Geographic Names officially named the pass Shrine Pass, for the view of the Mount of the Holy Cross from near the top.

The route was originally an Indian trail. Daggett discovered the prominent or outstanding view about a mile northwest of the pass in 1921. He proposed to build a large outdoor amphitheater where thousands could gather to worship — with camping areas, golf course, parking, and an airport. He intended to make this area a shrine, hence the name that was eventually chosen for the pass. In 1931, hundreds of people gathered for the grand opening of his Shrine Pass road, which had been improved just for the view offered here.

Many calendar pictures of wildflowers taken in Colorado are from the sides of the slopes along the Shrine Pass roadway. In mid-July the fields look like a child's coloring book, with all colors and many flowers. Visitors head toward the various viewing spots along the road of the Mount of the Holy Cross, to the southwest.

In the wintertime, this is a good place for cross-country skiing. The pass is one and a half miles northeast of Sloane Mountain, which was previously named Shrine Mountain.

SILVER PASS

Elevation: 10,780 feet
Location: T37N R2E, Map 8
County: Mineral
Topo: Elwood Pass

National forest: Rio Grande/
San Juan
On the Continental Divide

Silver Pass is accessible by foot on forest service trail #567. It divides the waters of Pass Creek to the north and Silver Creek to the south.

The pass is named for nearby Silver Peak and for Silver Creek, which it heads. Hayden's survey party crossed and mapped the pass in the 1870s.

The view is spectacular from the top — the San Juan mountain range to the south along the Silver Creek Valley is a rugged, snowcapped vista. Equally great views abound to the north and northwest. The pass is one and a half miles northwest of Silver Peak.

Watch for elk moving in and out of the woods along the trail. There is some logging here, so watch road access carefully.

Silver Pass is just east of the Continental Divide Trail.

SILVER CREEK PASS

Elevation: 12,260 feet
Location: T11S R87W, Map 5
County: Gunnison
Topo: Snowmass Mountain
National forest: White River

Silver Creek Pass is accessible by foot on forest service trail #1959 in the Maroon Bells–Snowmass Wilderness Area. It divides the waters of the East Fork of Avalanche Creek to the north and North Fork Lost Trail Creek to the south.

A true saddle marks the site of Silver Pass in the San Juan mountain range.

The pass is in a relatively little used hiking area. It is a half-mile west of Meadow Mountain and a mile south of Mount Richey.

Silver Creek Pass is not named on current forest service or topo maps. It was identified by Len Shoemaker, an Aspen-area forest ranger. It was also named on a late-1950s White River forest service map.

SIMMONS PASS

Elevation: 11,060 feet
Location: T48N R9E, Map 6
County: Fremont/Saguache
Topo: Poncha Pass
National forest: Rio Grande/
  San Isabel

Other name: North Bear Creek

Simmons Pass is accessible by foot. It divides the waters of Lone Tree Creek to the west and Bear Creek to the east.

Indians used this crossing as a shortcut from the upper (north) reaches of the San Luis Valley to the Arkansas River at Salida, rather than the longer routes farther west.

The pass is about a half-mile northwest of Simmons Peak and southeast of Fremont Peak. It is a wide, fairly low gap, with an open meadow at the top. The area is now used by hunters.

The pass is not named on forest service or topo maps. James Grafton Rogers located and named it in his listing of Colorado's geographic features. Locals also know of and use the pass.

SLAGLE PASS

Elevation: 11,020 feet
Location: T47N R7W, Map 8
County: Gunnison/Ouray
Topo: Buckhorn Lakes
On private land

There is no access to Slagle Pass. It divides the waters of Billy Creek to the west and Coal Creek to the east.

The pass is shown on Uncompahgre forest service maps, but access is blocked by private landowners.

SLUMGULLION PASS

Elevation: 11,300 feet
Location: T43N R3W, Map 8
County: Hinsdale
Topo: Slumgullion Pass
National forest: Gunnison

Slumgullion Pass is passenger-car-accessible on forest route #788. It divides the waters of the Lake Fork Gunnison River to the west and Mill Creek to the east.

The pass was named by members of the Hayden survey party for an area rockslide's colors, which might be said to resemble slumgullion, a meat stew. This rockslide, which occurred many, many years ago (one geologist estimates A.D. 1258), is still barren and dead-looking. The slide dammed up the Lake Fork of the Gunnison River to create the beautiful Lake San Cristobal. The accompanying mudflow, which has now hardened into rock, was named a National Interest Point in 1966. Part of it is still moving – about a half-inch per day.

A trail was over the pass by the early 1870s, and miners toted their ore over for about fourteen years, until the railroad finally made it to Lake City in 1889.

The pass was crossed by the Hayden party in 1874. The route was developed as a toll road in 1879 and became the main route between Del Norte and Lake City. Many grizzly bears were here in the late 1800s.

This is near the site of the infamous Packer cannibalism incident. Alfred Packer is said to have partaken of five of his companions when they became lost in a snowstorm in 1874.

The highway sign indicating Slumgullion Pass is on CO149; however, the real pass is actually about a quarter-mile northeast of that point, along the secondary road. The topo map shows the pass saddle and identifies the pass in the correct location.

SNOW LAKE PASS

Elevation: 12,540 feet
Location: T5S R79W, Map 6
County: Eagle
Topo: Willow Lakes
National forest: White River

Snow Lake Pass is accessible by foot in the Eagles Nest Wilderness Area. It divides the waters of Deluge Creek to the west and Gore Creek to the east.

The pass is just off the trail to Deluge Lake from the East Vail campground trailhead.

Snow Lake Pass is not named on forest service or topo maps. It is identified in Vail-area hiking guides.

SNOWCAT PASS

Elevation: 12,510 feet
Location: T8S R79W, Map 6
County: Eagle
Topo: Leadville North
National forest: San Isabel/
 White River
On the Continental Divide

Snowcat Pass is accessible by foot, unless you can catch a ride in the snow cat that goes up here during ski season. It divides the waters of the East Fork Eagle River to the north and the Arkansas River to the south.

The pass is at the top of one of the Ski Cooper Ski Area hills. It's on the Chicago Ridge and has good views all around.

This pass is not named on forest service or topo maps. It is identified by local maps.

SONY PASS

Elevation: 10,510 feet
Location: T44N R2E, Map 8
County: Saguache
Topo: Elk Park
National forest: Gunnison/
 Rio Grande
On the Continental Divide

Sony Pass is 4WD-accessible on forest service route #776. It divides the waters of Cochetopa Creek to the north and North Fork Saguache Creek to the south.

This is an old Cochetopa Hills crossing; it could well have been an alternate crossing over this mountain range for westward-bound travelers in the days before roads were developed.

The area is used for hunting, and there are many signs. Good views to the north are of the Elk mountain range and to the southwest of the La Garita mountain range. The pass is about a mile northwest of the La Garita Wilderness Area. Table Mountain, a wide mesa, is three miles south.

Sony Pass is not named on forest service or topo maps. It is named on old Saguache County maps.

SOUTH PASS

Elevation: 10,656 feet
Location: T44N R2E, Map 8
County: Saguache
Topo: Saguache Park
National forest: Gunnison/
 Rio Grande
On the Continental Divide
Other names: Carnero, Salt House,
 Stone Cellar

South Pass is passenger-car-accessible on forest route #787. It divides the waters of Joe Gulch to the north and Horse Canyon to the south.

An alternate name, Salt House Pass, is for the old building (still standing) at the top of the pass, which was used for storing blocks of salt for the cattle grazing in the park.

This is an old crossing, used first by Indians, then by trappers and traders. Fremont in 1848 called the pass "Carnero" and used the low crossing to move through the mountains as he looked for a rail route west. This was just before he and his party were caught in a snowstorm and stranded in the mountains; eleven men died. Beale and Heap, in 1853, noted the pass when they crossed it, also seeking low routes for rails across the mountains.

The forest service has now named and posted this pass as "South Pass" (although it is not named on forest service or topo maps), perhaps to differentiate it from the "North Pass" at the other end of the Cochetopa Hills mountain range.

The pass is at the edge of a wooded area and overlooks the upper reaches of Saguache Park. Saguache Park Peak is just east of the pass.

SOUTH FORK PASS

Elevation: 11,840 feet
Location: T10S R82W, Map 5
County: Pitkin
Topo: Mount Champion
National forest: White River

South Fork Pass is accessible by foot on forest service trail #1940 in the Hunter Fryingpan Wilderness Area. It divides the waters of the South Fork of the Fryingpan River to the north and Lost Man Creek to the south.

There is no indication of much historic use of this trail.

High-country meadows in this area are glacially formed. The view from the pass is very good – to the south is the Continental Divide. This is an easy hike (even though it is at a high elevation) because it takes about four miles to gain twelve hundred feet, a gentle grade for hiking.

The pass is four miles west of Deer Mountain. Deadman Lake is a mile north.

SOUTH HALFMOON PASS

Elevation: 12,880 feet
Location: T11S R81W, Map 5
County: Lake
Topo: Mount Elbert
National forest: San Isabel
Other name: Halfmoon

South Halfmoon Pass is accessible by foot. It divides the waters of South Halfmoon Creek to the north and Echo Creek to the south.

The pass is on the Continental Divide Trail. It is an interesting destination point because it is possible here, with field glasses, to look to the top of Mount Elbert and count the climbers atop Colorado's highest mountain.

The pass is situated between Mount Elbert and Casco Peak. From the top look south to La Plata, another "fourteener," and across the two deep canyons below: Echo Canyon and Hayden Gulch.

The pass is not named on forest service or topo maps. Some newer maps do not even show a trail over the pass, but it can be approached on 4WD forest route #110.3A, which leads to a point near the base on the north side.

SPAR HILL PASS

Elevation: 9,358 feet
Location: T40N R1W, Map 8
County: Mineral
Topo: Spar City
National forest: Rio Grande

Spar Hill Pass is accessible by passenger car on forest route #528. It divides the waters of two different gulches off Lime Creek.

The pass was well used when mining activity around Spar City was good, in the 1870s to the early 1890s. The top is wide and open, with good views in all directions.

Spar Hill Pass is just west of the ghost town of Spar City, three miles southeast and above the Rio Grande River. It is not named on the forest service or topo maps, but there is a sign at the top.

SPRAGUE PASS

Elevation: 11,708 feet
Location: T4N R74W, Map 3
County: Grand/Larimer
Topo: McHenrys Peak
In Rocky Mountain National Park
On the Continental Divide

Sprague Pass is accessible by foot, but no established trail currently goes over the pass, which is in Rocky Mountain National Park. It divides the waters of Tonahutu Creek to the west and Spruce Creek to the east.

The pass is named for Abner Sprague, an early settler in Estes Park who wrote a history of Rocky Mountain National Park. His name was first applied to the Sprague Glacier, high up on the Continental Divide, then to the adjacent mountain and pass.

This area is remote, rugged, and not used much by hikers.

SPRING CREEK PASS

Elevation: 10,898 feet
Location: T43N R3W, Map 8
County: Hinsdale
Topo: Slumgullion Pass
National forest: Gunnison
On the Continental Divide
Other names: Cebolla, East, Pass of
** the Rio Del Norte, Summer,**
** Williams**

Spring Creek Pass is passenger-car-accessible on CO149. It divides the waters of Cebolla Creek to the north and Big Spring Creek to the south.

This is an old crossing in the San Juan mountain range. The pass is shown on the Kern army map of 1851 as the "Pass of the Rio Del Norte." It was often called Cebolla Pass due to the creek it heads. *Cebolla* is Spanish for "onion."

Lieutenant E. H. Ruffner noted and mapped the pass in 1873: He called it East Pass.

Utes originally used this crossing. It was a trail for many, many years. Then Otto Mears built a toll road over the pass in 1874 and 1875. It was used to move goods into the mining camps and ore to the smelters. Travelers often used this route to move from the northern end of New Mexico into the Gunnison River Valley. Some believe this may be the area where Fremont's disastrous 1848 winter journey ended.

Spring Creek Pass is on the Continental Divide Trail and the Colorado Trail.

SPRING CREEK PASS

Elevation: 12,020 feet
Location: T13S R84W, Map 5
County: Gunnison
Topo: Italian Creek
National forest: Gunnison
Other names: American Flag, Italian

Spring Creek Pass is 4WD-accessible on forest route #759. It divides the waters of South Italian Creek to the north and Spring Creek to the south.

The pass is named for one of the creeks it heads. It is located on the saddle between North Italian Mountain and American Flag Mountain. The Star Mine is north of the pass.

This Spring Creek Pass is not named on forest service or topo maps. It is identified on a map of the Gunnison area.

SPUD PASS

Elevation: 11,740 feet
Location: T12S R88W, Map 5
County: Gunnison
Topo: Marble
National forest: Gunnison

Spud Pass is accessible by foot, but no established trail goes over the pass, which is in the Raggeds Wilderness Area. It divides the waters of Deep Creek to the west and North Anthracite Creek to the east.

The pass is three-quarters of a mile south of Ragged Mountain and above the easternmost Deep Lake. It is not named on topo or forest service maps but is identified by locals. The Spud Pass Trail is named on Trails Illustrated maps.

SQUAW PASS

Elevation: 11,210 feet
Location: T39S R3W, Map 8
County: Hinsdale
Topo: Cimarrona Peak

**National forest: Rio Grande/
San Juan
On the Continental Divide**

Squaw Pass is accessible by foot on forest service trail #586 in the Weminuche Wilderness Area. It divides the waters of Squaw Creek to the north and Williams Creek to the south.

The pass is named for one of the creeks it heads.

The Continental Divide Trail goes nearby but stays on the north side of the pass. Several other backcountry trails are close and they lead to the few good campsites near the top. Very little other use is made of the pass. Hossick Mountain is a mile and a half to the west.

SQUAW PASS

**Elevation: 9,790 feet
Location: T4S R72W, Map 6
County: Clear Creek
Topo: Squaw Pass
National forest: Arapaho
Other names: Soda Creek, Soda Hill**

Squaw Pass is passenger-car-accessible on CO103. It divides the waters of Little Bear Creek to the north and Corral Creek to the south.

The pass was named Soda Creek Pass on an 1897 Colorado map. The alternate names are from nearby Soda Creek.

The first recorded use was as early as 1858, by miners. This pass was part of the first outing for the

fledgling Colorado Mountain Club in 1912. Today, many Front Range drivers take this route as a day trip to view fall colors.

The pass is between Bergen Park and Echo Lake. Nearby Squaw Mountain is a flat-topped 11,475-foot peak.

SQUIRREL PASS

**Elevation: 11,262 feet
Location: T8S R77W, Map 6
County: Park
Topo: Como
National forest: Pike**

Squirrel Pass is 4WD-accessible on forest route #194. It divides the waters of Tarryall Creek to the north and Trout Creek to the south.

The pass and the steep road to it are visible from US285. Look for the saddle between Mount Silverheels and Little Baldy Mountain.

The pass is not named on forest service or topo maps. It is identified by local usage.

ST. LOUIS PASS

**Elevation: 11,532 feet
Location: T3S R76W, Map 3
County: Grand
Topo: Byers Peak
National forest: Arapaho
Other name: Packard**

St. Louis Pass is accessible by foot on forest service trail #14 on the edge of the Fraser Experimental

Forest. It divides the waters of St. Louis Creek to the north and South Fork Williams Fork to the south.

In 1867 the pass was called Packard Pass. It is a nondescript crossing, buried in trees. St. Louis Lake is off to the north in a snow-bowl setting. The pass is a half-mile east of St. Louis Peak and two miles southwest of Mount Nystrom.

STAR PASS

Elevation: 11,900 feet
Location: T13S R87W, Map 5
County: Gunnison
Topo: Oh-be-joyful
National forest: Gunnison

Star Pass is accessible by foot on forest service trail #404. It divides the waters of Oh-be-joyful Creek to the west and Peeler Basin to the east.

The pass is on the southwest flank of Garfield Peak. It is not named on forest service or topo maps. A locally known and used hiking/biking trail exists over the pass.

STILLWATER PASS

Elevation: 10,620 feet
Location: T4N R77W, Map 3
County: Grand
Topo: Bowen Mountain
National forest: Arapaho

Stillwater Pass is passenger-car-accessible on forest route #123. It divides the waters of Willow Creek to the north and Stillwater Creek to the south.

This is an old crossing in Middle Park that goes by Lost Lake and provides access to some pretty backcountry. The top is marked, is tree-covered, and is an indistinct crossing. The area is used by snowmobilers and is well marked with diamond metal markers. The region has lots of logging; be sure to stay on the main roads.

The road is passable by passenger car except in very poor summer weather. The pass is not named on current forest service or topo maps; it is marked by a highway department sign on CO125. It was named on a late-1950s Routt forest service map.

STONE MAN PASS

Elevation: 12,500 feet
Location: T3N R74W, Map 3
County: Boulder/Grand
Topo: McHenrys Peak
In Rocky Mountain National Park
On the Continental Divide
Other name: Flattop

Stone Man Pass is accessible by foot, but no established trail currently goes over the pass, which is in Rocky Mountain National Park. It divides the waters of the North Inlet to the west and Glacier Creek to the east.

The pass was called Flattop Pass until it was renamed in 1922 for the forty-foot rock on the east side of the pass, which resembles the top half of a man if one has a good imagination.

The pass is on the saddle between Chiefs Head Peak and McHenrys Peak, just west of Longs Peak. The climb to the top is across scree and very dangerous.

STONEY PASS

Elevation: 8,562 feet
Location: T9S R71W, Map 6
County: Jefferson
Topo: Green Mountain
National forest: Pike
Other name: Webster

Stoney Pass is passenger-car-accessible on forest route #560, adjacent to the Lost Creek Wilderness Area. It divides the waters of Buffalo Creek to the north and Cabin Creek to the south.

A 1907 to 1908 Pike forest service map shows the crossing as Webster Pass.

Stoney Pass is near Wellington Lake. There are many good views around the lake, but the pass itself is an indistinct crossing in trees and without views.

The road over the pass serves as a bypass route for mountain bikers on the Colorado Trail (where the regular route goes through the Lost Creek Wilderness Area). The road is dirty and bumpy and has been used for logging activity. The route is also well used by mountain bikers who have discovered this remote but

For an easy, wooded backcountry drive close to the Front Range, visit Stoney Pass.

The Animas Forks area provides a wealth of 4WD roads, including this one over Stony Pass. (*Photograph courtesy Dannels collection*)

easy ride that is close to Front Range population centers.

STONY PASS

Elevation: 12,588 feet
Location: T41N R6W, Map 8
County: San Juan
Topo: Howardsville
National forest: Rio Grande/
** BLM land**
On the Continental Divide
Other names: Hamilton, Rio
** Grande**

Stony Pass is 4WD-accessible on forest route #520, adjacent to the Weminuche Wilderness Area. It divides the waters of Stony Gulch to the west and the Rio Grande River to the east.

The name "Stony" was commonly used to denote the rocky crossing. Lieutenant E. H. Ruffner's 1873 expedition called the pass Hamilton Pass in honor of the man who built the wagon road they were following. Another early name for the pass is from one of the rivers it heads, the Rio Grande. The pass name has been spelled "Stoney" erroneously by some writers.

The original crossing was an old Ute trail. A map of the 1778 expedition by Dominguez and Escalante shows the crossing. Spanish artifacts have been found near the pass. Later, fur traders moved through.

This old crossing served as an early route into the Animas River Valley. In 1860, prospector Charles Baker is believed to have discovered the pass while looking for a shorter route through the San Juan mountains. The area was all Ute territory at that time. To cross the pass took several teams of animals pulling a single wagon; sometimes the wagons had to be dismantled and "snubbed" over the worst parts of the trail at the top.

A wagon toll road was built in 1872 and improved in 1879. The wagon road was built by Major E. M. Hamilton and named the Silverton and Grassy Hill Toll Road.

By 1873, over four thousand mines were operating in the area. In August 1874, Franklin Rhoda and his explorers found the pass and noted it a "well-marked trail." At the summit itself, the terrain was open and rolling. Smelter machinery was moved in on burros in 1874.

The pass was well used from 1875 until 1882, when the railroad arrived in Silverton. Many wagon trains and much mining equipment crossed the pass. Stage lines crossed, with a snowshoe line used in winter months. Both sides of the pass were very steep.

The route was almost abandoned after the railroad arrived. In 1903 the road was still in good enough condition to be used for mining claims. The first automobile made it over the pass in 1910, but the vehicle had to be pulled over the top by a team of horses. By 1916 the route was considered a state highway. It was abandoned and then reopened again by the forest service in the early 1950s, with upgrading in the 1960s and again in the 1970s to provide a 4WD route into the high country. The newer 4WD route has smoothed out some of the steepness of the old road. The road is now opened each year by the San Juan County maintenance department by July 4.

The pass doesn't have really good views, but a small rise off to the south has a full vista of the Weminuche Wilderness Area. The route is a long 4WD road and not well used.

The pass is on the Continental Divide Trail and also is a detour route for mountain bikers on the Colorado Trail, in order to bypass the Weminuche Wilderness Area.

STORM PASS

Elevation: 10,250 feet
Location: T4N R73W, Map 3
County: Larimer
Topo: Longs Peak
In Rocky Mountain National Park

Storm Pass is accessible by foot in Rocky Mountain National Park. It divides the waters of Wind River to the north and Inn Brook to the south.

The USGS Board on Geographic Names officially named the pass in 1911, using a name suggested by Enos Mills for the inclement weather here.

The route to the pass provides a

good hike with views occurring at several places along the trail. The hike begins along the Longs Peak route.

STORM PASS

Elevation: 12,450 feet
Location: T15S R88W, Map 5
County: Gunnison
Topo: West Elk Peak
National forest: Gunnison

Storm Pass is accessible by foot on forest service trail #450 in the West Elk Wilderness Area. It divides the waters of South Castle Creek to the north and Mill Creek to the south.

Look for the good views of the Castles, and other West Elk mountain range features, off the Mill-Castle Trail. The pass is east of West Elk Peak and north of North Baldy Mountain.

STORM KING–SILEX PASS

Elevation: 12,820 feet
Location: T39N R6W, Map 8
County: San Juan
Topo: Storm King Peak
National forest: San Juan

Storm King–Silex Pass is accessible by foot, but no established trail currently goes over the pass, which is in the Weminuche Wilderness Area. It divides the waters of Tenmile Creek to the west and Trinity Creek to the east.

This is an old game-trail crossing between Storm King Peak and a ridge that contains Peaks #8 and #9. From the top, look east across Lake Silex to Mount Silex.

The pass is not named on forest service or topo maps. It is identified by Colorado Mountain Club hiking guides.

STORMY PEAKS PASS

Elevation: 11,660 feet
Location: T6N R73W, Map 3
County: Larimer
Topo: Pingree Park
In Rocky Mountain National Park

Stormy Peaks Pass is accessible by foot. It divides the waters of the South Fork of the Cache la Poudre River to the west and the North Fork of the Big Thompson River to the east.

The pass is a half-mile south of Stormy Peaks and a mile and a half east of Sugarloaf Mountain.

This is a good hike through forest that comes out into an open above-timberline meadow with good views in all directions. The pass is named on Rocky Mountain National Park maps.

STRIEBY PASS

Elevation: 8,100 feet
Location: T13S R68W, Map 6
County: El Paso
Topo: Cascade
National forest: Pike

Strieby Pass is accessible by foot. It divides the waters of Cusack Canyon to the west and Waldo Canyon to the east.

Manley Ormes named the pass for his good friend and colleague William Strieby, who headed the Colorado College Department of Chemistry and Metallurgy from 1880 to 1920. Strieby was known for allowing students to make candy in the chemistry lab in order to compensate for the odors emanating from the lab.

The 1918 Manley Ormes *Map of the Pikes Peak Region* shows and names the pass. It is not named on forest service or topo maps.

STROUP PASS

Elevation: 11,940 feet
Location: T4S R77W, Map 6
County: Grand/Summit
Topo: Loveland Pass
National forest: Arapaho

Stroup Pass is accessible by foot, but no established trail currently goes over the pass. It divides the waters of South Fork Williams Fork to the north and Straight Creek to the south.

This pass is about four miles west and three-quarters of a mile north of Loveland Pass, about a half-mile down on the west side of Coon Hill, in the Williams Fork mountain range. An access road on the west side of the I70 tunnel portals makes a good beginning for the hike.

The pass is not named on current forest service, topo, or other maps. It is named on the 1912 Arapaho National Forest Service map.

STUART HOLE PASS

Elevation: 7,710 feet
Location: T10N R72W, Map 3
County: Larimer
Topo: Haystack Gulch
National forest: Roosevelt

Stuart Hole Pass is accessible by foot, but no established trail currently goes over the pass. It divides the waters of the North Fork of Rabbit Creek to the north and Hole Canyon to the south.

The pass is framed by rocky outcrops interspersed with evergreens. No trails, not even game trails, exist over the pass. It can be seen from county road #82E and is located on a point just south of the Mobil water treatment plant.

The pass is two miles north of Sheep Mountain. It is named on the forest service map.

STUNNER PASS

Elevation: 10,541 feet
Location: T36N R4E, Map 8
County: Conejos
Topo: Platoro
National forest: Rio Grande
Other names: Alamosa, Celeste

Stunner Pass is passenger-car-accessible on forest route #250. It divides the waters of the Alamosa River to the north and the Conejos River to the south.

A toll road over the pass was built by the LeDuc and Sanchez Toll Road Company, which was chartered in July 1884. This was used as a freight route from Platoro to Alamosa or Del Norte. Mining activity started in the 1880s, and a post office was established at Stunner in 1890, but the area never really boomed as did many other mining communities. By the end of the 1800s, this area was mostly deserted, but this crossing has continued as access into the forest land.

The ghost town of Platoro (now only a tourist cabin and cafe) is southeast of the pass; the ghost town of Stunner, with a few buildings near a mine dump, is north.

The road is dirt, but is wide and well maintained. Platoro Reservoir is south and Klondike Mountain is west of the pass.

SUGARLOAF PASS

Elevation: 11,075 feet
Location: T9S R81W, Map 5
County: Lake
Topo: Homestake Reservoir
National forest: San Isabel

Sugarloaf Pass is accessible by foot on forest service trail #1776. It divides the waters of the Lake Fork of the Arkansas River to the north and Colorado Gulch to the south.

The pass is on the Leadville 100 trail, south of Turquoise Lake and north of the fish hatchery. The Mount Massive Wilderness Area begins just west of the pass.

Sugarloaf Pass is also on the Colorado Trail. The top is open, without signs, and located under power lines. The pass will be on the new section of the Continental Divide Trail. It is not named on forest service or topo maps.

SUMMIT PASS

Elevation: 11,780 feet
Location: T37N R3E, Map 8
County: Rio Grande
Topo: Elwood Pass
National forest: Rio Grande/
**   San Juan**
On the Continental Divide

Summit Pass is accessible by foot. It divides the waters of Elwood Creek to the west and Park Creek to the east.

Hayden's survey party located the pass in 1874. In 1888 a toll road was built over the pass between Summitville and Del Norte. Mail was carried between Del Norte and Pagosa Springs three times each week via horseback until the wagon road was built.

The pass is on the Continental Divide Trail (#813 in this area). There are signs on the top. An old wagon track runs up and over the pass, but the trail is indistinct in places. The pass is now crossed by the Western Slope pipeline.

SUNNYSIDE SADDLE

Elevation: 12,780 feet
Location: T42N R7W, Map 8
County: San Juan
Topo: Handies Peak
On private land

Sunnyside Saddle is accessible by foot, through private land, in an area of BLM land holdings. It divides the waters of Cement Creek to the west and Eureka Gulch to the east.

The pass is west of Hanson Peak, south of Hurricane Peak, and above Lake Emma. There is evidence of old mining here; the area is now used mostly for hiking. The pass is named on the topo map.

SUNSHINE SADDLE

Elevation: 7,490 feet
Location: T1N R71W, Map 3
County: Boulder
Topo: Boulder
On BLM land

Sunshine Saddle is passenger-car-accessible on county road #83. It divides the waters of Lefthand Creek to the north and Fourmile Canyon to the south.

The saddle is above the little community called Sunshine and at the top end of Sunshine Canyon. Some parking is available atop the saddle. It is not named on the Roosevelt forest service or BLM maps. It is named on the topo map.

SWAMPY PASS

Elevation: 10,365 feet
Location: T14S R87W, Map 5
County: Gunnison
Topo: Anthracite Range
National forest: Gunnison

Swampy Pass is accessible by foot on forest service trail #439 in the West Elk Wilderness Area. It divides the waters of Cliff Creek to the west and Pass Creek to the east.

The railroad was supposed to run over Swampy, but after the route got to the head of Ohio Creek the money ran out, and the railroad never continued over this pass.

The pass is regularly used by hunters and hikers who favor the West Elk Wilderness scenery, as exemplified by The Castles and other rock formations. The pass is northeast of Storm Ridge and southwest of Ohio Peak.   □

T

TAYLOR PASS

Elevation: 11,928 feet
Location: T12S R84W, Map 5
County: Gunnison/Pitkin
Topo: Hayden Peak
National forest: Gunnison/
  White River

Taylor Pass is accessible by 4WD via forest routes #761 from the east and #122 from the west. It divides the waters of Express Creek to the west and Taylor River to the east.

The USGS Board on Geographic Names officially named Taylor Pass in 1940 for the creek it heads, which, in turn, was named for Jim Taylor, a local mining pioneer. He was here looking for "color" as early as 1860.

This was one of the earliest crossings to serve Ashcroft, a major mining area. Crossing the pass was so hard that wagons had to be "snubbed" over the top (taken apart and carted in pieces).

Stevens and Company, owned by H. B. Gillespie, built a wagon road over the pass in 1880. Later, the same company started the first stage route over this road. Use of the pass declined when other routes opened up. Telegraph lines crossed in November 1881.

Use of the pass was almost non-existent by the 1890s except for local foot traffic and sportsmen who desired to reach the good fishing spots in the nearby high country. The road today is as it was in the late 1800s: often closed by snow- or rock slides. In 1901 there was discussion about building a rail line over the pass, possibly with a tunnel near the top, but nothing ever came of the railroad. Mining ores were still shipped over the pass in the early 1900s via wagon or sleds to the railroad in Aspen from the Taylor River Valley.

Taylor Pass is still one of the more popular (and roughest) 4WD roads in the state, even though the road was improved in 1969. This route is sometimes called the Express Creek Road. Taylor Lake, just to the south of the pass top, is worth the trip. The top has signs and views in all directions.

TAYLOR PASS

Elevation: 12,300 feet
Location: T12S R84W, Map 5
County: Gunnison
Topo: Pearl Pass
National forest: Gunnison

Taylor Pass is accessible by foot on forest service trail #406. It divides the waters of East Brush Creek to the west and the Taylor River to the east.

The pass is located at the saddle between Star Peak and Crystal Peak and is east of Carbonate Hill. It is not named on current forest service or topo maps. It is named on a 1918 forest service map.

TAYLOR CREEK PASS

Elevation: 9,980 feet
Location: T7S R85W, Map 5
County: Eagle
Topo: Toner Reservoir
National forest: White River

Taylor Creek Pass is accessible by foot on forest service trail #1909. It divides the waters of Cattle Creek to the north and Taylor Creek to the south.

The pass is marked in the wrong place on the 1961 topo and 1991 White River National Forest Service maps. The pass is not adjacent to Toner Reservoir; it is actually one and a half miles northeast of the reservoir, at the head of Taylor Creek, for which the pass is named. The pass is shown in the correct location on the 1979 (revised 1985) White River forest service map.

Even before the Red Table Mountain Road was developed, this trail served as the main access. The top is tree-covered, mostly with aspen and some pines. No views are available,

This zigzag fence is an interesting discovery for the hiker who reaches Taylor Creek Pass.

but a very pretty zigzag log fence is at the southeast side of the pass.

It is difficult to locate the trail-head, even more difficult to locate this pass, but worth the effort. Taylor Creek Pass makes a good hike; it is unusual, though, in that when approached from the north, the hike in is downhill and the hike out is uphill.

TELLURIUM PASS

Elevation: 12,620 feet
Location: T11S R83W, Map 5
County: Gunnison/Pitkin
Topo: New York Peak
National forest: Gunnison/
** White River**

Tellurium Pass is accessible by foot in the Collegiate Peaks Wilderness Area. It divides the waters of Brooklyn Gulch to the north and Tellurium Creek to the south.

Prospectors used this old route. It was never more than a pack trail, but it was an easier crossing for their animals than other close passes and so was well used.

Truro Peak is about two miles east of the pass and above Tellurium Lake. Forest service maps show Ptarmigan Lake between the wilderness boundary and the pass. A 1960 topo map names the lake "Tellurium Lake."

The pass is not named on forest service or topo maps. Forest route #584 north of Dorchester provides southern access to the pass via a road spur up into the wilderness area.

TENDERFOOT PASS

Elevation: 10,200 feet
Location: T15S R69W, Map 6
County: Teller
Topo: Cripple Creek North
Public access through private land

Tenderfoot Pass is passenger-car-accessible on CO67. It divides the waters of Spring Creek to the north and Cripple Creek to the south.

This is one of the more interesting little-known passes, and it is easily accessible by automobile. The highway goes over the pass at a point a little east of the lowest part of the saddle.

Drive over from the north for an outstanding and breathtaking view of the Sangre de Cristos serving as a backdrop to the Cripple Creek mining district. In the fall, the snow-capped Sangre de Cristo range is especially attractive.

Drive over the pass from the south to the north for a close-up view of the back (south) side of Pikes Peak.

Gillett is the little crossroads north of Cripple Creek, and Tenderfoot Pass is closer to Gillett than to Cripple Creek. A small ski area was built on the east side of the pass in the early 1950s. The pass is not named on the Pike forest service or topo maps.

TENNESSEE PASS

Elevation: 10,424 feet
Location: T8S R80W, Map 6

County: Eagle/Lake
Topo: Leadville North
National forest: San Isabel/
  White River
On the Continental Divide
Other names: Arkansas, Tenth
  Mountain

Tennessee Pass is passenger-car-accessible on US24. It divides the waters of the South Fork of the Eagle River to the north and Tennessee Creek to the south.

The pass was named by prospectors who hailed from the southern state of Tennessee.

An old Indian trail, the pass was well known and used extensively by trappers and traders as early as the 1830s. In 1869, Edward Berthoud surveyed the pass for a railroad route. He recommended it as the most practicable and lowest crossing through the main range of the Rockies, with a maximum grade of seventy-five feet per mile. In 1879 a wagon toll road was opened over the pass between Leadville and Redcliff and stage service began.

After some "color" was found atop the pass in the early 1880s, a small community, also called Tennessee Pass, was started. It had been abandoned by 1885 and no sign of it remains.

A narrow gauge railway was built over the pass in 1881; a third rail, which allowed standard gauge trains to use this track, was added in 1891. The tunnel under the pass was built in 1890 and enlarged in 1945. This

tunnel had been opened by the Denver and Rio Grande Railway when they wanted to provide service to Aspen. Passenger rail service ceased in 1964.

Photographer William H. Jackson, with the Hayden survey party, crossed the pass in 1873 and 1874 seeking good views for his photos of the Mount of the Holy Cross.

In 1902, an auto first crossed the pass without having to be towed over. The Ocean-to-Ocean Trail crossed the pass when roads were known as trails, before numbers were assigned to routes. In 1913 and 1914 the road was graded and surfaced. The road used an abandoned railroad bed with an easy four percent grade over the top part of the pass, where the current railway now goes through the tunnel.

In 1928, Tennessee was the first Continental Divide pass crossed by a highway to be kept open all year by the state. This was mainly due to the efforts of Orion W. Daggett, an editor and publisher in Redcliff during the 1920s.

This gentle crossing is not well used compared to other major highway crossings in the state, because it connects Leadville and Redcliff, two towns that can be served more directly by other routes from the Front Range. The pass is adjacent to the Ski Cooper Ski Area.

Camp Hale was located at the north end of the pass, at the little community of Pando. The Tenth Mountain Battalion trained here in

WWII and a monument to their memory is erected at the pass summit. The road was closed during WWII to keep the public out of the training area at Camp Hale, which was used as a detention camp for captured German soldiers. The camp was used again by the army in 1950 to train GIs for Korea. It was decommissioned in 1965.

The northwest side of the pass is marked with a shelf road that snakes down the side of Battle Mountain and overlooks the Eagle River far below the highway.

Tennessee Pass is on the Continental Divide Trail and the Colorado Trail.

THREE STEP PASS

Elevation: 12,820 feet
Location: T45N R11E, Map 9
County: Custer
Topo: Electric Peak
National forest: Rio Grande/
  San Isabel

Three Step Pass is accessible by foot via forest service trails #856 on the west side and #1355 on the east side. It divides the waters of Cotton Creek to the west and South Brush Creek to the east.

The pass is named for the nearby Three Step Mine.

Three Step Pass is southeast of Electric Peak. Banjo Lake is north.

The trail over this pass is shown on the San Isabel forest service map. Three Step Pass is named on an historical map of Custer County.

THUNDER PASS

Elevation: 11,331 feet
Location: T6N R76W, Map 3
County: Grand/Jackson
Topo: Fall River Pass
National forest: Routt and Rocky
  Mountain National Park
On the Continental Divide
Other name: Lulu

Thunder Pass is accessible by foot. It divides the waters of the Michigan River to the north and the Colorado River to the south.

The USGS Board on Geographic Names officially named Thunder Pass in 1932. The alternate name of the pass, Lulu, honored the daughter of an early settler.

The Indians called the pass *bohah ah ah netheson* ("Thunder Pass") because, as they said, a black cloud always hung over the vicinity. That name has stayed with the pass.

An old stage road led over the pass between the communities of Lulu City and Teller City. A stagecoach crossed twice weekly.

The old town of Lulu City is at the south end and makes an interesting stop en route to the pass top. The pass is on the Continental Divide Trail.

TIMBERLINE PASS

Elevation: 11,484 feet
Location: T5N R74W, Map 3

County: Larimer
Topo: Trail Ridge
In Rocky Mountain National Park

Timberline Pass is accessible by foot. It divides the waters of the Big Thompson River to the west and Windy Gulch to the east.

The pass was named by Roger Toll in 1914 when he noted it was the only pass on the old Ute trail through Rocky Mountain National Park that is above timberline.

The route to Timberline makes for an interesting hike, following the trail that many moccasins have taken over the years.

The pass is on a saddle between two rocky areas, and although the trail is indistinct, it is well marked by cairns. Many interesting but low rock formations are along the Tombstone Ridge.

TINCUP PASS

Elevation: 12,154 feet
Location: T15S R81W, Map 5
County: Chaffee/Gunnison
Topo: Cumberland Pass
National forest: Gunnison/
    San Isabel
On the Continental Divide
Other name: Alpine

Tincup Pass is 4WD-accessible via forest route #267 on the west and county road #267 on the east. It divides the waters of East Willow Creek to the north and North Fork of Chalk Creek to the south.

The pass was named because a prospector used a tin cup while looking for "color" here in 1879. He found gold instead.

First used by Indians (arrowheads and flint tools have been found here), then as a pack trail, the pass contains much history.

In 1879, a railroad route was projected, and both the Elk Mountain Railroad Company and the Colorado Southern Railroad Company were incorporated, but neither ever got over the pass.

In 1880, a hydroelectric plant from St. Elmo ran power lines to provide power to the mining area around Tincup. A wagon road was built in 1881 by the Chalk Creek and Elk Mountain Toll Road Company. By 1882, three stage lines were operating daily over the pass. The road was not well used, however, after the Denver and Rio Grande Railway got to the Western Slope in 1887.

In 1902 other railroad surveys were done, but no rails were ever laid. A railroad tunnel was started under the pass but soon abandoned.

This route was never anything but a rough road. It was usually a softer and easier ride to cross in winter on a sled than it was in summer, when the wooden wagon wheels bounced and clattered on the rocks of the road.

The route was considered a state highway in the 1910s. In 1954, prison labor was used to construct an improved roadbed over the pass. In recent years counties have done some maintenance to keep the road passable for 4WD enthusiasts.

The pass is a good back-road drive through pretty country and past a pretty lake (Mirror Lake, first called Lake Catherine) on the north side. The pass is a narrow spot at the road crest, open and with good views.

Tincup Pass was used in WWI to train a cavalry squadron. The road is now used for winter activities such as cross-country skiing and snowmobiling and provides a summer weekend getaway for 4WD fans. This route between Taylor Park and St. Elmo is well used. It is on the Continental Divide Trail.

TOLL PASS

Elevation: 12,100 feet
Location: T5N R74W, Map 3
County: Larimer
Topo: Trail Ridge
In Rocky Mountain National Park

Toll Pass is accessible by foot, but it can be nearly reached by passenger car via US34. It divides the waters of the Fall River to the north and the Big Thompson River to the south.

The pass is named to honor Roger Toll, the third superintendent of Rocky Mountain National Park, who was killed in an automobile accident in 1936. Just to the west of the pass is a memorial to honor Toll. The old trail to the memorial is now fenced off, and visitors to the memorial are routed from the parking area at Rock Cut just to the west on US34.

The pass is not named on forest service or topo maps. It is identified by Doris B. Osterwald in her book about Rocky Mountain National Park.

TOMICHI PASS

Elevation: 11,979 feet
Location: T50N R5E, Map 5
County: Gunnison
Topo: Whitepine
National forest: Gunnison

Tomichi Pass is accessible by 4WD on forest route #888. It divides the waters of Quartz Creek to the north and Tomichi Creek to the south.

Tomichi is the Ute word for "hot water." There are many hot springs nearby.

The road over the pass was used to move between the mining areas of Tomichi and White Pine. It was never anything but a rough road most suited to stock drives, but wagons did cross after the road was rebuilt to cover the mud holes that would develop after each rain or snow.

The pass road over Tomichi is a very narrow shelf road—an abandoned 4WD vehicle litters the valley below. A plank bridge covers a marshy area on the road. This is a remote area, and not many travelers visit it. The pass is between Paywell Mountain and Van Wirt Mountain.

TRAIL RIDER PASS

Elevation: 12,410 feet
Location: T11S R87W, Map 5
County: Gunnison/Pitkin
Topo: Snowmass Mountain
National forest: White River
Other name: Snowmass

Trail Rider Pass is accessible by foot on forest service trail #1973 in the Maroon Bells–Snowmass Wilderness Area. It divides the waters of the North Fork of the Crystal River to the west and Snowmass Creek to the east.

The pass was named in 1938 by the Trail Rider of the Wilderness, an informal club of equestrians. The riders put their names on a paper in a bottle that was buried in a cairn at the top. Another story is that the name came from the local outfitters, who often conducted pack trips here in the late 1940s. A favorite packhorse collapsed and died at the pass and is buried in an unmarked grave at the top. The pass was then named "Trail Rider" in honor of the horse. The spot is called Snowmass Pass by some area residents because it is above Snowmass Lake and adjacent to Snowmass Peak.

There is no indication that this route has ever been anything but a hiking trail, because other, more direct routes provided better mining-claim access.

Until recently, no established trail existed, but the route has been used for many years by fishing enthusiasts to go from Snowmass Lake to Geneva (also called Little Snowmass) Lake. The forest service has now constructed a good trail over the pass.

It is a very long hike to reach Trail Rider Pass, but the view is well worth the effort. The hike can be combined with other passes for a backpack trip of several days.

The pass is south of Hagerman Peak. The top is usually windy.

TREASURE PASS

Elevation: 11,740 feet
Location: T37N R2E, Map 8
County: Mineral
Topo: Wolf Creek Pass
National forest: Rio Grande/
**   San Juan**
On the Continental Divide

Treasure Pass is accessible by foot on forest service trail #565. It divides the waters of Lane Creek to the west and Pass Creek to the east.

The pass is named for the treasure buried on nearby Treasure Mountain. Supposedly, early French explorers in the 1770s penetrated this area of the West and buried millions of dollars (maybe thirty-three million) worth of gold on the mountain. The members of the exploration party all met with untimely deaths or, for some reason or another, were never able to return and claim the fortune.

A large search party was put together in 1844 to look for the gold stash; this party was set upon by

Indians, so they fled the area. The treasure is said to be in a deep, well-hidden grave, and although many shafts have been dug and several thousands of dollars have been spent in searching, it has not yet been located.

The pass is near the Continental Divide Trail (#813 in this area). The nearby ski area provides a good trail access to the summit of the pass, which is a mile northwest of Alberta Peak.

TRIANGLE PASS

Elevation: 12,900 feet
Location: T12S R85W, Map 5
County: Gunnison/Pitkin
Topo: Gothic
National forest: Gunnison/
  White River

Triangle Pass is accessible by foot via forest service trails #1981 on the north and #981 on the south in the Maroon Bells–Snowmass Wilderness Area. It divides the waters of Conundrum Creek to the north and Copper Creek to the south.

The USGS Board on Geographic Names officially named the pass in 1973 to honor the convergence of three ridges at a nearby peak, which is also named Triangle.

A wagon road to the pass was built in 1883 by the commissioners of Gunnison County. Pitkin County was to construct a road on their side, but it didn't ever get done, so eventually the Gunnison side fell into

disuse. This route served as a crossing between Gothic, located above Crested Butte, and Aspen.

Len Shoemaker, an Aspen forest ranger, built a new trail over the pass in the late 1920s. While on the south side his horse fell, then he got caught in a snowdrift. Afterward, although he enjoyed riding the trail, he never could forget the rough day he'd had atop Triangle Pass.

A hike to Triangle makes a good round trip when combined with other passes; Triangle is the highest of the four passes in the immediate vicinity.

The area is used for winter ski-touring trips. The top of the pass is just above a long switchback that rises above a rock-covered cirque. Castle Peak is to the east. Approximately two miles below the pass (on the northeast) is the Conundrum Hot Springs, a popular hiking destination.

TRIMBLE PASS

Elevation: 12,860 feet
Location: T38N R7W, Map 8
County: La Plata
Topo: Columbine Pass
National forest: San Juan

Trimble Pass is accessible by foot on forest service trail #534 in the Weminuche Wilderness Area. It divides the waters of Johnson Creek to the north and the Florida River to the south.

The pass is named for Frank

Trimble, a rancher who pioneered here and who discovered the Trimble Hot Springs.

Trimble Pass is located in the Needles mountain range section of the San Juan mountains.

Florida (pronounced Flow-ree'-da) Mountain is to the east and Bullion Mountain is to the northwest of the pass. The pass is a crossing between the Crystal Valley and Chicago Basin.

TROUBLESOME PASS

Elevation: 10,027 feet
Location: T4N R79W, Map 3
County: Grand/Jackson
Topo: Parkview Mountain
National forest: Arapaho/Routt
On the Continental Divide

Troublesome Pass is accessible by foot via forest service trail #55, also called the Haystack Creek Trail. It divides the waters of Willow Creek to the north and Haystack Creek to the south.

The pass is named for the difficulty ranchers have in moving their animals across the old stock trail.

An old wagon road once crossed the pass, which was originally mapped by the Hayden survey party in 1873.

The pass is in the Rabbit Ears mountain range. Many logging roads are now cut throughout the area. The top is tree-covered, with signs, and has good valley views to the south.

Sheep Mountain, just to the west, has good vistas into the mountains southwest toward Kremmling. Parkview Mountain is just to the east; look for the old fire lookout.

The pass is on the Continental Divide Trail.

TROUGH ROAD PASS

Elevation: 8,329 feet
Location: T1S R81W, Map 2
County: Grand
Topo: Sheephorn Mountain
Public access through private land

Trough Road Pass is accessible by passenger car on county road #1. It divides the waters of the Colorado River to the west and Beaver Creek to the east.

Although virtually unknown now, this route almost became part of the major east-west route through Colorado's mountains. The pass is named on a 1924 auto trails road map as Trough Road Pass, and the road that crosses it is now called Trough Road, Grand County Road #1. In the spring of 1913, Grand County began developing the road as a major crossing. It was an extension of the Midland Trail that was heading toward Salt Lake City. The road was improved and widened; however, until 1925, driving this highway required opening and closing cattle gates.

The route was a cutoff between Kremmling and Dotsero, and because it was much lower than snowy crossings farther north, it would make a better year-round route to the west. Other interests prevailed eventually, and this route was not further developed.

The top of the pass is open and in grazing country. It is marked by a small lake to the south and a communications tower on the mountain to the north. A trip over the old potential highway route makes for a fine diversion through the central mountains. For several miles, the west side is a shelf road above the spectacular Gore Canyon.

The pass is not named on current forest service or topo maps.

TROUT CREEK PASS

Elevation: 9,487 feet
Location: T13S R77W, Map 6
County: Chaffee/Park
Topo: Antero Reservoir
National forest: San Isabel/Public access through private land
Other names: Bath, Hilltop

Trout Creek Pass is accessible by passenger car on US24/US285. It divides the waters of Salt Creek to the north and Trout Creek to the south.

The USGS Board on Geographic Names officially named the pass in 1906 for the Trout Creek it heads. The alternate names of Bath and Hilltop refer to the stations that existed at the top of the pass when the railroads were running; one station was called Bath by the Colorado Midland, and the other Hilltop by the South Park Railroad. The

population of the little stations was never more than about twenty-five.

This very old Indian crossing was used as passage between the Elk mountains and South Park. It was used by Zebulon Pike in 1806, and by many other explorers who headed west out of South Park into the Collegiate Valley. The crossing was used by fur trappers and traders, then by prospectors.

In September 1866, the Lake County Commissioners (Chaffee County had not yet been divided away from Lake County) designated the road a public highway.

Two railroads crossed the pass, the Denver and South Park (narrow gauge), and the Colorado Midland (standard gauge). Both came over the pass in the 1880s, racing to the west. The Denver, South Park and Pacific (a later incarnation of the Denver and South Park) discontinued service in 1910 over the pass; the Colorado Midland operated until 1921. The rails were removed in 1926. The railroad grades can still be seen in places along the west side of the pass.

In 1930 a rock with the inscription "PIKE EXP" was claimed to have been found atop the pass. Look for the old railroad trestle still standing at the top.

The view of the Collegiate Range from the highway on the west side of the pass is described by many as the best view in the whole state. Mount Princeton is the main massif looming ahead.

Natural salt springs at the east end of the pass once drew many visitors. Indians and settlers alike needed the salt for their own use and for their animals. Most of the table salt in early Denver came from these saltworks. Dolomite (a type of limestone) was also mined at the pass.

TWELVEMILE PASS

Elevation: 6,380 feet
Location: T17S R71W, Map 6
County: Fremont
Topo: Rice Mountain
Public access through private land

Twelvemile Pass is accessible by passenger car on CO9. It divides the waters of Twelvemile Hole Creek to the west and Bumback Gulch to the east.

According to locals, the pass and other features are named "Twelve-mile" because they are twelve miles from Cañon City.

The top of the pass is a nondescript crossing of a small ridge in open farmland. There are pines running down the ridge and down and across the saddle.

From the top, look south to the Royal Gorge bridge. Cactus Mountain is to the west of the saddle. Just north of the pass is an old building called the Twelvemile Schoolhouse.

The pass is not named on forest service or topo maps. It is named in the BLM maps book.

TWENTYMILE DIVIDE

Elevation: 7,219 feet
Location: T6N R85W, Map 2
County: Routt
Topo: Cow Creek
Public access through private land

Twentymile Divide is accessible by passenger car on county road #33. It divides the waters of Cow Creek to the east and Trout Creek to the west.

The pass is in open ranching country—a minor divide in a remote area. It is located southeast of Saddle Mountain and northeast of Appels Pond. Twentymile Divide is not named on forest service or topo maps. It is identified in a Routt County historical guide.

TWIN CREEK PASS

Elevation: 8,579 feet
Location: T13S R71W, Map 6
County: Teller
Topo: Lake George
Public access through private land
Other name: Divide

Twin Creek Pass is passenger-car-accessible on county road #1. It divides the waters of Grape Creek to the north and Fourmile Creek to the south.

Some historians believe Zebulon Pike crossed this way to go from the valley of the Arkansas River to the South Platte River Valley. Thomas Farnham crossed the pass in 1839, seeking to stay out of sight of Indians who were hunting buffalo nearby.

An 1882 map of Colorado shows and names the pass, but some later maps confused the pass with the better known Ute Pass at Divide.

The top of this unmarked pass is about one-quarter mile south of the southern end of the Florissant Fossil Beds National Monument grounds. The pass is a wide, open crest of a ridge; it's not spectacular, but it gives good views of rolling hills and Pikes Peak, to the east. It is not named on the Pike forest service or topo maps.

TWIN THUMBS PASS

Elevation: 13,060 feet
Location: T39N R7W, Map 8
County: La Plata
Topo: Storm King Peak
National forest: San Juan

Twin Thumbs Pass is accessible by foot, but no established trail currently goes over the pass, which is in the Weminuche Wilderness Area. The pass divides the waters of No Name Creek to the north and Needle Creek to the south.

The pass is just northeast of North Eolus and provides a crossing between No Name Basin and Chicago Basin in the rugged Needles mountain range. It is located between the Twin Thumbs and Glacier Point. Technical gear is required to descend north from the pass in any but the driest years.

The pass is not named on forest service or topo maps. James Grafton Rogers located and named this pass in his listing of Colorado's geographic features.

TWO ELK PASS

Elevation: 10,970 feet
Location: T5S R80W, Map 6
County: Eagle
Topo: Red Cliff
National forest: White River
Other name: Peck

Two Elk Pass is accessible by foot on forest service trail #2005. It divides the waters of Two Elk Creek to the west and Black Gore Creek to the east.

The pass is named for one of the creeks it heads. The alternate name of Peck Pass was to honor an early supervisor of the Holy Cross National Forest, Colonel A. S. Peck. It was assigned by Orion W. Daggett, editor and publisher of the *Holy Cross Trail* newspaper in Redcliff. He proposed a route over the pass to serve as an alternative to the existing highway.

Two Elk makes an excellent hike between the east side of the town of Vail and the top of Vail Pass. It makes a good weekend getaway from the highway bustle, because the area is not well used in the summer months.

The top is well marked with a stone monument in trees. An open saddle is just off to the west of the top. The back bowls of Vail's ski area

Various markers identify the tops of passes; Two Elk Pass has an elaborate rock cairn with a post.

are above the pass, to the west, but an opening to the northeast along a saddle gives great views into the Eagles Nest Wilderness Area. The south side of the pass is well used in the winter for ski touring along the Commando Run.

Two Elk Pass is a National Scenic Trail. It has views of the Mount of the Holy Cross from its top. Also, look for lots of wildflowers in season.   □

U

UNAWEEP DIVIDE

Elevation: 7,048 feet
Location: T14S R101W, Map 4
County: Mesa
Topo: Snyder Flats
Public access through private land

Unaweep Divide is passenger-car-accessible on CO141. It divides the waters of West Creek to the west and East Creek to the east.

Unaweep is a Ute word meaning "dividing of waters," which well describes the area: It is a high

Unaweep Divide in western Colorado marks the beginnings of two creeks.

plateau with river drainages on each side.

The pass is marked at the top with a sign and is located between Whitewater and Gateway. This section of Colorado is an informative study for individuals interested in the geology evident in the canyon and the water erosion that occurred there. The divide is an uplift through the old canyon.

UNEVA PASS

Elevation: 11,900 feet
Location: T6S R79W, Map 6
County: Summit
Topo: Vail Pass
National forest: Arapaho

Uneva Pass is accessible by foot on forest service trail #60 (the Gore Range Trail) in the Eagles Nest Wilderness Area. It divides the waters of North Tenmile Creek to the north and Officers Gulch to the south.

The pass is located above well-known fishing spots Wheeler Lakes and Lost Lake. Lost Lake is deemed by many hikers one of the prettiest high-mountain lakes in our state.

The top is open, a large, flat area that has good views to the south overlooking Copper Mountain Ski Area. Views to the north, to the Gore Range, are also spectacular. From various points on the south access, views of the Mount of the Holy Cross can be seen by looking southwest.

Saddles, such as this one at Uneva Pass, are often gentle in slope and covered with grass.

Just under the top is a scree-covered slope on a long switchback that requires some careful stepping. The pass could be bushwhacked from the top of Vail Pass by experienced map readers.

Uneva Peak is to the west; a dude ranch was once located nearby. Even though the pass is not on the Continental Divide, it is on the Continental Divide Trail.

UTAH PASS

Elevation: 12,820 feet
Location: T8S R81W, Map 5
County: Eagle/Lake
Topo: Homestake Reservoir

National forest: San Isabel/
** White River**
On the Continental Divide

Utah Pass is accessible by foot above forest service trail #1499 in the Holy Cross Wilderness Area. It divides the waters of the East Fork of Homestake Creek to the west and West Tennessee Creek to the east.

This is the pass that Captain John Fremont is believed to have crossed on his 1845 expedition into the Rockies. He went down the Eagle River and headed into Utah territory.

Some historians have claimed that "Utah" was an earlier name for Tennessee Pass, but the more direct route would have been over this pass, and no mention of taking a roundabout way is made by the journalists who accompanied Fremont's trips. Kit Carson was Fremont's guide on this trip, and he knew all the short routes through the mountains.

The pass is now used as a shortcut; it has never been more than a foot and pack trail.

Utah Pass is not named on forest service or topo maps. It is located a half-mile southwest of Homestake Peak.

UTE PASS

Elevation: 9,165 feet
Location: T13S R70W, Map 6
County: Teller
Topo: Divide
Public access through private land
Other names: Divide, Hayden Divide, Twin Creek, Yute

Ute Pass is accessible by passenger car on US24. It divides the waters of Twin Creek to the west and Trout Creek to the east.

The USGS Board on Geographic Names officially named Ute Pass in 1982, after some controversy about the location of the pass. Although some residents believe the actual pass should be located closer to Manitou Springs (and old maps show it at various places along US24), the true watershed divide is reached at the now-official location near Divide.

The alternate name of Hayden Divide is to honor Ferdinand Hayden for his exploration work in the Rockies. He crossed here during his survey trip of 1873. And "Twin Creek" is to remember one of the streams the pass heads.

The pass is on the old Ute trail that goes along the north side of Pikes Peak. The Utes came down from their "shining mountains" to the hot springs, where they believed the Great Spirit lived; his breath made the bubbling spring water roil. Enemies of the Utes also used the pass.

In 1829, Stephen Long went up the pass. He noted that bison used the pass more than did the Indians. Kit Carson led trappers into South Park to find beaver. "Old Bill" Williams was guiding parties through the pass as early as 1842.

A forest fire that lasted for three weeks at the end of 1853 and into 1854 wiped out most of the timber in the canyon. In 1865 a grasshopper plague here was so severe that almost all traffic and all construction on the road through the pass had to be halted.

In 1858, ore finds brought prospectors to this area in droves. All of these people used the old Indian route. In August 1862, the Colorado Territory issued a charter for the Ute Pass Wagon Road Company to build a toll road. Stage and freight service began at once and the road was so well used that many settlers never made it to the mining towns but set up farming in the Ute Pass.

Homesteading in the area was opened, with 160-acre tracts advertised to eastern U.S. residents. Because earlier routes through the pass had been free, there was much opposition to the initiation of tolls at this time. Three charters for toll roads were issued; all ended in bankruptcy. Then, in 1872, a wagon road was built along Fountain Creek, which bypassed part of the Indian trail just above Manitou Springs.

A famous traveler of this era, H.A.W. Tabor, moved through the pass on his way to the mining communities where he later made his fortune. In the 1870s, this route west was a continuous stream of wagons pulled by mules or oxen.

Colorado City residents turned out in large numbers in 1875 to witness a twenty-four-wagon freight train, pulled by more than 150 yoke of oxen, go through the pass. By 1876, an average of fourteen wagons and twenty-four travelers each day were going up and five others were coming down the pass toward Colorado City.

The Colorado Midland Railroad ran a line up through this Fountain Creek Canyon in 1887. In 1916 the

Before the modern road was developed up Fountain Creek, this route served travelers heading west out of Colorado Springs through Ute Pass. (*Photo courtesy Denver Public Library, Western History Department*)

trains discontinued regular service over the pass. Between 1916 and 1949, special trains were sometimes run. These were often Sunday excursions that took Colorado City and Colorado Springs residents up Ute Pass to open meadows where wildflowers were especially abundant.

The pass was well used in the mid-1800s because it was lower, an easier climb, and more open going than heading west out of Denver and over higher passes. Merchants in Colorado City eagerly sought the miners' business and worked to keep the road in good shape.

The county name of El Paso refers to "the pass" part of Ute Pass, which indicates the importance this crossing had in the history of this area.

In 1871, county commissioners issued the first bond issue for work on this road. A flood in 1902 wiped out the road, all its bridges, and some railroad track. In the early 1910s, convict labor was used to rebuild part of the road. The road was named part of the Ocean-to-Ocean Highway; when numbers were assigned to highways in 1932 it became US24. The state took over responsibility for the road in the 1930s; they closed and then completely rebuilt it. It was reopened to public use in 1937. The road has been upgraded often since then. In 1963 the four-lane highway on the lower portion was started; it was finished by 1965.

Since the earliest days of the pass road, visitors have made communities such as Cascade, Green Mountain Falls, Woodland, and Chipeta Park their summer residences. At the pass itself, the town of Divide grew up. First it was a lumber center, then potatoes and lettuce were raised here and shipped all over the country. It was a major stop on most stage lines into South Park. Cattle were driven over the pass to provide fresh meat to the mining communities in and beyond South Park. Now Divide is best known as the place visitors turn south in order to get to the gambling casinos at Cripple Creek.

UTE PASS

Elevation: 9,568 feet
Location: T3S R78W, Map 3
County: Grand/Summit
Topo: Ute Peak
National forest: Arapaho

Ute Pass is accessible by passenger car on forest route #15. It divides the waters of Pass Creek to the west and Williams Fork to the east.

The pass is named for the nearby Ute Peak.

Following an old Indian trail across the mountains east of the Blue River, early prospectors and settlers moved across this high-country crossing. There is no indication that a road was built over the pass until the 1900s; earlier users followed the pack trail.

A journal kept by a traveler in 1862 tells of the boggy marsh on the east side of the pass, the open dry west side, and the views from the top. Much wildlife lived at the pass, providing provisions for the writer's party.

Today this is a graded dirt road in good shape, mostly because the road provides access to the west portal of the Henderson molybdenum mine. Good views await the visitor atop the pass, particularly the views west, of the Gore Range.

The pass is in the Williams Fork mountain range. It is a mile southeast of Prairie Mountain and three miles northwest of Ute Peak.

UTE PASS

Elevation: 9,944 feet
Location: T45N R8E, Map 9
County: Saguache
Topo: Klondike Mine
National forest: Rio Grande

This Ute Pass is accessible by 4WD on forest route #842. It divides the waters of Ute Creek to the north and Findley Gulch to the south.

A rough, bumpy road crosses the pass in a short climb. Look for the good views back into the west part of the San Luis Valley from the top, which is unmarked. On the east side of the pass a power line runs across the road.

This Ute Pass is an interesting backcountry road that is rarely used except as access to the grazing areas on BLM land.

The road north of the pass leads to the old mining district of Bonanza.

The pass is two miles northwest of Saguache Peak.

UTE PASS

Elevation: 11,000 feet
Location: T9N R82W, Map 2
County: Jackson/Routt
Topo: Mount Zirkel
National forest: Routt
On the Continental Divide

Ute Pass is accessible by foot via forest service trails #1150 from the west and #1128 from the east, in the Mount Zirkel Wilderness Area. It divides the waters of Gold Creek to the west and Bear Creek to the east.

The pass was used by Indians to cross between North Park and the Elk River Valley.

Many people hike into Gold Creek Lake, fewer go on to the pass, which crosses the Continental Divide at a low spot. The pass is in the Sierra Madre mountain range. One of the Slavonia mines, a trail landmark, is near the top.

UTE PASS

Elevation: 9,869 feet
Location: T10N R77W, Map 3
County: Jackson/Larimer
Topo: Shipman Mountain
National forest: Roosevelt/
    Colorado State Forest

This Ute Pass is accessible by foot from the east via forest service trail #971, and by 4WD from the west when permission is arranged with the landowner (try during hunting season). The pass divides the waters of East Sand Creek to the west and the South Fork of La Garde Creek to the east.

This is an old Indian trail that connected the Laramie River Valley and North Park. Later, a rough wagon road was built over the pass.

Back in 1861, an interesting event occurred here after Utes had stolen settlers' horses. The settlers set out and caught the Indians at the pass, killing many of them and recovering the stolen horses.

The pass is in the Medicine Bow mountain range and is located behind the Upper Sand Hills. Good hiking access is available to the pass via the McIntyre Creek Trail through Shipman Park; this is a long hike. The Medicine Bow Trail intersects McIntyre Creek Trail at the timbered pass. The views into North Park are worth the trip.

UTE PASS

Elevation: 7,420 feet
Location: T35N R9W, Map 7
County: La Plata
Topo: Durango East
Public access through private land

Ute Pass is accessible by passenger car via county road #240. It divides the waters of Spring Creek to the west and the Florida River to the east. The river name is pronounced Flow-ree'-da by locals.

This old Indian crossing was used by military groups moving northwest from New Mexico Territory by the mid-1860s. Then it was used by trappers and prospectors. A wagon-road charter was issued in June 1887 to the Animas City, Pagosa Springs and Conejos Wagon Road Company. That road developed into the road still used today.

The pass is now crossed by a paved road that heads east out of Durango en route to Vallecito or Lemon Reservoir. It is unmarked with no indication of the pass and no distinct views from the top. The pass top is at the entrance to a housing subdivision.

Locally, the road over the pass is called the Florida Road, but it is not named on forest service or topo maps.

UTE PASS

Elevation: 12,702 feet
Location: T40N R6W, Map 8
County: San Juan
Topo: Rio Grande Pyramid
National forest: Rio Grande
Other name: Starvation

This Ute Pass is accessible by foot on forest service trail #787 in the Weminuche Wilderness Area. It divides the waters of Bear Creek to the west and West Ute Creek to the east.

The alternate name of "Starvation" exists because the pass heads Starvation Gulch.

The route over the pass is called

the West Ute Creek Trail. It also serves as part of the La Garita stock drive way. Look for elk nearby. The pass is southeast of Beartown and on a saddle between two peaks, each over thirteen thousand feet. The pass is not named on forest service or topo maps.

UTE CREEK PASS

Elevation: 11,340 feet
Location: T28S R72W, Map 9
County: Costilla/Huerfano
Topo: Blanca Peak
National forest: San Isabel and
  private land

Ute Creek Pass is not accessible via the private land on its south side; foot access is via forest service trail #1306 on its north side. It divides the waters of South Huerfano River to the north and Ute Creek to the south.

The pass is not used now except for hiking, but old maps of the San Luis Valley show a mail route once ran over it. This was used in the summer months only. The pass is between Slide Mountain (which was called Greyback Mountain earlier) and Mount Blanca.

The pass is not named on forest service or topo maps. It is identified by Luther Bean in his history of the San Luis Valley.   □

VAIL PASS

Elevation: 10,603 feet eastbound;
  10,662 feet westbound
Location: T6S R79W, Map 6
County: Eagle/Summit
Topo: Vail Pass
National forest: Arapaho/
  White River
Other names: Black Gore, Low
  Divide, Pottery

Vail Pass is accessible by passenger car on I70. It divides the waters of Black Gore Creek to the west and West Tenmile Creek to the east.

The USGS Board on Geographic Names officially named the pass

in 1950 to honor Charles Vail, the chief engineer of the Colorado Highway Department. He died in 1945, after this route was planned and developed.

The top of the pass was used by Utes as a camping area. While the highway was being constructed, many shards of pottery were found at some of these old camps, thus the alternate name of "Pottery." The current highway rest area is built over this old camping site.

In his letter to the USGS, Charles Vail indicated that the pass was called "Black Gore" by locals for one of the creeks it heads.

Although this was not a major

crossing historically, the route was used because it was a low-divide route into the Eagle Valley and beyond.

In 1879, a major forest fire cleared out about twenty thousand acres of trees near the top of the pass and created the open wildflower meadows now existent. By 1955, all the standing dead timber had fallen, and the forest began regrowing. Slowly, the trees are creeping down and across the pass again.

No wagon road was ever built over the pass; it served as a low-use trail only until 1940, when another, lower, route that would reach the west side of Colorado and replace Shrine Pass was desired. The Vail Pass route was converted to the interstate system in the mid-1970s.

Vail Pass is now well traveled by mountain bikers, hikers, and cross-country skiers who use the twenty-seven-mile Vail Pass/Ten Mile Canyon National Recreation Trail, in addition to the traffic carried on the interstate. Each winter the threat of avalanches is great, and during wet years the interstate must sometimes be closed to clear away fallen snow and soil.

VASQUEZ PASS

Elevation: 11,700 feet
Location: T3S R75W, Map 3
County: Clear Creek/Grand
Topo: Berthoud Pass
National forest: Arapaho

On the Continental Divide
Other name: New

Vasquez Pass is accessible by foot on forest service trail #13. It divides the waters of Vasquez Creek to the north and the West Fork of Clear Creek to the south.

Vasquez Pass is named for Louis Vasquez, an early trader more famous in the area north of Denver (Vasquez Fort is along US87 north of Brighton). The alternate name, New Pass, was the original name of the pass.

An old Indian trail ran over the pass. Vasquez was already being used regularly when the crossing just to the east, Berthoud Pass, was noted. Vasquez was then used as an alternate crossing of the Continental Divide when Berthoud Pass was too muddy or during periods of construction, but it was never a major crossing.

Stanley Mountain is on the east side and Vasquez Peak on the west side of the pass. Each of these is about fifteen-hundred feet higher than the pass top. Because weather is often bad on this part of the Continental Divide, prospectors called the area "Camp Foulweather."

A charter was granted by Colorado Territory to William H. Russell and the Central Overland California and Pikes Peak Express in 1862 for a wagon road over the pass. Russell was thwarted by the steepness of the route once he reached the foot of the pass.

In March 1864, The Denver and Pacific Wagon Road Company was granted a charter for a toll road over Vasquez Pass and to the western boundary of Colorado Territory. The pass is shown on an 1872 map of the state.

For a good drive on a back road out of Winter Park, take forest route #148, also called the Vasquez Road, to its end, which differs from time to time depending upon which culverts have been washed out. A long hike up the old wagon road provides access to the top of the pass, which is an indistinct crossing of the ridge. Look for the nice view of Red Mountain to the south from the pass top, which is open and has wide vistas.

Some hikers like the shorter route, which is to bushwhack up from the south side, climbing the mountain alongside a little feeder stream to the West Fork of Clear Creek.

The pass is on the Continental Divide Trail, although it is not marked well. Another trail here, the Mount Nystrom Trail, uses access from the ski area atop Berthoud Pass but is nearly obliterated.

Part of the pass is used today for a water tunnel, owned by the Denver Water Board, to provide Western-Slope water to the population centers on the Front Range.

VENABLE PASS

Elevation: 12,780 feet
Location: T44N R12E, Map 9

County: Custer/Saguache
Topo: Rito Alto Peak
National forest: Rio Grande/ San Isabel

Venable Pass is accessible by foot via forest service trails #859 on the west side and #1347 on the east side. It divides the waters of the North Fork of North Crestone Creek to the west and Venable Creek to the east.

The USGS Board on Geographic Names officially named the pass in 1962 for Jack Venable, an early homesteader in the Wet Mountain Valley.

Pike noted the pass in 1806 but did not climb it. It has never been more than just a good horseback trail.

The area is well used each summer and fall by pack animals; it is often combined with a trip to other passes and to the Marble Cave, which is at the eastern foot of the pass. The forest service has, in past years, used this area for a fire lookout. The pass is about a mile north of Venable Peak.

VETA PASS

Elevation: 9,220 feet
Location: T29S R70W, Map 9
County: Costilla/Huerfano
Topo: McCarty Park
On land owned by the Denver and Rio Grande Railroad
Other names: Middle Creek, Wagon Creek

There is no access to Veta Pass because it is where the railroad crosses the divide. The top is marked by no-trespassing signs erected by the Denver and Rio Grande Railroad. The pass divides the waters of Wagon Creek to the west and South Middle Creek to the east.

The USGS Board on Geographic Names officially named Veta Pass in 1965. The alternate names for the pass refer to the two creeks the pass heads. *Veta* means "vein" in Spanish.

In early days the pass was well used by Indians who had discovered this good crossing, then by traders, trappers, and prospectors moving west. It was called Middle Creek Pass, and a wagon toll road had been constructed over it in the early 1870s.

The railroad used to cross, with a narrow-gauge track, the nearby La Veta Pass. In 1899 the railroad moved the route to this lower crossing, built it as standard gauge, and assigned it such a similar name that much confusion has existed ever since. The rail station at the top was named Fir.

Explorers such as Gwinn Heap in 1853 and Captain John Gunnison in 1854 crossed the pass and noted its low altitude. The pass is three miles southwest of Cross Mountain.

VICTOR PASS

Elevation: 10,201 feet
Location: T15S R69W, Map 6

County: Teller
Topo: Big Bull Mountain
Public access through private land

Victor Pass is accessible by passenger car. It divides the waters of Grassy Creek to the north and Wilson Creek to the south.

The Colorado Midland built a railroad over the pass and connected the mining towns of Victor and Cameron in 1894. Before that, a wagon road provided service. This route was a bit longer than other more direct routes, but it allowed for a more gradual grade.

The pass is located northeast of Victor, past the old mining community of Goldfield. At the top is another dirt road that heads west to the ghost town of Independence.

President Theodore Roosevelt exclaimed about the view of "a trip that bankrupts the English language" when he visited here in the early 1900s.

The pass is not named on the Pike forest service or topo maps. It is named on the XYZ maps.

VIRGINIUS PASS

Elevation: 13,100 feet
Location: T43N R8W, Map 7
County: Ouray/San Miguel
Topo: Telluride
National forest: Uncompahgre
Other name: Mendota

Virginius Pass is accessible by foot. It divides the waters of Sneffels

Creek to the north and Marshall Creek to the south.

The pass is named for the Virginius Mine, discovered by William Freeland in 1877, above the mining community of Sneffels. The Virginius Mine is believed to be the first one to use underground electric power for lighting. The alternate name is from Mendota Peak, which is just west of the pass.

This route provides an alternate crossing between Telluride and Ouray and goes through the Marshall Basin. The crossing was never more than a burro trail; it was very narrow but used by miners to move between the Virginius and Smuggler mines.

Each year there are many avalanches here, and the pass is safe only for a short period each summer.

Virginius Pass is not named on forest service or topo maps. □

WAGON GAP

Elevation: 4,747 feet
Location: T28S R53W, Map 10
County: Las Animas
Topo: Brown Canyon
On private land

There is no access to this pass. It divides the waters of Smith Canyon to the west and Muddy Creek to the east.

The pass can be seen from a nearby road. However, all access is now on fenced private land.

The pass is not named in the BLM maps book. It is named on the topo map.

WATSON DIVIDE

Elevation: 7,582 feet

Location: T9S R86W, Map 5
County: Pitkin
Topo: Woody Creek
Public access through private land

Watson Divide is passenger-car-accessible on county road #8. It divides the waters of Snowmass Creek to the west and the Roaring Fork River to the east.

Watson Divide Road is marked by a sign as a nonmaintained road: "Travel at your own risk, 4WD required during snow and wet periods." It is, however, a good gravel-based road that is a little narrow in a few spots. This pass road parallels CO82 and makes a good backroad trip into some pretty country that the state highway bypasses.

From the top, the views to the west of the twin peaks on Mount

Sopris are outstanding. Other Snowmass Wilderness Area peaks are visible. A house (what a view!) is on the ridge north of the pass and communications equipment is in view on the peaks north of that house.

WAUNITA PASS

Elevation: 10,260 feet
Location: T50N R4E, Map 5
County: Gunnison
Topo: Pitkin
National forest: Gunnison

Waunita Pass is passenger-car-accessible on forest route #763. It divides the waters of Quartz Creek to the north and Hot Springs Creek to the south. The pass is above the scenic resort area of Waunita Hot Springs.

Early travel across the pass shortened the distance between mining districts. Then, after the railroad reached Pitkin, the road over the pass was kept up to provide freight service into the silver mines on Tomichi Creek.

In the 1880s, Waunita Hot Springs was a favorite tourist spot. Visitors would take the train to Pitkin (via the Alpine Tunnel under Altman Pass) and then take a stage to Waunita Hot Springs. Gold was discovered at the pass in the late 1890s, and a mining town (named Bowerman in honor of the miner J. C. Bowerman) sprang up. It lasted only a few years. Today's tourists use the pass road as a backcountry diversion.

The top is heavily tree-covered with no views, but it is marked. The pass is a mile and a half west of Little Baldy Mountain.

WEBSTER PASS

Elevation: 12,096 feet
Location: T6S R76W, Map 6
County: Park/Summit
Topo: Montezuma
National forest: Arapaho/Pike
On the Continental Divide
Other names: Handcart,
    Montezuma

Webster Pass is 4WD-accessible via forest routes #121 on the south side (in Pike National Forest) and #285 on the north side (in Arapaho National Forest). It divides the waters of the Snake River to the north and Handcart Gulch to the south.

The alternate name of Montezuma Pass is what David Moffat called the crossing when he was considering it as a potential railroad route. He surveyed it in the early 1890s.

A small mining community named Montezuma existed on the north side of the pass. Today, Montezuma is a small community with a pleasant inn.

The pass is named for the Webster brothers, who developed a wagon road in 1878 over this old Indian crossing between the Snake River Valley and the South Platte River Valley. The area had been explored by prospectors in the 1860s, when a couple of Norwegians brought their handcart loaded with supplies up the valley and found "color" in the streams. The Webster brothers' wagon road, called Post Road #40, was heavily used for freighting the ores to smelters and for stage lines— as many as three routes per day over the pass. Residents of Montezuma, the little town of Webster, and other parts of the Hall Valley on the south side used the road to go back and forth for social events.

The pass is sometimes mistakenly called Handcart Pass, but the real Handcart Pass is on the same Continental Divide ridge and about one and a half miles south of Webster. To confuse the issue, Webster Pass is at the head of Handcart Gulch, while Handcart Pass is at the head of another gulch off Hall Valley. And both crossings were called Handcart way back, when no wagon road had been built over either pass. When the Webster brothers built the road over this crossing, their name was assigned to it and remains.

Webster Pass provided a shortcut into the mining communities around Peru Creek from the South Platte supply towns. It quickly became the favorite route of miners, trappers, and settlers going west. Father Dyer, the itinerant parson, used the pass to carry the mail and to go between his preaching engagements on either side of the Continental Divide.

The route over the pass was not used after mining activity in this area declined. It was reopened in 1971 through the combined efforts of forest service personnel and 4WD clubs.

Part of the upper reaches of the road across the talus-covered slopes on the south side can be seen from the east side of Kenosha Pass. Look across to the north for the bright red rocky slopes and the cut for 4WDs across the rocks. In a couple of places there are stretches of road where there is no room for passing another vehicle, so make sure no one else is on that stretch before starting out.

The north side is open, above timberline, and has great views into the Saints John area. On weekends in the summer, Webster Pass is a favorite drive of 4WD enthusiasts from the Front Range cities. Some drivers like to take an alternate crossing by going east and then north, up and over Red Cone Mountain, then descending back to the Webster Pass road at the top of the pass. The Red Cone route was the crossing for Webster Pass until the road across the talus slopes was reopened in 1971.

The $40,000 stolen by the Confederate Reynolds Gang is supposed to be buried somewhere in this region. Some wreckage from a 1930s airplane crash can still be found along the ridge west of Webster Pass. Handcart Peak is on the west side of the pass and Red Cone Peak is on the east.

WEMINUCHE PASS

Elevation: 10,622 feet
Location: T40N R4W, Map 8
County: Hinsdale
Topo: Weminuche Pass
National forest: Rio Grande/
    San Juan
On the Continental Divide

Weminuche Pass is accessible by foot on forest service trail #523 in the Weminuche Wilderness Area. It divides the waters of Weminuche Creek to the north and the Los Piños River to the south.

Weminuche is often mispronounced with an extra syllable on the end; it should be pronounced Wim-a-newch. The pass is named after a Ute tribe.

This old buffalo route and Ute trail is now a pack and foot trail through some pretty country. James Pattie, in 1827, crossed the pass and wrote about it in his journal. He saw Utes camped close to where Bayfield is today and noted the height of the snowdrifts atop the pass. Franklin Rhoda's group of the Hayden survey party camped here in late 1874. By October of that year the snow was already "two to three feet deep." He thought the pass would be a pleasant and easy crossing in summer months.

In 1900, consideration was given to building a standard gauge line across "Wimmenuche" pass. The pass is now crossed by a couple of water ditches (Raber Lohr and Fuchs) that carry water to the Rio Grande Reservoir.

The Continental Divide Trail (although it's not currently well marked) uses the pass, which is marked by a large meadow. It is difficult to determine the true pass top. The trail is on higher ground to the west of the pass, which bypasses the marshy area lower down. Recent trail work has been done here.

This is a low crossing below timberline; the peaks on either side of the pass are less than 13,000 feet in elevation. An easy four-mile hike southwest from the Rio Grande Reservoir dam leads to the pass with only a twelve-hundred-foot elevation gain.

WEST GAP

Elevation: 7,670 feet
Location: T34N R10W, Map 7
County: La Plata
Topo: Basin Mountain
On the Southern Ute Indian
    Reservation

There is no public access to this pass. It divides the waters of Basin Creek to the north and Indian Creek to the south.

The pass is on the west side of a cone-shaped peak and is visible from the Wildcat Canyon road (county road #141), but access to the gap is blocked by private land holdings.

West Gap is on a rolling grassy hillside with some pines on the north side. The pass is not named in the BLM maps book. It is named on the topo map.

WEST MAROON PASS

Elevation: 12,500 feet
Location: T12S R86W, Map 5
County: Gunnison/Pitkin
Topo: Maroon Bells
National forest: White River

West Maroon Pass is accessible by foot on forest service trail #1970 in the Maroon Bells–Snowmass Wilderness Area. It divides the waters of the East Fork of the Crystal River to the west and West Maroon Creek to the east.

The pass is named for the deep purple-red color, said to look "maroon," of the rocks.

This crossing was used by prospectors in the 1880s to go between the Lead King mining basin and the upper Crested Butte region.

The trail is now used by some for winter ski-touring. The southern approach is a shorter hike than the northern; each approach provides a beautiful excursion into the southern end of the Maroon Bells–Snowmass Wilderness Area.

WESTON PASS

Elevation: 11,921 feet
Location: T10S R79W, Map 6
County: Lake/Park
Topo: Mount Sherman
National forest: Pike/San Isabel

Weston Pass is passenger-car-accessible in good weather via county roads #7 on the west side and #22 on the east side. It divides the waters of Big Union Creek to the west and the South Fork of the South Platte River to the east.

The pass is named for either Algernon or Philo Weston. Algernon established the Weston ranch on the west side of the pass and raised beef cattle to supply meat to the mining towns. He was also an attorney and had a law practice in Lake County. Philo had a wayside house on the east side of the pass and later moved to Granite.

The route over Weston Pass was developed over an old Indian trail. It is a lower, although longer, way between the South Park mining region around Fairplay and the area around what is now Leadville.

A wagon road was built over the pass in the 1860s. At that time, the route was called The Ute Trail. The stage-service town of Weston grew on the east side of the pass, where the railroad reached. There, travelers met and rested in order to tackle the hard crossing. Mail was carried over the pass once each week beginning in 1861.

This first road was operated by the Central Overland California and Pikes Peak Express Company. In 1862 the Tarryall and Arkansas River Wagon Road Company built its own trail between Fairplay and the California Gulch. A third line, the Park Range Road Company, started another route and ran it for about three years in the late 1870s. There was enough business, until the railroads came, to keep all three road companies busy. The Wall and Witter Stage Company kept four hundred horses, eleven freight wagons, and seven stage coaches in use at its peak.

With the twin threats of the railroad reaching Leadville and the road over Mosquito Pass being upgraded, the town of Weston crumbled and the pass traffic fell off considerably. Some local use was still made of the road, which had been the most heavily traveled route into the upper Arkansas River Valley for almost twenty years.

Hayden's survey party thoroughly explored this region in 1873. They noted the good wagon road with easy access on each side. Father Dyer crossed the pass, often at night, delivering mail and his word of God to the mining communities. He was caught in a severe blizzard at the pass late in 1861 and almost lost his life.

Silver mines at the pass continue to be worked off and on, but the main use of the pass top in more recent times has been for animal grazing. One mystery remains about the pass: A rich mine is said to exist on the pass, and a hermit-miner once brought rich ores out, then disappeared. No one has been able to find his workings.

In the 1950s, both surrounding counties upgraded their sections of the pass road, and it has been in good shape since. The top is open and above timberline but gives no spectacular views. Better views are on the west side. Near the top but on the east side is an old cabin with a mine beside it.

WET CANYON PASS

Elevation: 8,651 feet
Location: T32S R68W, Map 9
County: Las Animas
Topo: Herlick Canyon
Public access through private land

Wet Canyon Pass is passenger-car-accessible on county road #42.0. It divides the waters of Jarosa Canyon to the north and Wet Canyon to the south.

Look for the good views of the Spanish Peaks (to the north) from the top. The saddle has some pines but is mostly open, and cattle are grazed here. An old snow fence remains up all year in most snowy years.

The road over the pass is Wet Canyon Road. The southern access is a better road than is the northern access, but each will take passenger cars in good weather. The pass is not named on forest service or topo maps.

WETTERHORN PASS

Elevation: 12,540 feet
Location: T44N R6W, Map 8
County: Ouray
Topo: Wetterhorn Peak
National forest: Uncompahgre

Wetterhorn Pass is accessible by foot on forest service trail #226, at the southern edge of the Big Blue Wilderness Area. It divides the waters of Cow Creek to the north and Mary Alice Creek to the south.

The pass is about one and a half miles south of Wetterhorn Peak. The Wetterhorn Basin Trail, also called the West Fork Trail, crosses the pass. Wetterhorn Pass is not named on forest service or topo maps. James Grafton Rogers located and named it in his listing of Colorado's geographic features.

WHISKEY PASS

Elevation: 12,540 feet
Location: T33S R70W, Map 9
County: Costilla
Topo: El Valle Creek
On private land
Other name: Whiskey Creek

Unfortunately, there is no access to this old pass that almost became a highway. The pass divides the waters of El Valle Creek to the west and Whiskey Creek to the east.

Colonel William Payton claims his father, Kit Payton, and Kit Carson blazed the original trail over this pass in 1865. They were building a shortcut route to haul military goods between Trinidad and Fort Garland. The pass and the creek the pass heads were named by the senior Payton and Carson when, in August of 1865, an ox wagon overturned on the pass, spilling all but two barrels

of whiskey en route to the soldiers at Fort Garland. The two barrels were hidden on the pass, and the two Kits returned two years later for them.

A Works Progress Administration (WPA) state highway was planned to cross this pass in the late 1930s, with a tunnel under the very top. It was begun but never completed. A 1933 state road map shows CO152 traveling all the way over the pass; a 1934 state road map shows the road making it to the top from the west side, with a proposed route down the east side. A 1936 map shows roads on each side with a 4WD section over the very top. But a 1941 map shows a trail on the east side and a road on the west side. Sometime after that, all map references to any type of road over the pass ceased.

Today, all access to the pass is on private land. Interest in the pass continues to crop up from time to time by southern central Colorado residents who would like another crossing into the San Luis Valley south of La Veta Pass. As late as 1964, residents around Trinidad asked for a route over this pass.

Whiskey Pass is located between Scotch Mountain and Beaubien Peak. Recent landowners prosecute trespassers. The pass is not named on current forest service maps, but it is named on the topo map.

WILDHORSE CREEK PASS

Elevation: 12,680 feet
Location: T43N R7W, Map 8

County: Ouray
Topo: Wetterhorn Peak
National forest: Uncompahgre

Wildhorse Creek Pass is accessible by foot on forest service trail #215 in the Big Blue Wilderness Area. It divides the waters of Difficulty Creek to the west and Wildhorse Creek to the east.

The pass is on the Horsethief Trail, a very old Ute crossing that is believed to be the earliest trail into the San Juans and considered one of the most scenic trails in America. The pass is located one and a half miles west of Wildhorse Peak, and it overlooks the wide meadow expanse called American Flats.

Wildhorse Creek Pass is not named on forest service or topo maps. James Grafton Rogers located and named it in his listing of Colorado's geographic features.

WILKERSON PASS

Elevation: 9,502 feet
Location: T12S R73W, Map 6
County: Park
Topo: Glentivar
National forest: Pike
Other names: Badger, Pulver
 Divide, Puma

Wilkerson Pass is passenger-car-accessible on US24. It divides the waters of the South Platte River to the west and Link Creek to the east.

The USGS Board on Geographic Names officially named the pass in 1963. The name honors the Wilkerson family, headed by John W. Wilkerson, who had a ranch at the west end of the pass in the mid-1800s; he decided to call the pass after himself. Some reports suggest that Mrs. Wilkerson and a son kept a roadhouse for travelers.

The pass crosses the Puma Hills, leading to one alternate name for the pass. A 1912 Colorado highway map calls the pass Pulver Divide. Hayden's survey party and a 1919 Pike National Forest map named the pass "Puma." The alternate name of Badger comes from the proximity to Badger Mountain.

The Utes crossed this divide repeatedly on their way between South Park and the Great Spirit at Manitou, at the hot springs. The route was heavily used during the mining boom days, but freighting continued after the mining novelty had worn off, in order to keep the supply towns farther west in goods.

In late 1853 and early 1854 a devastating three-week forest fire burned up the east side of the pass.

H.A.W. Tabor and his equally famous first wife, Augusta, made their way west to the mining fields around Leadville over Wilkerson Pass.

One mine, right at the top of the pass, did contain zinc and lead. It was worked only about one season. The stage station on the pass was called Illinois House; it was still in existence in 1898.

When the Colorado Midland abandoned its rail line through

Elevenmile Canyon in 1921, the highway was rerouted over that road grade. Then in 1931, when Elevenmile Reservoir was built, the old route over Wilkerson Pass was reopened.

One of the nicest rest stops in the Colorado mountains is found at the forest service visitor center atop the pass, which is staffed by volunteers and open only during the summer months.

WILLIAMS PASS

Elevation: 11,766 feet
Location: T51N R5E, Map 5
County: Chaffee/Gunnison
Topo: Cumberland Pass
National forest: Gunnison/
San Isabel
On the Continental Divide

Williams Pass is accessible by foot via forest service trail #539 on the west side, and an unnumbered forest service trail on the east side. It divides the waters of Tunnel Gulch to the north and Middle Quartz Creek to the south.

A couple of stories exist about the naming of the pass. The first is that it is named for Robert Williams, an assistant engineer for the Denver and South Park Railroad who developed the wagon road here. The second is that it is named for an eccentric trapper who crossed over this route in the 1840s.

The pass road was developed to provide access to both ends of the

Alpine Tunnel while it was under construction. In November 1880, stages ran over the pass via the Alpine and South Park Toll Road between Gunnison and the eastern divide supply towns.

Today, a 4WD road takes travelers near the top on the east side (about one-quarter mile), but the very top is a foot trail only, because of marshy road conditions. It is a flat swampy top. The west side access to the pass takes off close to the rock palisades built along the railroad grade. In recent years a 4WD club has been working with the forest service to upgrade the road, drying up boggy spots and defining the roadway. Keeping the road open when this work is completed will depend upon 4WD users not abusing the off-road property.

The pass is on the Continental Divide Trail and a half-mile east of Mount Poor.

WILLOW PASS

Elevation: 12,580 feet
Location: T11S R86W, Map 5
County: Pitkin
Topo: Maroon Bells
National forest: White River

Willow Pass is accessible by foot on forest service trail #1978 in the Maroon Bells–Snowmass Wilderness Area. It divides the waters of Willow Creek to the north and Minnehaha Gulch to the south.

Rugged peaks provide a striking vista from the Willow Pass summit.

The pass name comes from the willows that grow along the creeks leading to the pass.

The pass itself is a narrow crossing with a "top of the world" feeling. The top is above a steep area and open-sloped meadows. The view to the north overlooks Willow Lake and a secluded mountain valley. A descent to the north takes you to Snowmass Creek and the little community of Snowmass. The hike is worth it, just to say you've been to Minnehaha Gulch. (Say that gulch name fast, with lots of lilt to it.)

This area is hiked heavily in the summer months, which, in this part of the world, is only about six weeks long. Beautiful views abound. Watch for young bighorn sheep on the rocky slopes.

The pass is on the southeast flank of Buckskin Peak.

WILLOW CREEK PASS

Elevation: 9,621 feet
Location: T4N R78W, Map 3
County: Grand/Jackson
Topo: Radial Mountain
National forest: Arapaho/Routt
On the Continental Divide
Other names: Good, Middle Park

Willow Creek Pass is accessible by passenger car on CO125. It divides the waters of Snyder Creek to the north and Willow Creek to the south.

The pass is named for one of the

streams it heads. In the 1873 Hayden survey report, the pass is called Good Pass, but no reason is given for this name. The name "Middle Park" is because the pass crosses from Middle Park into North Park.

An old Indian trail, the road over Willow Creek Pass was not developed until fairly late by other pass-development standards—1902. Early in the twentieth century, a stage line went over the pass and connected the towns of Granby and Walden. This line was owned by H. Loucks of Walden. Consideration was given about this same time to running a rail line over the pass.

A Willow Lodge roadhouse was opened at the pass top. It was owned and operated by Dave and Mrs. A. L. Gresham, who provided meal service for stage travelers.

The pass is a gentle tree-lined approach from either side and is well marked. Parkview Mountain can be glimpsed from the road at times. Moose have been transplanted here; keep an eye out for them in the willows. The pass is on the Continental Divide Trail.

WILLOW DIVIDE

Elevation: 10,300 feet
Location: T40N R12W, Map 7
County: Dolores
Topo: Groundhog Mountain
National forest: San Juan

Willow Divide Pass is 4WD-accessible on forest route #727. It divides the waters of Fish Creek to the west and West Dolores River to the east.

Willow Divide is a long ridge; the road travels from one end of the ridge to the other. The views of peaks in the Lizard Head Wilderness Area are beautiful, especially at the north end of the ridge.

The divide is in prime hunting country. Numerous dips in the road make 4WD desirable for traveling to this remote spot. There are some shelf roads and narrow places on the north side of the divide. Watch for elk that summer near here.

This backcountry route provides a good way to get away from people: It's a long way to or from anywhere.

WIND RIVER PASS

Elevation: 9,130 feet
Location: T4N R73W, Map 3
County: Larimer
Topo: Longs Peak
Public access through private land

Wind River Pass is accessible by passenger car on CO7. It divides the waters of Fish Creek to the north and Tahosa Creek to the south.

Utes crossed back and forth to the Tahosa Valley through this pass. They have a story about the naming of the valley: A log fell on a woman and killed her at the pass, so they named the valley with their word for the event, which, transliterated into English, is "tahosa."

The pass top is not marked, but it is wide, with a notch through a rocky area.

THE WINDOW

Elevation: 12,857 feet
Location: T39N R5W, Map 8
County: Hinsdale
Topo: Rio Grande Pyramid
National forest: Rio Grande/
  San Juan
On the Continental Divide

The Window is accessible by foot, but no established trail currently goes over the pass, which is in the Weminuche Wilderness Area. It divides the waters of East Ute Creek to the west and the Rincon La Vaca to the east.

This opening in the rock ridge was named by eighteenth-century Spanish gold-seekers. The passage is steep and narrow, with many switchbacks. It is sometimes also called The Devil's Gateway. It is located south of another outstanding geological feature, the Rio Grande Pyramid.

WINDY GAP

Elevation: 10,995 feet
Location: T37N R11W, Map 7
County: Montezuma
Topo: La Plata
National forest: San Juan

Windy Gap is accessible by 4WD via forest routes #561 and #565. It divides the waters of Bear Creek to the north and Crystal Creek to the south.

The top is tree-covered, with no really good views, but it is marked with a small sign. Many logging roads in the area can confuse travelers. This is a backcountry road that does not see much public use.

WINDY PASS

Elevation: 9,940 feet
Location: T37N R1E, Map 8
County: Mineral
Topo: Wolf Creek Pass
National forest: San Juan

Windy Pass is accessible by foot on forest service trail #566. It divides the waters of Wolf Creek to the west and the East Fork of the San Juan River to the east.

The trailhead is marked on the west side of Wolf Creek Pass on US160. The trail is narrow but designed for horses. It has lots of undergrowth foliage that holds moisture, therefore the route tends to be boggy.

A part of US160 is visible from the pass, and there are good views of the San Juan mountain range. This is a beautiful pass between two mountains that is defined by a typical saddle-shaped top.

The top is partially tree-covered and provides good views. And it is not always windy!

Windy Pass is located on a ridge spur that runs west off the Continental Divide. It is on the Windy Pass

Trail. About a half-mile east off the top of the pass, Treasure Mountain Trail (#565) takes off northeast.

WINDY PASS

Elevation: 9,100 feet
Location: T36N R2W, Map 8
County: Archuleta
Topo: Pagosa Peak
National forest: San Juan

Windy Pass is accessible by foot on forest service trail #569. It divides the waters of Martinez Creek to the west and Cade Creek to the east.

The view from the top to the northeast is toward the Continental Divide. Cade Mountain is to the south. The pass is easily reached by a two-mile hike northeast from forest route #634.

WINDY POINT PASS

Elevation: 9,450 feet
Location: T48N R15W, Map 4
County: Montrose
Topo: Windy Point
National forest: Uncompahgre

Windy Point Pass is passenger-car-accessible via forest route #600. It divides the waters of Campbell Creek to the west and the North Fork of Tabeguache Creek to the east.

The pass is just southeast of a butte also called Windy Point. It is not named on forest service or topo maps.

WINDY SADDLE

Elevation: 6,900 feet
Location: T4S R70W, Map 6
County: Jefferson
Topo: Morrison
Public access through private land

Windy Saddle is passenger-car-accessible on county road #68, also known as the Lariat Loop Road. It divides the waters of Clear Creek to the west and Chimney Gulch to the east.

The saddle is on the Lookout Mountain road, above Golden. A parking area at the saddle provides access to Mount Zion, where the big "M" for Colorado School of Mines is located.

The pass is aptly named: It is windy most of the time. Many bikers and joggers use the trails that head off this trailhead. On some Jefferson County hiking guides, this location is called Windy Gap. Windy Saddle is named on the topo map.

WIXSON DIVIDE

Elevation: 9,379 feet
Location: T22S R70W, Map 9
County: Custer
Topo: Deer Peak
Public access through private land

Wixson Divide is passenger-car-accessible on CO165. It divides the waters of the South Fork of Hardscrabble Creek to the north and South Hardscrabble Creek to the south.

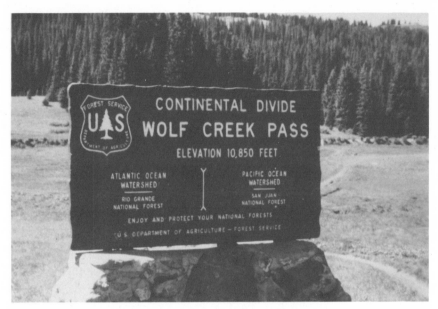

The backbone of the North American continent is formed by the Continental Divide. Passes in Colorado along the Divide are often marked with signs, such as this one at Wolf Creek Pass, indicating that waters flowing east from the Divide go to the Atlantic Ocean and waters flowing west enter the Pacific Ocean.

The pass is named for nearby Wixson Mountain.

A paved road goes over this minor crossing. It is a wide, open area – not a severe pass – on the Greenhorn Highway. The top is not marked and is located a mile and a half northeast of Wixson Mountain.

WOLF CREEK PASS

Elevation: 10,850 feet
Location: T37N R2E, Map 8
County: Mineral
Topo: Wolf Creek Pass
National forest: Rio Grande/
    San Juan

On the Continental Divide

Wolf Creek Pass is passenger-car-accessible on US160. It divides the waters of Wolf Creek to the west and Pass Creek to the east.

Some people believe the pass is named for one of the creeks it heads, which in turn is named for the wolves that used to live here. Others believe the pass is named for a William Wolf, who was an early settler.

The heaviest snowfall in the state is traditionally in this area. In 1978 to 1979, over 835 inches fell at the pass. That is seventy feet of snow!

Many Indian tribes used the pass as a regular route from their southwestern lower-elevation camps into the San Juan mountains. In the 1820s, trappers began using the pass, then prospectors trailed over it. In 1873, the Hayden survey party mapped the region. A wagon road was never built over the pass, even though an army lieutenant was assigned to design a road in the 1870s. He gave up because the area was just too rough; the state highway department tackled the job in the 1910s. This was the first auto road to cross the Continental Divide; it was called The Spanish Trail. The modern highway was opened in 1916. By 1939 the road was kept open year-round, and in 1950 it was widened and paved.

A ski resort near the pass top brings visitors to the area. A snowshed opened in 1965 on the east side of the pass and provides protection from the Alberta Slide, where some of the heavy winter flakes are known to pile up and slide down.

The pass is tree-covered. Views come as a descent is made on one side or the other. The pass has a song named after it, made popular by the former mayor of Ouray, C. W. McCall. It tells about the truck driver who lost his load of chickens after a brake failure and wound up in front of a store in downtown Pagosa Springs.   □

Y

YELLOW JACKET PASS

Elevation: 7,428 feet
Location: T4N R85W, Map 2
County: Routt
Topo: Blacktail Mountain
Public access through private land

Yellow Jacket Pass is passenger-car-accessible on county road #14. It divides the waters of Dry Creek to the north and the Yampa River to the south.

The pass is named for the wasps in the area – or for a burglar who hid out in the pass, wearing a yellow jacket!

Yellow Jacket Pass can be reached via a paved road through sagebrush country. The nondescript top is not marked, but it is open with some views in each direction.

The road over the pass runs parallel to CO131 and is located just north of the Stagecoach State Recreation Area. The pass is the saddle between Thorpe Mountain and Blacktail Mountain.

YELLOW JACKET PASS

Elevation: 7,538 feet
Location: T2N R92W, Map 2
County: Rio Blanco
Topo: Thornburgh
Public access through private land

Yellow Jacket Pass is passenger-car-accessible on county road #15. It divides the waters of Milk Creek to the north and Coal Creek to the south.

The pass is on the old government road that ran between Meeker, Colorado, and Rawlins, Wyoming. It follows an old Ute trail through the rolling countryside.   •

In 1861, Colorado Territory authorized a charter for the Colorado and Pacific Wagon, Telegraph and Railroad Company to cross the pass; in March of 1864, the Denver and Pacific Wagon Road Company was also issued a charter. This second route was called the Berthoud Salt Lake Wagon Road. Hayden's survey party mapped the area in 1873. Maps of 1876 show and name the pass; it was already well used by then.

The top is open and a mile and a half southeast of Yellow Jacket Peak.

Just to the north of the pass is a historical site marker commemorating where, in August 1879, Utes killed fifteen and injured thirty-five members of a U.S. cavalry force led by Major Thomas Thornburg. Thornburg was attempting to reach the Indian agent Nathan Meeker, who

was under attack in another assault by Utes at the White River Indian Agency near Meeker.

YELLOW JACKET PASS

Elevation: 7,780 feet
Location: T35N R5W, Map 8
County: Archuleta
Topo: Baldy Mountain
National forest: San Juan

Yellow Jacket Pass is passenger-car-accessible on US160. It divides the waters of Hayden Creek to the west and Squaw Creek to the east.

The pass is an unmarked crossing between Piedra and Bayfield. Approaches to the pass are gentle and the top is wide and open. A ranch near the top on the east side (named Yellow Jacket Ranch) is the only landmark.

YULE PASS

Elevation: 11,700 feet
Location: T12S R87W, Map 5
County: Gunnison
Topo: Snowmass Mountain
National forest: Gunnison/
**   White River**

Yule Pass can be reached by foot on forest service trail #2083 on the west side, and an unnumbered forest service trail on the east side, on the eastern edge of the Raggeds Wilderness Area. It divides the waters of Yule Creek to the west and the Slate River to the east.

The pass is named for George Yule, who found marble deposits here. Early prospectors used the route to cross between Crested Butte and the Crystal River Valley.

In 1880, then again in 1908, a railroad was planned to move the marble from quarries near the pass to Crested Butte, where it could be freighted east. Track was laid and some marble was moved. Many important buildings, both government and private, used marble from the quarries near Yule Pass.

A wagon road was built in 1905. The pass lies on the south shoulder of Treasury Mountain and north of Purple Mountain.

YURI PASS

Elevation: 5,900 feet
Location: T1S R70W, Map 3
County: Boulder
Topo: Eldorado Springs
Public access through private land

Yuri Pass is accessible by foot. It divides the waters of two different sections of Bear Canyon.

The pass is on a short unmarked trail in the Boulder Mountain Trails system. It is located between Yuri Point, to the south, and the National Center for Atmospheric Research Mesa, to the north.

The pass is not named on forest service or topo maps. It is identified in Boulder-area hiking guides.

YVONNE PASS

Elevation: 12,740 feet
Location: T43N R6W, Map 8
County: Hinsdale/San Juan
Topo: Handies Peak
Public access through private land
Other name: South Engineer

Yvonne Pass is accessible by 4WD via a particularly difficult route from the east side of the pass. It divides the waters of Mineral Creek to the west and Schafer Gulch to the east.

It is located on the south and opposite side of Engineer Mountain from Engineer Pass, which explains the alternate name that is sometimes used: South Engineer.

This pass has little history of its own; it served as just another of the many routes through this mining country. The meadow below the pass, on the east, was often used for grazing livestock and for camping. The newer crossing over what is now Engineer Pass has been kept up, and the older crossing, now Yvonne Pass, has deteriorated, because no need to keep up two crossings existed. Mining communities used whatever route was open; this route, located on the south side of a major peak, was open earlier each year than the more northerly crossing.

The pass is north of Siegal Mountain. Current forest service and topo maps do not name the pass. A 1902 map shows the road over the pass.

Z

ZAPATA PASS

Elevation: 11,860 feet
Location: T28S R73W, Map 9
County: Alamosa/Huerfano
Topo: Mosca Pass
National forest: Rio Grande/
**   San Isabel**

Zapata Pass may be reached on foot on forest service trail #853. It divides the waters of North Zapata Creek to the west and the Huerfano River to the east.

The pass is two miles north of California Peak. From the pass, look west into the San Luis Valley and east to the headwaters of the Huerfano River.

Zapata Pass is not named on current forest service or topo maps. James Grafton Rogers located and named this pass in his listing of Colorado's geographic features.   □

APPENDIX 1:
Maps

KEY TO MAPS

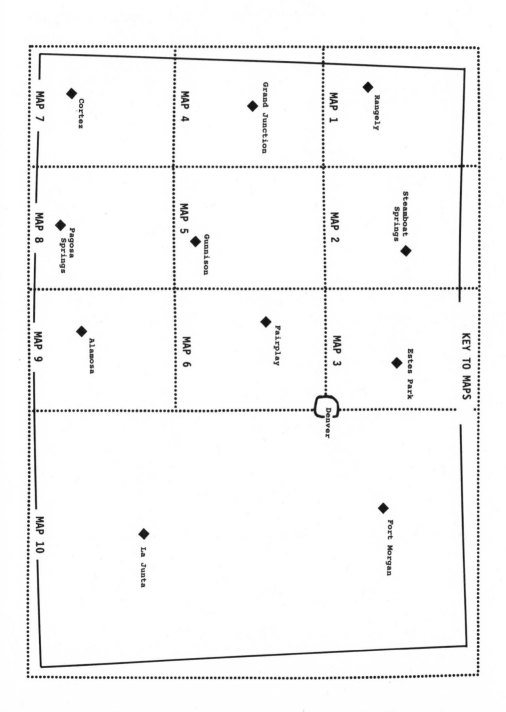

KEY TO MAPS

MAP 1 — Rangely

MAP 2 — Steamboat Springs

MAP 3 — Estes Park, Denver

MAP 4 — Grand Junction

MAP 5 — Gunnison

MAP 6 — Fairplay

MAP 7 — Cortez

MAP 8 — Pagosa Springs

MAP 9 — Alamosa

MAP 10 — La Junta, Fort Morgan

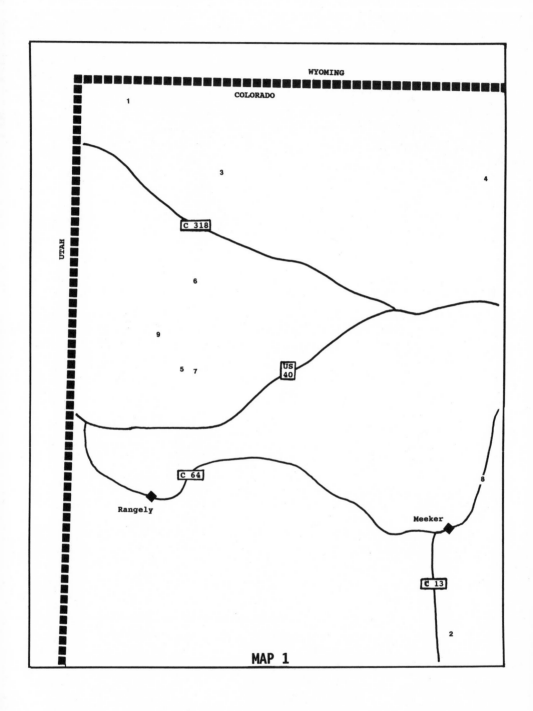

WYOMING

COLORADO

UTAH

1

3

4

C 318

6

9

5 7

US 40

C 64

Rangely

Meeker

8

C 13

2

MAP 1

Map 1 Legend   261

MAP 1

1 Antone Gap
2 Dick
3 G Gap
4 Great Divide
5 Gunsight Gap
6 Iron Mine Gap
7 Jack Springs
8 Ninemile Gap
9 Serviceberry Gap

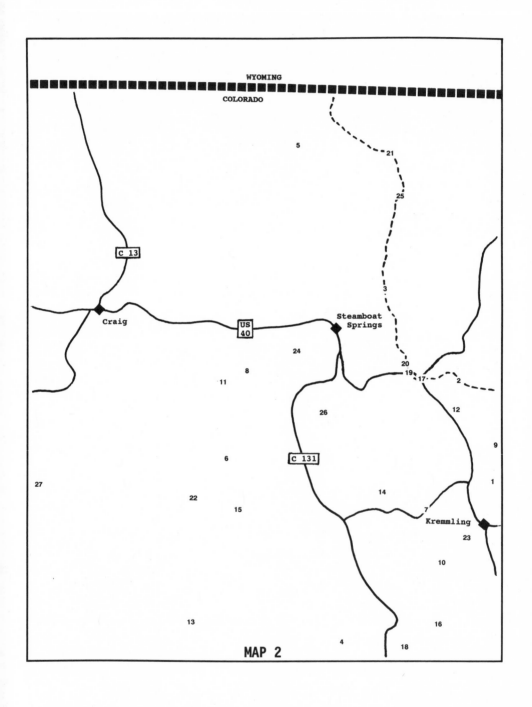

MAP 2

Map 2 Legend   263

MAP 2

The dashed line on this map marks the passage of the Continental Divide through the area.

1	Antelope	15	Mandall
2	Arapaho	16	McCord
3	Buffalo	17	Muddy
4	Coberly Gap	18	Muddy
5	Columbine	19	Rabbit Ears
6	Dunckley	20	Rabbit Ears-Old
7	Gore	21	Red Dirt
8	Grassy Gap	22	Ripple Creek
9	Gunsight	23	Trough Road
10	Hartman Divide	24	Twentymile Divide
11	Height Divide	25	Ute
12	Indian	26	Yellow Jacket
13	Indian Camp	27	Yellow Jacket
14	Lynx		

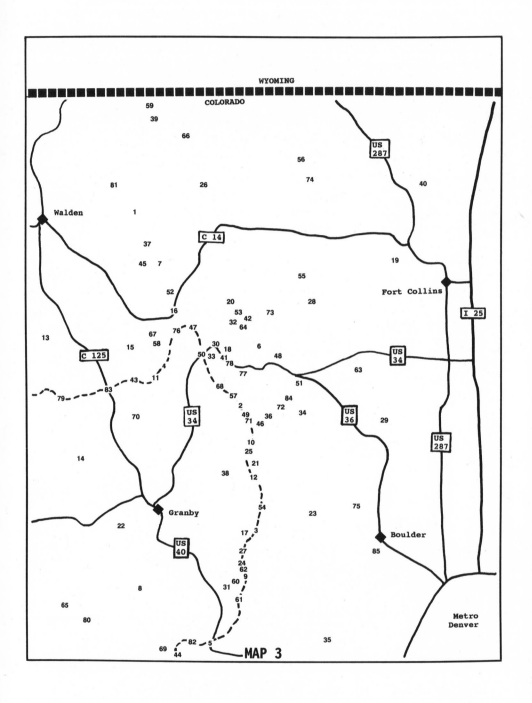

MAP 3

Map 3 Legend 265

MAP 3

The dashed line on this map marks the passage of the Continental Divide through the area.

1 Allen Creek	30 Fall River	59 Red Mountain
2 Andrews	31 Fawn Creek	60 Rifle Sight Notch
3 Arapaho	32 Flint	61 Rogers
4 Baker	33 Forest Canyon	62 Rollins
5 Berthoud	34 Game	63 Saddle Notch
6 Big Horn	35 Golden Gate	64 The Saddle
7 Blue Lake	36 Granite	65 The Saddle
8 Bottle	37 Grassy	66 Sand Creek
9 Boulder	38 Hell Creek Divide	67 Seven Utes
10 Boulder-Grand	39 Horse Ranch	68 Sprague
11 Bowen	40 Horsethief	69 St. Louis
12 Buchanan	41 Iceberg	70 Stillwater
13 Buffalo	42 Icefield	71 Stone Man
14 Cabin Creek Divide	43 Illinois	72 Storm
15 Calamity	44 Jones	73 Stormy Peaks
16 Cameron	45 Kelly	74 Stuart Hole
17 Caribou	46 Keyhole	75 Sunshine Saddle
18 Chapin	47 La Poudre	76 Thunder
19 Cloudy	48 MacGregor	77 Timberline
20 Comanche Peak	49 McHenrys Notch	78 Toll
21 Cony	50 Milner	79 Troublesome
22 Cottonwood	51 Moccasin Saddle	80 Ute
23 Culbertson	52 Montgomery	81 Ute
24 Dart	53 Mummy	82 Vasquez
25 Dead Man's	54 Pawnee	83 Willow Creek
26 Deadman Hill	55 Pennock	84 Wind River
27 Devil's Thumb	56 Prairie Divide	85 Yuri
28 Donner	57 Ptarmigan	
29 Dowe	58 Red Dog	

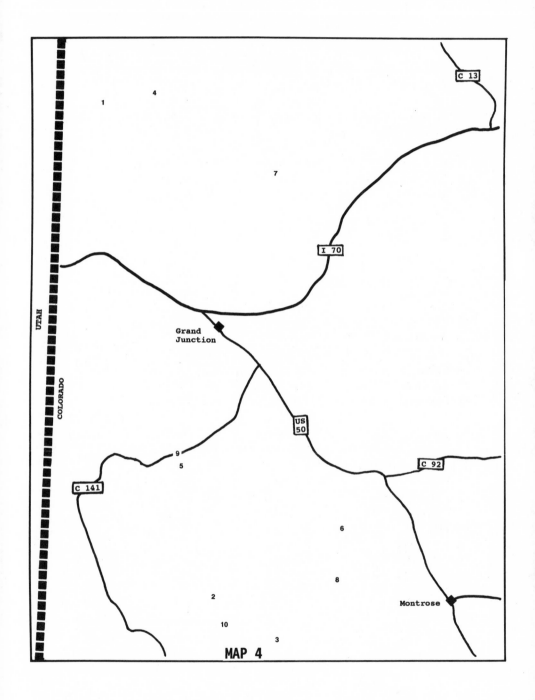

MAP 4

Map 4 Legend   267

MAP 4

The dashed line on this map marks the passage of the Continental Divide through the area.

 1 Baxter
 2 Chillycoat
 3 Columbine
 4 Douglas
 5 Gill Creek Divide
 6 The Narrows
 7 The Saddle
 8 The Saddle
 9 Unaweep Divide
10 Windy Point

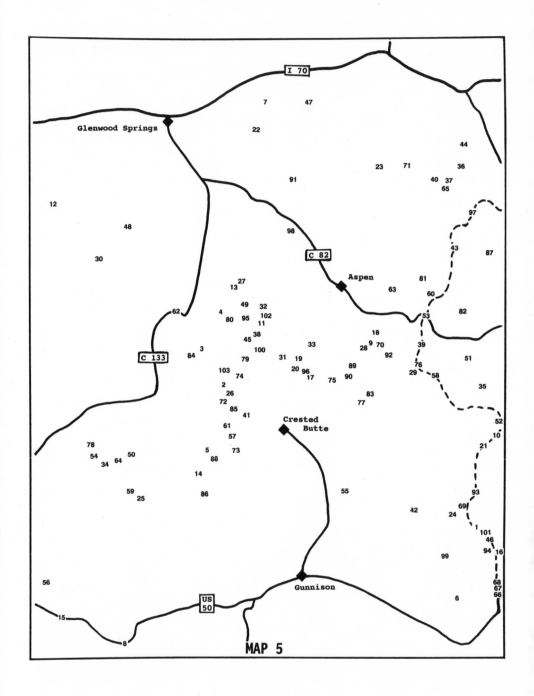

MAP 5

Map 5 Legend   269

MAP 5

The dashed line on this map marks the passage of the Continental Divide through the area.

1 Altman	35 Elkhead	69 Napoleon
2 Angel	36 Fall Creek	70 New York
3 Anthracite	37 Fancy	71 The Notch
4 Avalanche	38 Frigid Air	72 Oh-be-joyful
5 Beckwith	39 Graham	73 Ohio
6 Black Sage	40 Grassy	74 Paradise Divide
7 Blue Hill	41 Gunsight	75 Pearl
8 Blue Mesa Summit	42 Gunsight	76 Red Mountain
9 Bowman	43 Hagerman	77 Reno Divide
10 Browns	44 Halfmoon	78 Sams Divide
11 Buckskin	45 Halsey	79 Schofield
12 Buzzard	46 Hancock	80 Silver Creek
13 Capitol	47 Hardscrabble	81 South Fork
14 Castle	Saddle	82 South Halfmoon
15 Cerro Summit	48 Haystack Gate	83 Spring Creek
16 Chalk Creek	49 Heckert	84 Spud
17 Coffeepot	50 Hoodoo Gap	85 Star
18 Columbia	51 Hope	86 Storm
19 Conundrum	52 Horn Fork	87 Sugarloaf
20 Copper	53 Independence	88 Swampy
21 Cottonwood	54 Inter Ocean	89 Taylor
22 Cottonwood	55 Jack's Cabin	90 Taylor
23 Crooked Creek	56 Jones Summit	91 Taylor Creek
24 Cumberland	57 Kebler	92 Tellurium
25 Curecanti	58 Lake	93 Tincup
26 Daisy	59 Lone Pine	94 Tomichi
27 Daly	60 Lost Man	95 Trail Rider
28 Difficult	61 Marcellina	96 Triangle
29 Dorchester	62 McClure	97 Utah
30 East Hightower	63 Midway	98 Watson Divide
Mountain	64 Minnesota	99 Waunita
31 East Maroon	65 Missouri	100 West Maroon
32 East Snowmass	66 Monarch	101 Williams
33 Electric	67 Monarch, Old	102 Willow
34 Elk Basin	68 Monarch, Original	103 Yule

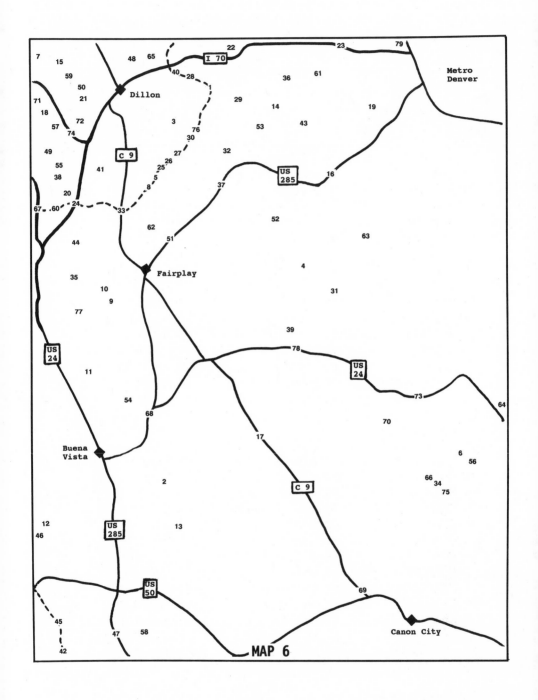

7   15   48 65   22   23   79
        59   40 28   Metro
          50   21   1   36   61   Denver
71   18   29
        57 72   14   19
    74   53   43
49   [C 9]
    55   41   32
    38   US 285   16
    20   24   37
67 .60   33   62   52
        44   51   63
    35   4
        10   31
        9
    77   39
                78
US   US 24
24   11   73   64
        54   70
        68
Buena   17   6
Vista   56
    2   C 9   66 34
                        75
12   US   13
46   285
        US
        50   69
45   Canon City
    47 58   MAP 6
42

Map 6 Legend   271

MAP 6

The dashed line on this map marks the passage of the Continental Divide through the area.

1 Argentine	28 Grizzly	55 Searle
2 Bassam Park	29 Guanella	56 Seven Lakes
3 Bear	30 Handcart	57 Shrine
4 Bison	31 Hankins	58 Simmons
5 Black Powder	32 Hepburn's	59 Snow Lake
6 Blizzard	33 Hoosier	60 Snowcat
7 Booth Creek	34 Hoosier	61 Squaw
8 Boreas	35 Horseshoe	62 Squirrel
9 Breakneck	36 Juniper	63 Stoney
10 Browns	37 Kenosha	64 Strieby
11 Buffalo Meadows	38 Kokomo	65 Stroup
12 Calico	39 La Salle	66 Tenderfoot
13 Cameron Mountain	40 Loveland	67 Tennessee
14 Campion	41 Lucas	68 Trout Creek
15 Central	42 Marshall	69 Twelvemile
16 Crow Hill	43 Meridian	70 Twin Creek
17 Currant Creek	44 Mosquito	71 Two Elk
18 Daggett	45 Pahlone	72 Uneva
19 Dix Saddle	46 Pomeroy	73 Ute
20 Eagle River	47 Poncha	74 Vail
21 Eccles	48 Ptarmigan	75 Victor
22 Empire	49 Ptarmigan	76 Webster
23 Floyd Hill	50 Red Buffalo	77 Weston
24 Fremont	51 Red Hill	78 Wilkerson
25 French	52 Rock Creek Trail	79 Windy Saddle
26 Georgia	53 Rosalie	
27 Glacier	54 Salt Creek	

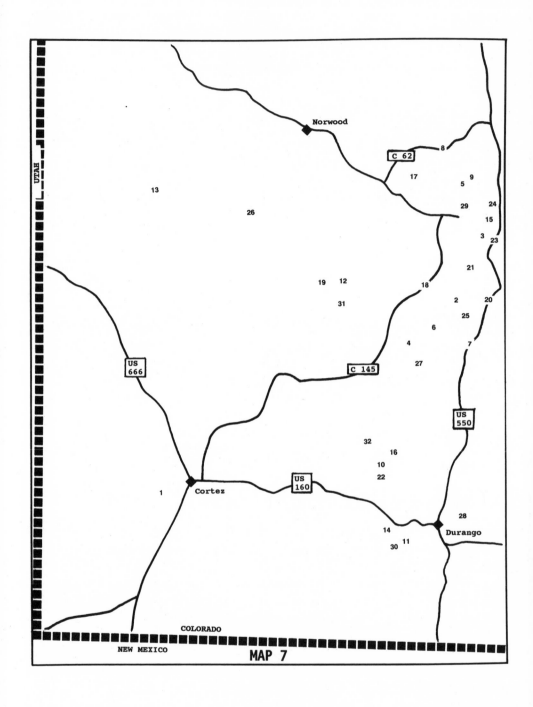

UTAH

Norwood

C 62   8

17   9
              5

13   29   24
                                15
      26   3
                             23

                        21
  19   12   18
                              20
  31   2
                     25
                           6
                  4
                      7
  US   C 145   27
  666

                        US
                        550

                  32
                      16
                  10
                  22

  1   Cortez   US   28
                160   Durango

                  14
                  30 11

COLORADO

NEW MEXICO
MAP 7

Map 7 Legend   273

MAP 7

1 Aztec Divide
2 Bear Creek
3 Black Bear
4 Blackhawk
5 Blue Lakes
6 Bolam
7 Coal Bank
8 Dallas Divide
9 Dyke Col
10 Eagle
11 East Gap
12 East Lone Cone
13 Gypsum Gap
14 Hesperus
15 Imogene
16 Kennebec

17 Last Dollar
18 Lizard Head
19 Lone Cone
20 Molas
21 Ophir
22 Puzzle
23 Red Mountain
24 Richmond
25 Rolling Mountain
26 Sandy's Fort
27 Scotch Creek
28 Ute
29 Virginius
30 West Gap
31 Willow Divide
32 Windy Gap

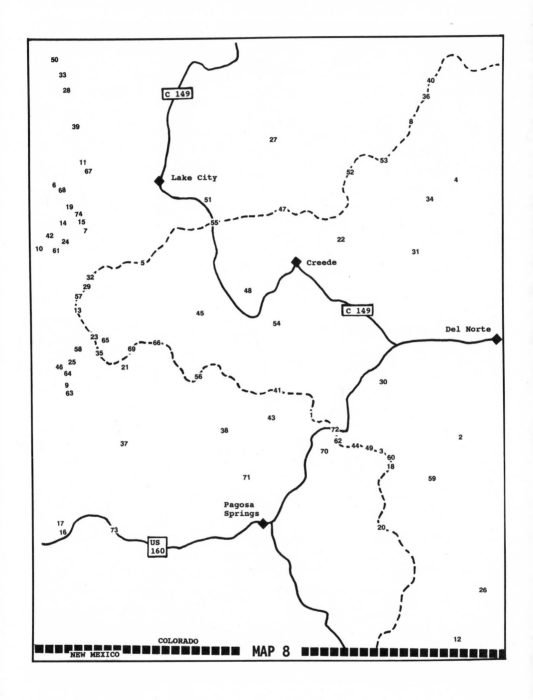

Map 8 Legend   **275**

MAP 8

The dashed line on this map marks the passage of the Continental Divide through the area.

1 Big Horn	26 La Manga	51 Slumgullion
2 Blowout	27 Los Piños	52 Sony
3 Bonito	28 Lou Creek	53 South
4 Carnero	29 Maggie Gulch	54 Spar Hill
5 Carson	30 Meadow	55 Spring Creek
6 Cascade	31 Milk Cow	56 Squaw
7 Cinnamon	32 Minnie Gulch	57 Stony
8 Cochetopa	33 Monument	58 Storm King-Silex
9 Columbine	34 Moon	59 Stunner
10 Corkscrew	35 Nebo	60 Summit
11 Coxcomb	36 North	61 Sunnyside Saddle
12 Cumbres	37 The Notch	62 Treasure
13 Cunningham	38 The Notch	63 Trimble
14 Denver	39 Owl Creek	64 Twin Thumbs
15 Denver	40 Peon	65 Ute
16 Dunham Gap	41 Piedra	66 Weminuche
17 Durant Gap	42 Poughkeepsie	67 Wetterhorn
18 Elwood	43 Puerto Blanca	68 Wildhorse Creek
19 Engineer	44 Railroad	69 The Window
20 Gunsight	45 River Hill	70 Windy
21 Gunsight	46 Ruby	71 Windy
22 Halfmoon	47 San Luis	72 Wolf Creek
23 Hunchback	48 Santa Maria	73 Yellow Jacket
24 Hurricane	49 Silver	74 Yvonne
25 Knife Point	50 Slagle	

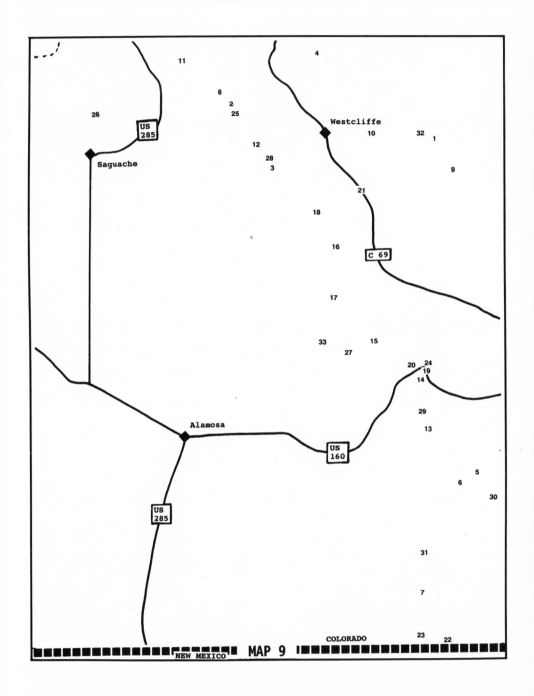

11

4

8
2
25

26

US
285

Westcliffe

10   32   1

Saguache   12
                   28
                   3   9

21

18

16   C 69

17

33   15
27

20 24
   19
14

29

13

Alamosa

US
160

5
6
30

US
285

31

7

23
22

COLORADO

MAP 9

NEW MEXICO

Map 9 Legend   277

MAP 9

The dashed line on this map marks the passage of the Continental Divide through the area.

 1 Bigelow Divide
 2 Brush Creek
 3 Comanche
 4 Copper Gulch
   Divide
 5 Cordova
 6 Cucharas
 7 Culebra
 8 Garner
 9 Greenhill Divide
10 Hardscrabble
11 Hayden
12 Hermit
13 Indian Creek
14 La Veta
15 Manzanares
16 Medano

17 Mosca
18 Music
19 North La Veta
20 Pass Creek
21 Promontory Divide
22 San Francisco
23 San Francisco
24 Sangre de Cristo
25 Three Step
26 Ute
27 Ute Creek
28 Venable
29 Veta
30 Wet Canyon
31 Whiskey
32 Wixson Divide
33 Zapata

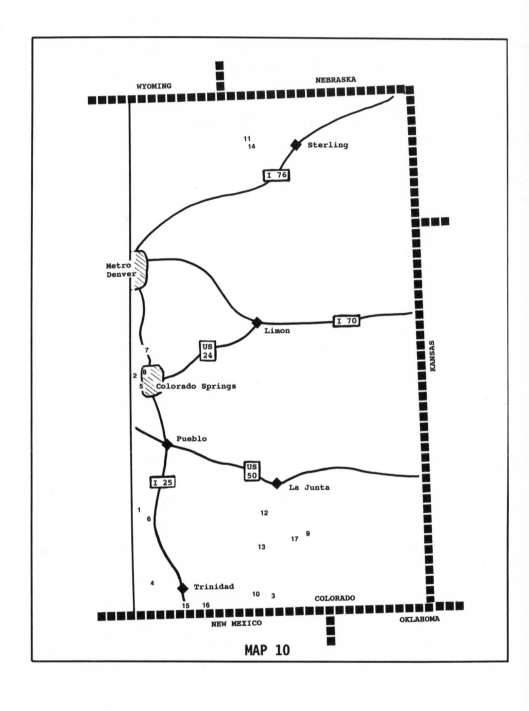

MAP 10

Map 10 Legend   279

MAP 10

1 Bells Gap
2 Buckhorn
3 Cotton Gap
4 Cottontail
5 Daniels
6 Long Saddle
7 Monument Hill
8 Mountain Shadows
9 Muddy Gap
10 The Narrows
11 North Pawnee
12 Packers Gap
13 Pamena Gap
14 Pawnee
15 Raton
16 San Francisco
17 Wagon Gap

APPENDIX 2:
Continental Divide Passes

Many of Colorado's passes are not on the Continental Divide; these ninety-two passes are. From (generally) north to south, the names of the Continental Divide passes are:

Red Dirt	Vasquez	Monarch
Ute	Jones	Pahlone
Buffalo	Loveland	Marshall
Rabbit Ears-Old	Grizzly	Peon
Rabbit Ears	Argentine	North
Muddy	Webster	Cochetopa
Arapaho	Handcart	South
Troublesome	Glacier	Sony
Willow Creek	Georgia	San Luis
Illinois	French	Spring Creek
Bowen	Black Powder	Carson
Baker	Boreas	Minnie Gulch
Thunder	Hoosier	Maggie Gulch
La Poudre	Fremont	Stony
Milner	Snowcat	Cunningham
Sprague	Tennessee	Hunchback
Ptarmigan	Utah	Nebo
Andrews	Hagerman	The Window
McHenrys Notch	Independence	Weminuche
Stone Man	Graham	Squaw
Boulder-Grand	Red Mountain	Piedra
Dead Man's	Lake	Big Horn
Buchanan	Horn Fork	Wolf Creek
Pawnee	Browns	Treasure
Arapaho	Cottonwood	Railroad
Devil's Thumb	Tincup	Silver
Dart	Altman	Bonito
Rollins	Williams	Summit
Boulder	Hancock	Elwood
Rogers	Monarch, Original	Gunsight
Berthoud	Monarch, Old	

THE CONTINENTAL DIVIDE THROUGH COLORADO

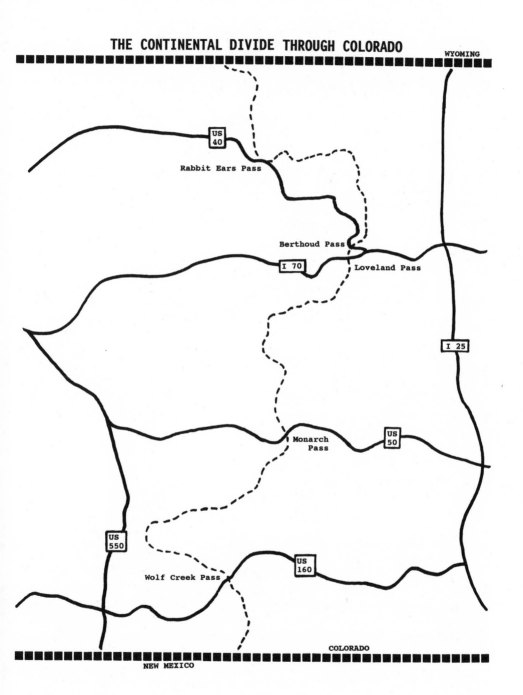

APPENDIX 3:
Colorado Gaps

These are gaps, not passes, identified on various maps of the state. Some are geographic features where a river runs through a ridge, such as Cat Creek Gap. Others are wind gaps, where only an opening in a ridge occurs with no river, trail, or road through it, such as Dipper Gap.

Name: **ANTELOPE GAP**
Location: T5N R48W
County: Yuma
Topo: Clarkville
On private land

Name: **CAT CREEK GAP**
Location: T33N R3W
County: Archuleta
Topo: Pagosa Junction
On Southern Ute Indian Reservation

Name: **DEVILS GAP**
Location: T18S R71W
County: Fremont
Topo: Royal Gorge
Public access through private land

Name: **DIPPER GAP**
Location: T11N R55W
County: Logan
Topo: Dipper Spring
Public access through private land

Name: **THE GAP**
Location: T30S R69W
County: Huerfano
Topo: Cuchara
Public access through private land

Name: **THE GATE**
Location: T46N R3W
County: Gunnison
Topo: Alpine Plateau
Public access through private land

Name: **THE GATE**
Location: T48N R7E
County: Saguache
Topo: Bonanza
National forest: San Isabel

Name: **GATES OF LODORE**
Location: T9N R102W
County: Moffat
Topo: Canyon of Lodore North
In Dinosaur National Monument

Name: **HARVEY GAP**
Location: T5S R92W
County: Garfield
Topo: Silt
Public access through private land

Name: **HELL GATE**
Location: T9S R82W
County: Pitkin
Topo: Nast
National forest: White River

Name: **HELLGATE**
Location: T42N R6E
County: Saguache
Topo: Twin Mountains SE
Public access through private land

Name: **HELLS GATE**
Location: T3S R86W
County: Eagle
Topo: Dotsero
Public access through private land

Name: **LIMESTONE GAP**
Location: T11N R101W
County: Moffat
Topo: Big Joe Basin
On private land

Name: **MARTIN GAP**
Location: T3N R101W
County: Moffat
Topo: Lazy Y Point
On private land

Name: **MORMON GAP**
Location: T2N R104W
County: Rio Blanco
Topo: Dinosaur
On BLM land

Name: **THE NARROWS**
Location: T11S R90W
County: Gunnison
Topo: Bull Mountain
National forest: Gunnison

Name: **RIFLE GAP**
Location: T5S R92W
County: Garfield
Topo: Rifle
Public access through private land

Name: **STONEWALL GAP**
Location: T33S R68W
County: Las Animas
Topo: Stonewall
Public access through private land

Name: **TEMPLETON GAP**
Location: T13S R66W
County: El Paso
Topo: Falcon NW
Public access through private land

Name: **WAGON WHEEL GAP**
Location: T41N R1E
County: Mineral
Topo: Wagon Wheel Gap
National forest: Rio Grande

Name: **WINDY GAP**
Location: T2N R77W
County: Grand
Topo: Hot Sulphur Springs
On land owned by the state of
  Colorado

Name: **WINDY GAP**
Location: T1N R73W
County: Boulder
Topo: Nederland
National forest: Roosevelt, and
  private land

GLOSSARY

Bushwhacking. To hike without benefit of a trail. Comes from "whacking through the bush."

Cirque. A deep basin on a mountainside that is shaped like a half-bowl.

Coney or Cony. A pika. Has a high-pitched squeak and likes to live in rocky areas with a sunny exposure.

Cribbing. A supporting structure under a roadway, rail bed, or trail. May be made of stones or wood.

Divide. A dividing ridge between drainage areas, also known as a "watershed divide."

Flank. The shoulder of a mountain.

Front Range. The easternmost edge of the Rocky Mountains in Colorado.

Gap. A cut through mountains or rock. A gap may allow a wind, water, or road passage.

Hayden Survey Party. In the mid-1870s, Ferdinand V. Hayden led a large party of explorers into the mountains of Colorado Territory to map the area and make geographic identifications. Many of the geological features in the Rocky Mountains were named by the party. The party broke up into smaller groups to explore more area.

Massif. A principal mountain mass, usually standing apart from others.

Mountain park. A high valley rimmed by mountains. In Colorado, the major mountain parks are: the North, Middle, South, Collegiate, and San Luis parks.

Mountain range. A series of mountains running in a line.

Pass. A low place in a mountain range where stream waters divide.

Petroglyph. A carving into rock.

Pictograph. An ancient or prehistoric painting on a rock wall.

Ptarmigan. A northern mountain bird that changes plumage color for camouflage: white in winter, mottled brown in summer.

Rock-scrambling. To walk across rocks without benefit of a trail; may also be called "rock-crawling." Rock-crawling may also refer to the slow movement of a 4WD vehicle across sloping rocks.

Saddle. The narrow ridge that connects two higher points in a mountain range.

Scree. An accumulation of loose stones lying on a slope; also called "talus."

Snub. To move wagons or goods over obstructions or steep areas by tying ropes to trees and the wagons, blocking the wagon wheels, and pulling or lowering the wagons or goods over the obstruction.

Talus. Large rock debris on a slope or base of a mountain; sometimes referred to as "scree."

Topo. Topographic map issued by the United States Geological Survey showing geographic positions and elevations by the use of contour lines.

Vole. A small rodent common in the Rocky Mountains.

Watershed divide. See **Divide.**

Wye. A Y-shaped set of tracks used by rail engines to turn around; used in place of a roundhouse.

SOURCES AND SUGGESTED READING

The following is a listing of the major works used by the authors in compiling the material presented in this book, as well as other suggested reading.

BOOKS

Akers, Carl. *Carl Akers' Colorado.* Fort Collins, Colo.: Old Army Press, 1975. A general overview of Colorado's history in a very easy to understand format by one of Denver's leading newscasters of the 1970s and early 1980s.

Arps, Louisa Ward, and Elinor Eppich Kingery. *High Country Names.* Boulder, Colo.: Johnson Publishing Company, 1972. A listing of places and how they were named in the Rocky Mountain National Park area.

Backus, Harriet Fish. *Tomboy Bride.* Boulder, Colo.: Pruett Publishing Company, 1969. A memoir of living above Telluride near Imogene Pass.

Bartlett, Richard A. *Great Surveys of the American West.* Norman: University of Oklahoma Press,1962. Tells about the various survey expeditions into Colorado of the nineteenth century.

Bean, Luther E. *Land of the Blue Sky People.* Monte Vista, Colo.: Monte Vista Journal, 1962. An account of the San Luis Valley and the passes that rim it.

Benham, Jack L. *Silverton & Neighboring Ghost Towns.* Ouray, Colo.: Bear Creek Publishing Company, 1977. This little book is a history of the area.

Bird, Isabella L. *A Lady's Life in the Rocky Mountains.* Norman: University of Oklahoma Press, 1960. An account of an 1873 tour into the Colorado mountains.

Black, Robert C., III. *Island in the Rockies: The History of Grand County to 1950.* Boulder, Colo.: Pruett Publishing Company, 1969. A reprise of the development of Grand County.

———. *Railroad Pathfinder: The Life and Times of Edward L. Berthoud.* Evergreen, Colo.: Cordillera Press, 1989. An account of how Berthoud scouted many locations throughout the Rocky Mountains as potential railroad routes.

Boddie, Caryn, and Peter Boddie. *The Hiker's Guide to Colorado.* Billings, Mont.: Falcon Press Publishing Company, Inc., 1984. A hiking guide to various areas of Colorado.

Borneman, Walter R. *Marshall Pass.* Colorado Springs: Century One Press, 1980. A book about Marshall Pass that is mostly related to its railroad history.

Brandon, William. *The Men and the Mountain: Fremont's Fourth Expedition.* New York: William Morrow and Company, 1955. A good and complete review of the expedition.

Brown, Robert L. *Colorado Ghost Towns—Past and Present.* Caldwell, Id.: The Caxton Printers, Limited, 1972. A good review of many of our state's old towns.

———. *Colorado on Foot.* Caldwell, Id.: The Caxton Printers, Limited, 1991. A day-trip hiking guide to various locales throughout Colorado.

———. *Holy Cross—The Mountain and the City.* Caldwell, Id.: The Caxton Printers, Limited, 1970. All about the old area around Holy Cross, made famous by Jackson's photograph of the Mount of the Holy Cross.

———. *Jeep Trails to Colorado Ghost Towns.* Caldwell, Id.: The Caxton Printers, Limited, 1981. How to find ghost towns that are accessible by 4WD vehicles.

———. *Uphill Both Ways: Hiking Colorado's High Country.* Caldwell, Id.: The Caxton Printers, Limited, 1972. A good hiking book.

Brunk, Ivan W. *Shattered Dreams on Pikes Peak.* Colorado Springs: Pulpit Rock Press,1989. A quick history of the communities on the slopes of Pikes Peak.

Carter, Carrol Joe. *Pike in Colorado.* Fort Collins, Colo.: The Old Army Press, 1978. A study of Pike's exploration trip into the state, including information about the old stockade.

Colorado State Board of Immigration. *Year Book of the State of Colorado 1931.* Denver: Bradford-Robinson Printing Company, 1931. General information about the state, including a listing of passes and a good map showing many of them.

Conard, Howard Lewis. *"Uncle Dick" Wootton.* Chicago: W. E. Dibble and Company, 1890. One of Colorado's colorful people, Wootton helped establish Raton Pass.

Cornell, Virginia. *Doc Susie.* New York: Ballantine Books, 1991. This is the story of the first female doctor in Grand County.

Crofutt, George A. *Grip-Sack Guide of Colorado.* Omaha: The Overland Publishing Company, 1885. Thumbnail sketches of towns and other geographic locations in the state.

Crossen, Forest. *The Switzerland Trail of America.* Boulder, Colo.: Pruett Publishing Company, 1962. The mountains west of Boulder were mining empires, and railroads rushed to serve the area. A fine history of the era.

Dannen, Kent, and Donna Dannen. *Rocky Mountain National Park Hiking Trails.* Charlotte, N.C.: Fast and McMillan Publishers, Inc., 1985. A good hiking guide for Rocky Mountain National Park passes.

Dawson, Louis W., II. *Colorado High Routes.* Seattle: The Mountaineers, 1986. A guide to cross-country ski trips in the Vail and Aspen areas.

Dyer, John Lewis. *Tracking the Snow-shoe Itinerant.* Breckenridge, Colo.: Snowstorm Publications, 1981. Father Dyer's own story about early days in Colorado.

Edmondson, Clyde, and Chloe Edmondson. *Mountain Passes.* Boulder, Colo.: Estey Printing Company, 1963. A listing of various passes.

Eichler, George R. *Colorado Place Names: Communities, Counties, Peaks, Passes.* Boulder, Colo.: Johnson Publishing Company, 1977. The stories of how many of the places in Colorado were named.

Fielder, John, and M. John Fayhee. *Along the Colorado Trail.* Englewood, Colo.: Westcliffe Publishers, Inc., 1992. A newer book about the Colorado Trail, with pictures.

Flynn, Norma L. *History of the Famous Mosquito Pass.* Privately published, 1959. A short but good history of this historic pass.

Fossett, Frank. *Colorado—Tourists Guide to the Rocky Mountains.* New York: C. G. Crawford, 1880. This old book is an interesting review of the Colorado mountain areas.

Gebhardt, Dennis. *A Backpacking Guide to the Weminuche Wilderness.* Durango, Colo.: Basin Reproduction and Printing Company, 1986. A good review of the trails and passes in this wilderness area.

Gilliland, Mary Ellen. *The Summit Hiker.* Silverthorne, Colo.: Alpenrose Press, 1983. A good resource about Summit County.

———. *The Vail Hiker.* Silverthorne, Colo.: Alpenrose Press, 1988. Includes information about passes around Vail.

Gregory, Lee. *Colorado Scenic Guide Northern Region.* Boulder, Colo.: Johnson Publishing Company, 1983. A hiking guide that includes some of the passes in the northern part of the state.

———. *Colorado Scenic Guide Southern Region.* Boulder, Colo.: Johnson Publishing Company, 1984. A hiking guide that includes some of the passes in the southern part of the state.

Gregory, Marvin, and P. David Smith. *Mountain Mysteries.* Ouray, Colo.: Wayfinder Press, 1984. A good overview of the northern San Juan mountain area.

Hagen, Mary. *Hiking Trails of Northern Colorado.* Boulder, Colo.: Pruett Publishing Company, 1979. How to find some of the passes.

Harrison, Louise C. *Empire and the Berthoud Pass.* Denver: Big Mountain Press, 1964. All about the development of the pass that is the gateway to the ski slopes.

Helmers, Dow. *Historic Alpine Tunnel.* Denver: Sage Publishing, 1971. All about the tunnel under Altman Pass.

Ingersoll, Ernest. *The Crest of the Continent.* Chicago: R. R. Donnelley and Sons, Publishers, 1887. An old but good review of the mountains of Colorado.

Jacobs, Randy. *The Colorado Trail.* N.p.: FreeSolo Press, 1988. A mile-by-mile guide to the trail, written just after it opened.

Keener, James, and Christine Bebee. *Unaweep to Uravan.* Grand Junction, Colo.: Grand River Publishing, 1988. The history of this little-known and rarely visited part of Colorado.

Kindquist, Cathy E. *Stony Pass.* Silverton, Colo.: San Juan County Book Company, 1987. A master's thesis about the history and geographic importance of Stony and Cunningham passes.

Koch, Don. *The Colorado Pass Book.* Boulder, Colo.: Pruett Publishing Company, 1980. A listing of several 4WD passes in Colorado and how to find them.

Lecompte, Janet. *Pueblo, Hardscrabble, Greenhorn—The Upper Arkansas 1832–1856.* Norman: University of Oklahoma Press, 1978. A very good history of the area around Pueblo, Colorado.

Lowe, Don, and Roberta Lowe. *80 Northern Colorado Hiking Trails.* Beaverton, Ore.: The Touchstone Press, 1973. A hiking guide to some passes in the northern part of the state.

————. *50 West Central Colorado Hiking Trails.* Beaverton, Ore.: The Touchstone Press, 1976. How to get to, and what to expect from, several other passes.

McTighe, James. *Roadside History of Colorado.* Boulder, Colo.: Johnson Books, 1984. Every mountain driver should keep a copy of this book in his or her vehicle.

McConnell, Virginia. *Ute Pass—Route of the Blue Sky People.* Denver: Sage Books, 1963. A good review of early usage of the Ute Pass just west of Colorado Springs.

Marshall, Muriel. *Uncompahgre.* Caldwell, Id.: The Caxton Printers, Limited, 1981. A good guide to the Uncompahgre Plateau area.

Martin, Bob. *Hiking the Highest Passes.* Boulder, Colo.: Pruett Publishing Company, 1984. Martin hikes to fifty of the high passes in our state.

————. *Hiking Trails of Central Colorado.* Boulder, Colo.: Pruett Publishing Company, 1983. How to find and use trails in the West Elk, Sawatch, and Elk mountain ranges.

Muller, Dave. *Colorado Mountain Hikes for Everyone.* Denver: Quality Press, 1987. Includes information on how to reach 105 different summits.

Murray, John A. *The Indian Peaks Wilderness Area.* Boulder, Colo.: Pruett

Publishing Company, 1985. Hikes into several passes of the wilderness area are covered.

Ohlrich, Warren. *Aspen-Snowmass Trails: A Hiking Trail Guide.* Aspen, Colo.: Who Press, 1988. Tells how to reach several passes in the high country near Aspen.

Ormes, Robert M. *Colorado Skylines. Books I, II, III, and IV.* Colorado Springs, Colo.: Privately published, 1967 to 1974. These show-and-tell books display Ormes's sketches of the skylines and name each peak (and some passes in between) on the sketch.

————. *Guide to the Colorado Mountains.* Colorado Springs, Colo.: Privately published, 1952. Eight editions of this excellent mountain guide have been published, the last couple in conjunction with the Colorado Mountain Club. This hiking guide covers the whole state, describes how to access the various mountains, and lists trouble spots to watch out for.

Osterwald, Doris B. *Rocky Mountain Splendor—A Mile by Mile Guide for Rocky Mountain National Park.* Lakewood, Colo.: Western Guideways, Limited, 1989. The best reference book to have in your hands while traversing Trail Ridge Road through the park.

Pearson, Mark, and John Fielder. *Colorado BLM Wildlands.* Englewood, Colo.: Westcliffe Publishers, Inc., 1992. Covers areas proposed for wilderness status.

Peknik, George. *The Cheyenne Cañon and Broadmoor Guidebook & Almanac.* Colorado Springs: Hoopoe Publications, 1992. A hiking guide, and more, to the popular areas west and southwest of Colorado Springs.

Perry, Eleanor. *Taylor Park—Colorado's Shangri-La.* Buena Vista, Colo.: Privately published, 1989. A lot of history of Taylor Park.

Pettit, Jan. *Ute Pass.* Colorado Springs: Little London Press, 1979. Jan calls this a quick history, but it is very complete.

Pixler, Paul. *Hiking Trails of Southwestern Colorado.* Boulder, Colo.: Pruett Publishing Company, 1981. Hiking in the San Juan and Uncompahgre national forests.

Rhoda, Franklin. *Summits to Reach.* Boulder, Colo.: Pruett Publishing Company, 1984. An annotated edition of Rhoda's *Report on the Typography of the San Juan Country,* edited by Mike Foster. This is the description of how Rhoda found the area in 1874.

Rinehart, Frederick R., ed. *Chronicles of Colorado.* Boulder, Colo.: Roberts Rinehart, Inc. Publishers, 1984. A selection of essays about Colorado.

Ringrose, Linda Wells, and Linda McComb Rathbun. *Foothills to Mount Evans.* Evergreen, Colo.: The Wordsmiths, 1980. Trails to hike in the area.

Rosson, Douglas R. *Colorado's Browns Pass Trail Guide.* Arlington, Tex.: Wilderness America Adventures, 1983. All you ever wanted to know about Browns Pass on the Continental Divide.

Ruhoff, Ron. *Colorado's Continental Divide.* Evergreen, Colo.: Cordillera Press, Inc., 1989. Until the Continental Divide Trail is renovated, hikers need this guide.

Shaputis, June, and Suzanne Kelly. *A History of Chaffee County.* Buena Vista, Colo.: Buena Vista Heritage, 1982. A good history, in easy-to-read form, of the little-known but beautiful county in the upper Arkansas Valley.

Shoemaker, Len. *Roaring Fork Valley.* Denver: Sage Books, 1958. Written by the man who helped shape the history of this area.

Simmons, Virginia McConnell. *Bayou Salado.* Boulder, Colo.: Fred Pruett Books, 1992. A good history of South Park and the passes that rim the area where buffalo once roamed.

———. *The Upper Arkansas.* Boulder, Colo.: Pruett Publishing Company, 1990. This is the most complete modern work done on the headwaters of the Arkansas River.

Sprague, Marshall. *Newport in the Rockies.* Athens: Ohio University Press,1987. Everything about the beginnings of Colorado Springs, in one volume.

———. *The Great Gates: The Story of the Rocky Mountain Passes.* Boston: Little, Brown and Company, 1964. This is *the* book about how the mountain area along the Rockies from New Mexico into Canada was settled. It is easy to read, and even the most informed historian will find something new hidden in the pages of this book every time it is picked up.

Taylor, Bayard. *Colorado: A Summer Trip.* Niwot: University Press of Colorado, 1989. This eastern journalist was known as the "Great American Traveler." He visited Colorado in 1866 and wrote about it in this book.

Tighe, Ronald. *Journey to the Top of the Divide.* Denver: Golden Bell Press, 1979. One man's account of following the Continental Divide from its southern end into Canada, on horseback.

Upham, Charles Wentworth, ed. *Life, Explorations and Public Services of John Charles Fremont.* New Haven, Conn.: Ticknor & Fields, 1856. Fremont tells his own story in letters he sent home to his wife.

Wainwright, A., and Derry Brabbs. *Wainwright on the Lakeland Mountain Passes.* London: Michael Joseph, 1989. This wonderful book tells all about the passes in the lake country of England and helped the authors realize that people all over the world like passes.

Warren, Scott S. *Exploring Colorado's Wild Areas.* Seattle: The Mountaineers, 1992. A quick review of various hiking areas, arranged by sections of the state.

Wolf, James R. *Guide to the Continental Divide Trail,* vols. 4 and 5. Bethesda, Md.: Continental Divide Trail Society, 1982 and 1986. Volume 4 covers the northern part of Colorado and Volume 5 the southern part of the state. Good maps, trail mileage, and descriptions of flora accompany the general text.

Wolle, Muriel Sibell. *Stampede to Timberline*. Boulder, Colo.: University of Colorado, 1949. This extensive volume describes the author's personal experiences in and historic data concerning parts of the state.

Wood, Stanley. *Over the Range to the Golden Gate*. Chicago: R. R. Donnelley & Sons, Publishers, 1891. A tourist's guide to the western states from an 1890s point of view.

Works Progress Administration. *The WPA Guide to 1930s Colorado*. Topeka: University of Kansas Press, 1987. This older work has a new introduction written by Tom Noel of the history department, University of Colorado, Denver Center.

PERIODICALS AND OTHER

Brown, Ralph H. "Colorado Mountain Passes," *The Colorado Magazine* 6, no. 6 (1929). Brown was assistant professor of geography at the University of Colorado in Boulder when he compiled this listing of the 135 passes then known in the state, sectioned by the mountain range in which the passes were located.

Carhart, Arthur H. "Passes over the Blood of Christ," in *The 1957 Denver Westerners Brand Book*. Boulder, Colo.: Johnson Publishing Company, 1957. A review of the better-known passes in the Sangre de Cristo mountain range.

Gill, William H. "Mountain Passes of Colorado," compiled for the Map Information Office, *Federal Board of Surveys and Maps,* United States Geological Survey, 1940. This listing of 158 passes was the most complete in its time.

Gunnison, John W. *Reports of Explorations and Surveys to Ascertain the Most Practicable and Economical Route for a Railroad from the Mississippi River to the Pacific Ocean*. Report prepared for the 33rd Cong., 2d sess., 1855. A long and very detailed report written by Gunnison and his explorers of their trip through Colorado in 1853–1854.

Helmuth, Edward S. "Sangre de Cristo: Colorado's Forgotten Pass," *The Denver Westerners Roundup* (September-October 1991). This detailed study of the historic pass includes rare documentation by an 1870s traveler who sketched the stage station at the top of the pass.

Lecompte, Janet. "The Mountain Branch: Raton Pass and Sangre de Cristo Pass," *Essays and Monographs in Colorado History, Essays* 6 (1987). One of the Santa Fe Trail branches came over these routes.

Mathews, Ruth Estelle. "A Study of Colorado Place Names." Master's thesis, Stanford University, 1940. An unpublished thesis describing many locations in Colorado not found in other references.

Myers, Rex. "Rails to Taylor Park." *The Colorado Magazine* 45, no. 3 (1968). A good review of the rail lines that crossed the passes into the upper Taylor River valley.

Richmond, Patricia Joy. "Trail to Disaster." *Essays and Monographs in Colorado History, Monograph 4* (1989). The story of Fremont's Fourth Expedition, in 1848–1849.

Rogers, James Grafton. "Mountain Passes," in *Places in Colorado.* Unpublished notebooks of Colorado locations categorized by mountains, passes, streams, gulches, and so on, and written into notebooks, which now reside at the Colorado Historical Society in Denver. These listings were accumulated from map study, reading, and personal observations.

Ruffner, Lieutenant E. H. *Report of a Reconnaissance in the Ute Country, Made in the Year 1873.* Report prepared for the War Department, 1874. Lieutenant Ruffner and his exploration group studied various passes, particularly those rimming the San Luis Valley.

Shoemaker, Len. "The Wheeler Geologic Area and Passes of the Elk Mountain Range," in *The 1967 Denver Westerners Brand Book.* Boulder, Colo.: Johnson Publishing Company, 1968. A comprehensive review of the areas in which Shoemaker spent much of his professional life.

Sprague, Marshall. "First Cars over the Rockies." *Empire Magazine, Denver Post,* 16 August 1964. This amusing article tells how Colorado drivers propelled themselves and their weak-willed vehicles over the mountains early in the twentieth century.

MAPS

A Complete Set of BLM Land Ownership Maps. Sports Publishing, Inc., Cody, Wy., 1983. In this 144-page, 11-inch by 16.5-inch paperback volume, the entire state is covered in ninety-six area maps. The book also includes camping, hunting, fishing, and state recreation area data, as well as various other outdoor information items.

Colorado Atlas and Gazetteer. DeLorme Mapping, Freeport, Me., 1991. This 104-page, 11-inch by 15.5-inch paperback book covers the entire state with ninety-two area maps with topographical data on each. Various listings of state information are also included.

Forest Service Recreation Maps. U.S. Department of Agriculture, 1972 to the present. These maps of the national forests of Colorado provide detailed information about roads and trails within the national forests and adjacent areas.

Shaded Relief Mountain Road Maps. XYZ Map Company, Denver, Colo.,

1969–1970. These out-of-print maps provide some unique information about the central Colorado mountains area.

Topographic Maps. 7.5 Minute Series, U.S. Geological Survey, 1900 to the present. These maps contain a variety of data, of which the elevations were valuable to the authors. Newer topo maps take advantage of aerial photography, which has increased their usefulness.

Trails Illustrated Topo Maps. Trails Illustrated, Evergreen, Colo., 1989 to the present. These plastic-coated maps withstand the elements and also contain up-to-date road and trail type, placement, and access information.

INDEX

297

Continental Divide Trail, 13, 15, 20, 27, 43, 44, 46, 50, 57, 79, 86, 98, 100, 102, 103, 109, 110, 112, 114, 116, 120, 124, 125, 127, 133, 137, 141, 145, 146, 153, 156, 158, 162, 166, 167, 173, 174, 177, 186, 191, 197, 198, 202, 204, 205, 209, 212, 218, 220, 222, 223, 229, 237, 242, 247, 249

Conundrum Hot Spring, 222

Coon Hill, 211

Cooper, William, 88

Copper Basin, 54, 77, 165

Copper Canyon, 76

Copper Mountain Ski Area, 196, 228

Corona Trail, 66, 67, 68

Costilla, New Mexico, 190

Cottonwood Canyon, 156

Counties: Boulder, 10, 12, 13, 30, 35, 59, 66; Chaffee, 56, 57, 71, 102, 110, 127, 144, 224; Clear Creek, 94; Custer, 20, 34, 218; Delta, 117; El Paso, 232; Fremont, 105; Garfield, 116; Grand, 12, 32, 66, 68, 171, 182, 223; Gunnison, 56, 57, 71, 222; Jackson, 40, 113, 121; Jefferson, 251; Lake, 99, 111, 115, 224, 243; Larimer, 81, 112; Las Animas, 55; Pitkin, 71, 222; Rio Grande, 138; Routt, 37, 106, 133, 225; Saguache, 201; San Juan, 209; San Miguel, 114, 128, 129; Summit, 86; Teller, 109

Cow Canyon, 156

Coyote Basin Spring, 158

Cramer, Maurice Browning, 145

Creeks: Abrams, 104; Agate, 162; Agate–North Fork, 144; Ahogadero, 189; Alder, 128; Alkali, 38, 49; Allen, 7; Alpine Brook, 92; Andrews, 9; Antelope, 96, 170; Anthracite–West Fork, 14; Apishapa, 55; Arapaho, 10, 42; Archuleta, 49; Avalanche, 42; Avalanche–East Fork, 198; Badger, 116; Basin, 75, 242; Bear, 17, 36, 70, 80, 105, 106, 112, 199, 233, 234, 250; Beaver, 10, 53, 76, 129, 223; Beaver Brook, 84; Beaver Dam, 120; Beaver–East

Fork, 24; Bennett, 24; Big Atkinson, 47; Bigelow, 20; Big Horn, 45; Big Spring, 204; Big Union, 243; Billy, 200; Black Canyon, 20, 134; Black Gore, 226, 235; Blacktail, 90; Blue, 26; Boehmer, 24; Booth, 27; Boulder Brook, 92, 123; Bowman, 32, 70, 156; Box Prairie, 166; Browning, 142; Bruin, 32, 58, 96; Buchanan, 35; Buck, 117, 159; Buckhorn, 70; Buffalo, 207; Bull, 169; Burrows, 67; Busk, 99; Butte, 18, 129; Buzzard, 38; Cabin, 68, 207; Cabin–North Fork, 39; Cade, 251; Cals, 16; Campbell, 251; Cantonment, 49; Capitol, 42, 66; Carbonate, 14; Carnero–Middle Fork, 43; Carnero–South Fork, 148; Cascade, 44, 53, 164, 184, 190; Castle, 44; Cataract, 124; Cattle, 215; Cedar, 45; Cement, 55, 169, 180, 213; Chacuaco, 156, 163; Chalk, 45, 102; Chalk–North Fork, 219; Chaparral, 55; Chedsey, 37; Cinnamon, 47; Clear, 80, 84, 90, 132, 193, 251; Clear–West Fork, 18, 80, 119, 236; Cliff, 18, 44, 213; Coal, 48, 63, 96, 121, 135, 200, 254; Cochetopa, 201; Coleman, 140; Columbia, 51; Conundrum, 50, 53, 78, 222; Cony, 53; Copper, 54, 76, 165, 222; Corral, 39, 205; Cotton, 218; Cottonwood, 16, 24, 57, 64, 156; Cow, 225, 245; Cripple, 216; Criswell, 187; Crooked, 58, 178; Crooked Arroyo, 162; Cross, 82, 93, 142; Crystal, 30, 250; Cumbres, 61; Cunningham, 62; Curecanti, 63; Currant, 63; Curtis, 157; Cyclone, 40; Dallas–East Fork, 25; Deadman, 67; Deep, 62, 204; Deer, 59, 186; Deluge, 201; Denny–North Fork, 33; Diamond, 12; Difficult, 70; Difficulty, 44, 246; Disappointment, 98; Douglas, 71, 152; Dove, 98; Dry, 72, 253; Dry Fork, 187; Dry Fork Sand Wash, 87; Dry Sweetwater, 117; Duck, 94; East, 227; East Brush, 159, 165, 214; East Buffalo, 37;

Passes *(continued):*
Culbertson, 59–60; Culebra, 60; Cumberland, 60; Cumbres, 61–62, 125; Cunningham, 62–63; Curecanti, 63; Currant Creek, 63; Cyclone, 40; Daggett, 64; Daisy, 64, 65; Dallas Divide, 64–65, 128; Daly, 66; Daniels, 66; Dart, 66–67; Dead Lake, 196; Deadman Hill Divide, 67; Dead Man's, 67; Deer, 141; Denver, 67–68; Devil's Thumb, 68–69; Dick, 69–70; Difficult, 70; Divide, 225, 230; Dix Saddle, 70; Donner, 70–71; Dorchester, 71; Douglas, 71–72; Dowe, 72; Dunckley, 72; Dunham Gap, 72–73; Durant Gap, 73; Dyke Col, 73; Eagle, 74–75; Eagle River, 75; East, 203; East Gap, 75; East Hightower Mountain, 76; East Lone Cone, 76; East Maroon, 76–77; East River, 194; East Snowmass, 77; Eccles, 77–78; Electric, 78; Elk Basin, 78; Elkhead, 78–79; Elkhorn, 90, 91; Elk Mountain Divide, 157, 194; Elwood, 79; Empire, 79–80; Engineer, 80, 255; Eureka, 107; Fall Creek, 81; Fall River, 81–82; Fancy, 82, 83; Fawn Creek, 84; Fish, 55; Flat Top, 171; Flattop, 206; Flint, 84; Floyd Hill, 84; Fly, 148; Forest Canyon, 84–85; Fravert, 86; Fremont, 85–86; French, 86; Frigid Air, 86–87; Frying Pan, 99; Fryingpan, 99; G Gap, 87–88; Game, 88; Gap, The, 9, 118; Gap of the Sierra Blanca, 192; Garner, 88; Geneva, 94; Georgetown, 13; Georgia, 88–89; Gill Creek Divide, 89; Glacier, 89; Gold Hill, 59; Golden Gate, 89–90; Good, 248; Gore, 90–91, 173; Gore-Willow Creek, 175; Gothic, 194; Graham, 91–92; Granite, 92; Grassy, 92–93; Grassy Gap, 92; Great Divide, 93; Greenhill Divide, 93; Grizzly, 93–94; Guanella, 94–95; Gunnison's, 167; Gunshot, 96, 98; Gunsight, 95–98; Gunsight Gap, 95; Gunsight Notch, 96; Gun Site, 96; Guy's Hill, 90; Gyp-

sum Gap, 98; Hagerman, 99–100; Halfmoon, 100–101, 202; Halsey, 101; Hamilton, 28, 208; Hancock, 101–102, 159, 160; Handcart, 102–103, 240, 241; Hankins, 103; Hardscrabble, 103–104; Hardscrabble Saddle, 104; Hartman Divide, 104; Hayden, 104–105; Hayden Divide, 230; Haystack Gate, 105; Heckert, 105–106; Height Divide, 106; Hell Creek Divide, 106; Hepburn's, 106–107; Hermit, 107; Hermosa, 26; Hermosa Mountain, 26; Hesperus, 108; Hesperus Hill, 108; Hightower Mountain, 38; Hilltop, 224; Hite Divide, 106; Hoodoo Gap, 108; Hoosier, 108–109; Hope, 109–110; Horn Fork, 110; Horse Ranch, 110; Horseshoe, 111; Horsethief, 111–112; Howard, 160; Hunchback, 112; Hunter's, 30, 115; Hurricane, 112; Iceberg, 113; Icefield, 113; Illinois, 113–114; Imogene, 114; Independence, 115–116; Indian, 116, 117; Indian Camp, 116–117; Indian Creek, 117; Ingram, 21; Inter Ocean, 117–118; Iron Mine Gap, 118; Iron Springs Divide, 93; Irwin, 93, 94; Italian, 204; Jack Springs, 118; Jack's Cabin, 118–119; Jefferson, 88; Jones, 119–120; Jones Summit, 120; Juniper, 120; Keberg, 113; Kebler, 121; Kelly, 121; Kennebec, 121–122; Kenosha, 122–123, 241; Kenosha Hill, 122; Kenosha Summit, 122; Keyhole, The, 123; Knife Point, 123–124; Kokomo, 124; Lake, 127–128, 147, 180; Lake Creek, 127; Lake Fork, 47, 127; La Manga, 124–125; La Poudre, 125; La Salle, 125–126; Last Dollar, 128; La Veta, 126–127, 158, 238, 245; Leopard Creek Divide, 64; Leroux, 49; Lizard Head, 128–129; Lone Cone, 129; Lone Pine, 129; Long Draw, 125; Long Saddle, 129–130; Los Piños, 130; Lost Man, 130, 131; Lost Park Divide, 183; Lou Creek, 130–131; Loveland, 131–133,

Vasquez Fort, 236
Vasquez, Louis, 236
Venable, Jack, 237
Vermillion Basin, 88
Vernal, Utah, 71
Veterans of Foreign Wars, 109
Villasur, Pedro, 174
Violin music, 154
Virginius Mine, 239

Wagon Road Companies: Animas City,
  Pagosa Springs and Conejos, 234;
  Baldy Scott, 126; Breckenridge,
  Buckskin Joe and Hamilton, 109;
  Cañon City, Grand River and San
  Juan, 50; Cañon City and San Luis
  Valley, 105; Central Overland Cali-
  fornia and Pikes Peak Express, 236,
  243; Chalk Creek and Elk Mountain,
  219; Cheyenne and Beaver, 196;
  Colorado and California, 91, 119;
  Colorado and Pacific Wagon,
  Telegraph and Railroad, 90, 254;
  Cucharas and Sangre de Cristo, 126;
  Denver and Pacific, 237, 254;
  Empire City, New Pass and Mont-
  gomery City, 109; Empire City, New
  Pass, Breckenridge and Montgomery
  City, 119; Georgetown and Brecken-
  ridge, 94; Gore's Pass and White
  River, 91; LeDuc and Sanchez, 212;
  Middle and North Park, 10; Middle
  Park and South Boulder, 31; Mos-
  quito Pass, 151; Overland, 10, 30,
  182; Park Range, 243; Poncha Pass,
  168; Rollinsville and Middle Park,
  185; Saguache, Los Piños, Lake Fork
  and Upper Rio Los Animas, 157;
  Snake River, 14; Tarryall and
  Arkansas River, 243; Ten Mile, 94;
  Twin Lakes and Roaring Fork, 116;
  Ute Pass, 230
Waldo Canyon, 211
Wall and Witter stage line, 178, 244
Walsh, Tom, 114
Warm Springs Ranch, 33
Warrior's Mark Mine, 28
Washington, D.C., 50
Waunita Hot Springs, 240

Webster Brothers, 240
West Coast, 185
Western Slope Pipeline, 212
West Fork Trail, 245
Weston, Algernon, 243
Weston, Philo, 243
West Slope, 12, 45, 99, 109, 219, 237
West Ute Creek Trail, 235
Wet Canyon, 244
Wetterhorn Basin Trail, 245
Whale Mine, 103
Wheeler Geologic Area, 100, 101
Wheeler, Lieutenant George M., 100
Wheeler Survey Party, 135
"Where the Columbines Grow" song,
  79
White Desert movie, 185
White River Indian Agency, 254
Whitman, Walt, 122
Wildcat Canyon, 108, 242
Wild Irishman Mine, 17
Wilderness Areas: Big Blue, 58, 245,
  246; Collegiate Peaks, 32, 33, 51,
  70, 71, 78, 91, 110, 127, 156, 180,
  216; Comanche Peak, 53; Eagles
  Nest, 27, 45, 77, 175, 201, 227,
  228; Flat Tops, 117; Gore Creek,
  153; Holy Cross, 81, 82, 93, 100,
  142, 159, 229; Hunter Fryingpan,
  130, 140, 202; Indian Peaks, 10, 35,
  42, 57, 66, 106, 164, 186; La
  Garita, 100, 190, 201; Lizard Head,
  76, 249; Lost Creek, 20, 103, 207;
  Maroon Bells–Snowmass, 14, 36,
  42, 50, 53, 54, 66, 76, 77, 78, 86,
  101, 105, 165, 198, 221, 222, 243,
  247; Mount Evans, 41, 140, 186;
  Mount Massive, 212; Mount
  Sneffels, 25, 26; Mount Zirkel, 37,
  177, 233; Neota, 125; Never Summer, 15, 31, 177; Raggeds, 9, 10,
  159, 204, 254; Rawah, 7, 24, 92;
  West Elk, 18, 44, 63, 78, 108, 129,
  141, 160, 210, 213; Weminuche,
  20, 51, 62, 98, 112, 123, 156, 158,
  166, 172, 186, 205, 208, 209, 210,
  222, 226, 234, 242, 250
Wilkerson, John W., 246
Williams, Bill, 61, 139, 191, 230